Electronic Workflow

FOR INTERIOR DESIGNERS AND ARCHITECTS

Electronic Workflow

FOR INTERIOR DESIGNERS AND ARCHITECTS

ANDREW BRODY

Endicott College

AIA

FAIRCHILD BOOKS

NEW YORK

Executive Editor: Olga T. Kontzias

Assistant Acquisitions Editor: Amanda Breccia

Editorial Development Director: Jennifer Crane

Development Editor: Michelle Levy

Associate Art Director: Erin Fitzsimmons

Production Director: Ginger Hillman

Senior Production Editor: Elizabeth Marotta

Copyeditor: Peter Grennen

Cover Design: Chris Welch

Cover Art: Roberta DiGiovanni-Perkins

Text Design: Chris Welch

Library of Congress Catalog Card Number: 2008943617

ISBN: 978-1-56367-708-3

GST R 133004424

Printed in China

CH14, TP17

To Coleen, Nathan, Laena,
and the ever-patient Herschel the rabbit.

"Life is uncertain—eat dessert first."

—*Saying from Nepal*

CONTENTS

Unit 1: Predesign

Unit 2: Design in SketchUp

Unit 3: Schematic Design in Revit

EXTENDED TABLE OF CONTENTS

Unit 4: Working Drawings and Documentation

PREFACE

Learning a new piece of software can be a frustrating experience. It's often worse for professionals who have the experience to know what drawings and other documents are *supposed* to look like—they try to make the software produce results in the way that they're familiar with, rather than using the internal logic of the program. Students and others early in their career may be anxious to become productive as quickly as possible, foregoing the complete training that would make them most efficient. This book is meant to help everyone interested in (or being forced into) learning the software involved in the design and documentation of construction projects.

The different types of software currently used for architectural design are all similar in many ways, but they also have their own peculiarities and unique opportunities. Interior design in particular is often neglected in traditional technical manuals, favoring overall architectural design instead. The purpose of this text is to link the standard phases and processes of an interior design project with the capabilities of the software most commonly used to produce the deliverables, such as presentations, renderings, and construction drawings.

Sometimes a project requires quick studies and simple tests of layouts. A client may only need a feasibility study, with an emphasis on research and analysis. Sometimes a schematic rendering is needed to help generate interest in a project or to help with fund raising. Other projects might have a more traditional scope of services, from pre-design through construction drawings, bidding, and administration. Finally, projects must be distilled and packed into a portfolio, both as a means of reflection and to help generate future work. These very different tasks must be completed using different combinations of software, with care paid to the most efficient electronic workflow.

No designer wants to feel like they're a prisoner of the technology, limited in their creativity by the complexity of the software. Yet we often learn software without the holistic perspective on where an individual program fits within our overall goal of producing high-quality environments. Alas, no single piece of software can perform all the different tasks we designers require, and this forces us to makes choices about how we complete our work. By carefully considering how to best use the software currently available, designers can avoid frustrating dead ends and inefficient methodologies.

No single reference book can hope to completely explain all the software we use. Instead, this book explains strategies for managing different types of projects, and gives step-by-step instructions for the most common tasks. This should give a student or professional the framework of understanding on which to build further study and exploration.

ACKNOWLEDGMENTS

Without the encouragement and guidance of Olga Kontzias, the initial notion for this text would have remained just that. Guiding a new author through the process of pulling together an idea into a format that can be reviewed and approved is a mission that's part managerial, part psychology, and part diplomacy. The patient suggestions and good judgment of Michele Levy helped to keep the text on point and out of the woods. And the thorough, relentless precision of Chris Fortunato and Tina Henderson helped to create a polished final product.

Also, I'd like to acknowledge my students at Endicott College. Their constant questions have forced me to scramble to keep ahead of them and to revise my methods to be most applicable for what interior designers do. Their outlandish design ideas have forced the technology and my knowledge of it to expand and help to make every class surprising.

INTRODUCTION

What makes a good design good? And how do we recognize it when we get there? It's a synthesis of many skills—technical, interpersonal, organizational, managerial—and an ability to be understood by various audiences. Designers need to communicate in an accessible and accurate way, all the while evaluating and testing their design from a variety of perspectives. Computer technology is essential at every step of design, from initial research and modeling to construction drawings and project management. This book offers strategies for integration of different pieces of software into the traditional process of design, and with each other.

No single software package can capture all the different elements that go into a design project. Word processor and spreadsheet programs are most useful in researching precedents and developing an architectural program. Simple schematic designs are best modeled in SketchUp, which is quick, accurate, and flexible. Decent renderings can be created using internal "Styles," RPS IRender nXt, or Photoshop Elements. More complex designs need a Building Information Modeling (BIM) program like Revit, where schematics are linked more closely to DD- and CD-level drawings. Finally, presentation-quality renderings need to be developed in several programs, taking the flexibility and speed of SketchUp, the precision of Revit, and the material and texturing subtlety of Photoshop Elements. Public presentations and design portfolios are best done in a program such as PowerPoint, which can handle a variety of file-source types, such as rendered images, text boxes, simple graphics, spreadsheets, and hyperlinks.

Designers are holistic and visual thinkers, and need to see how specific problem-solving skills fit in with the ebb and flow of the design process. Thus, the goal of this book is twofold: to develop a strategic overview of the design process, examining how different software can best be woven into the traditional phases of an interior design project; and, to demonstrate technical tactics within those programs to optimize workflow and interoperability. This text is intended as a companion for a two-semester sequence in design technology for interior designers or architects. It is not, however, a complete technical reference manual for any of the software packages described—turn to more comprehensive manuals for the minutiae of program settings and tweaks. The central focus will address integrating technology across different phases of design, to produce well-composed and thorough designs quickly and efficiently.

Chapters are organized into Units that correspond to the traditional phases of an architectural project (predesign, schematic design, design development and construction drawings, and project documentation). Two projects are tracked through the text, to demonstrate the implications of design decisions across the whole length of the design process. Instructors may choose either a simpler, smaller project or a complex, multilevel one, depending on the design skill level of the students. Each chapter has Online Resources, such as files used for the illustrations, or base models. Term Project Assignments are meant to specify the progress expected of students working on single projects for the entire unit. Exercises and Further Study are an opportunity for the student to expand upon skills learned in the chapter, interpolating the lessons of the chapter to solve new problems. They are standalone and not tied together into a single project.

Finally, the ultimate goal of any designer should be to produce interesting, sophisticated, and compelling designs. Just as the techniques of using a paintbrush should not prove an impediment to a painter (and in fact can be a source of inspiration), so the use of software to explore and develop our designs can lead to an ever richer and more exciting built environment.

How to Use This Book

FOR STUDENTS

Each chapter is peppered with quick-reference mini-sections, such as Big Picture (describing how the lesson at hand fits into the overall design process), Magic Trick (for productivity tools), Under the Hood (for technical descriptions of how or why something works), and Look Out! (for things that can go horribly wrong). Key words are boldfaced the first time they appear, and are defined in the Glossary. Tools and options that occur within a drop-down or tabbed menu are indicated with an angled bracket, as in **Insert>Picture**. In addition, the active toolbars, menus, or palettes are indicated.

The step-by-step exercises should be followed very carefully, either in class or at home. They are meant to demonstrate the exact process for the core operations of the different software packages. You'll be getting intimately familiar with these programs over the course of your design career, so don't be shy. Explore the software beyond what is spelled out in this or any other book—open up menus, try out tools to see what they do, and always, always use the **Help** menu or tutorials. They are interactive and can guide you through the steps of new operations in as detailed a manner as this book.

Finally, you are all first and foremost designers, not technicians. All this software will not make your designs any better or worse—only your skills at design and evaluation can do that. Try to think about what the design wants to be, and find a way to evaluate if what you're creating actually follows that vision. Nothing motivates learning better than having something you'd like to draw, then needing to figure out how to draw it.

FOR PROFESSIONALS

The best thing you can do for your design business is to increase efficiency in your workflow. Many of you may already use some or all of the programs in this book, but without having given thought to the overall process. Read through this book and compare it with the software packages you're using and the types of drawings and presentations that your office does. Strive for efficiency, even if this means learning new software.

Electronic Workflow

FOR INTERIOR DESIGNERS AND ARCHITECTS

Unit 1

Predesign

The Electronic Design Process

LEARNING GOALS

- Understand the capabilities of different types of software
- Understand strategies for efficiently managing different types of projects
- Understand good file-management skills
- Develop organizational tactics for starting a new project

So you've just been handed a new design project—a site, a program, and maybe some general description of the clients and their dispositions. As an interior designer or architect, you're anxious to roll up your sleeves and start working, which probably means firing up your computer. Once you log in, though, what do you do first? Write a letter? Start a drawing? Write down your deadline? Like design in the physical world, there's a natural sequence for the different tasks you have to complete, if you want to be most efficient.

It's best to start an electronic project the same way you would back in ancient history when people used paper and pencils: with a clean desk and a fresh sheet of paper. In the old days, the main choice was white tracing paper or yellow—now there is an array of software choices, and it's never entirely clear which to use for what type of project or at which stage. Hours could be wasted unless you choose the most efficient drawing program, manage files consistently, create electronic correspondence, and set up a backup system.

Most interior design and architecture projects are now conceived and executed primarily using various drawing and modeling software. Yet

Here are the main tenets of good work habits:

- *Set up a logical filing system using folders and subfolders.*
- *Save **and** back up work frequently while working.*
- *Look at the scale and scope of the project to determine the most efficient software for each step.*
- *Create interstitial editions of the project for easy backward workflow.*
- *Keep sights on broad design themes and concept—avoid hyperdetailing or designing low-priority project elements.*
- *Pace yourself—evaluate each step in the design carefully before adding layers of complexity.*
- *Leave time for composition and printing—drawings straight out of the computer are cold and lifeless.*
- *Avoid too many steps outside of the electronic workflow (hand rendering on printed drawings, for example), as they must be re-created electronically to allow continued project development and collaboration.*
- *Document the physical parts of a design (models, hand sketches, and so forth) immediately.*
- *Add newly completed work to your design portfolio.*

there is often little consideration given to how these tools work together, or how the ebb and flow of the design process has changed because of their use. Students (as well as practitioners) are expected to be fluent in these software families, each of which is configured to address discrete tasks within the design process.

These new tools of the trade have different constraints and opportunities when compared with manual design techniques, especially when used together on more complex projects. If certain strategies are followed, the huge advantages of an electronic workflow can be realized. From the instructor's point of view, a successful design studio requires a solid understanding of the strengths and weaknesses of electronic visualization, and reasonable expectations regarding workflow and productivity.

To study how each of the usual professional tasks can be completed on the computer, we'll track two projects of differing scopes. They will be used to explore and explain workflow through the usual steps in the design process. For the first unit, we'll study the Chocolate Café, which is relatively small and simple.

The Twenty-first-Century Design Studio

Embracing the speed and power of electronic visualization tools requires greater discipline and planning when compared with manual techniques, but the end result is better communication and thus better designs. Contemporary students (and clients, for that matter) are used to sophisticated, rich 3D visualizations of virtual environments. After all, you can walk into Home Depot and get decent perspectives of your kitchen with different cabinet options in just an hour. Those designs are not particularly sophisticated, but they serve a purpose.

Good Work Habits

From the start of the design process, it cannot be emphasized enough that students (and practitioners) must be organized and consistent in their file organization. Saving interstitial versions of designs is important—just in case some notion from two A.M. a week ago turns out to be the key to the whole design. These steps are more critical with electronic media because the number of files can be huge. Luckily, we have electronic search tools that make staying organized easier than rifling through a physical filing cabinet.

Many students still feel more comfortable making initial conceptual sketches in hand-drawn or modeled form—there's something immediate and tangible about the physical interaction that makes abstract ruminations seem accessible. However, students cannot expect to exactly replicate these sketches in their computers, through modeling either from scratch or from a template. Once an electronic conceptual model has been created, it's much easier to evaluate it within that medium, developing and communicating the project fully within that virtual realm. Keep hand-drawn sketches for your portfolio and decide judiciously whether they are relevant to a final presentation.

Designs are never completely done, of course. One problem with electronic visualization is that the potential level of detail that can be studied is infinite. Great discipline is needed from all parties to design only what is appropriate for the particular stage of design at hand. Especially during schematics, I tell students not to bother fixing a problem in a model if you don't see it in any of the views of an upcoming presentation. It's akin to a singer ignoring one or two wrong notes, and instead continuing to keep the tune going—it's the continuity that gives the song meaning.

Software Families

The five basic types of architectural visualization software as they exist today have well-defined capabilities and limitations. It is my contention that, as of this writing, four of these are critical to producing a rich and successful design project. This is based both on my professional experience as an architect, and living vicariously through my students during and after their design education. I've chosen software based mainly on reasonable cost (to faculty and students) and interoperability. It makes teaching easier when most of the programs use similar strategies for organization, drawing composition, physical output, and rendering settings. Thus, media lessons can be applied across the software spectrum, emphasizing the design process over the specific requirements of one program or another.

OFFICE MANAGEMENT SOFTWARE

This is a suite of programs for word processing, spreadsheets, data management, and presentations. Clearly, Microsoft Office dominates the playing field, even on the Mac platform. Advantages are excellent integration of all programs within the entire suite, which means both ease of learning and use, and good interoperability. This suite also graphically looks much like the PC-embedded file-management program Windows Explorer (Macs have an entirely different-looking interface). Fortunately, other alternatives (like Open Office) use the same file formats and standards.

DRAFTING

This is software for two-dimensional drawing using lines, arcs, and the like, which have scaled geometric properties. AutoCAD is the big player, and we still teach it, although only for survival at internships. The advantage is mainly market saturation (although it's been losing ground steadily) and a vast, well-trained workforce. Recent integration of parametric objects (doors, walls, floors, and so forth) and an enhanced 3D interface are improvements, but it's a dinosaur in terms of workflow. The .dwg file format is common among most 3D modeling programs, Photoshop CS, and PowerPoint. Downsides are that it's much slower to build a whole project in three dimensions, and integrates poorly within the overall design process.

SKETCH MODELING

Solid or face-based 3D models are created with this type of software, which are to scale and visually representative of materials. We use SketchUp, which is the main player, because it's economical, fast, and has a rendering plug-in that uses the same "engine" as Revit. This software is quick and intuitive to learn, and generates simple but convincing models. It handles materials well (with a paint bucket) and has the capability for text, dimensions, scaled orthographic drawings, day-lighting, and nice perspective composition controls and view saving. The downsides are lack of the ability to model wall thicknesses easily, which makes anything beyond one or two rooms quite unpleasant, and difficulty handling reflected ceiling plan views and detail drawings.

BUILDING INFORMATION MODELING (BIM)

This software employs dimensionally precise, materials-based parametric objects to model the architecture. Using this type of software is more like defining a building through menus and settings than it is actually drawing one. We use Revit, a big player thanks mainly to backing from its parent company, Autodesk. Advantages include excellent integration across the phases of design; also, direct import of SketchUp models. Disadvantages are the complexity of the model, which slows down the modeling process significantly; 3D view controls are unwieldy at best; and materials are handled in a very complex and counterintuitive manner. Finally, the library of native components is tiny compared to SketchUp.

PHOTO MANIPULATION

This software is for raster-based image processing—no 3D geometry is used. Photoshop is the clear leader here. We use the pared-down version called Elements, partly for cost and partly to avoid unnecessary complexity. It handles all image formats well; uses tools and a layer strategy familiar from the other programs; and allows high-quality renderings to be produced with precise output control in both physical and electronic formats. The downside is that it's one way: Materials and lighting drawn in Photoshop Elements can't be imported back to other programs—they must be re-created.

Some programs are clearly stronger in one area (like SketchUp for speed modeling), or have a broader scope of capabilities (like Revit), but none can do everything. If you have the luxury of choosing a whole suite all at once, look for interoperability rather than some chimerical hope that one program can possibly meet all of your needs. Even a simple predesign presentation might use all four different types of software just to produce a decent-looking project.

Working efficiently involves knowing what each program can do *and* knowing your own strengths. You may be particularly good at one program, or have a slower computer that can't run big Revit models well. Be sure you plan your projects so that, when the time comes to switch programs, you'll experience the minimum loss of data.

The Design Process

The education of interior designers and architects has traditionally followed incremental phases of development. This process more or less matches the contractual phases of a real construction project. Projects start with research, then development of concepts, then graphic program analysis, and eventually those ideas and notions are transformed into a three-dimensional visualization. Finally, construction documents are prepared to communicate the design to the professional who will build it. Once everything is completed, designs (realized or not) are placed in a portfolio of work.

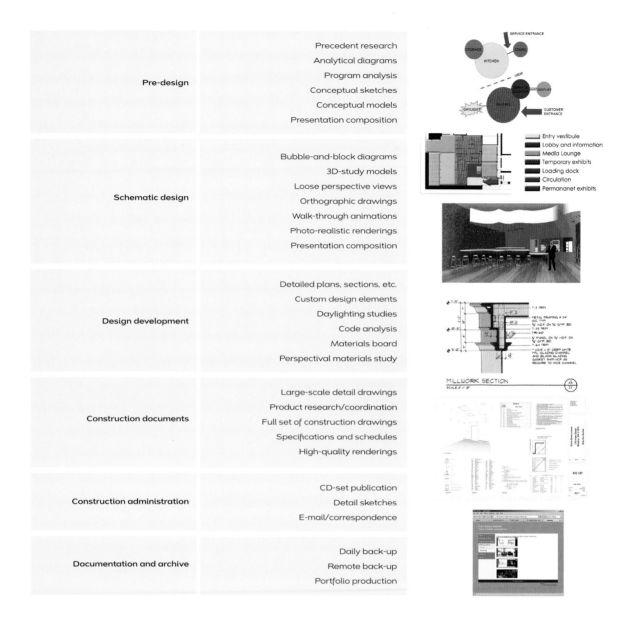

Pre-design	Precedent research	
	Analytical diagrams	
	Program analysis	
	Conceptual sketches	
	Conceptual models	
	Presentation composition	
Schematic design	Bubble-and-block diagrams	
	3D-study models	
	Loose perspective views	
	Orthographic drawings	
	Walk-through animations	
	Photo-realistic renderings	
	Presentation composition	
Design development	Detailed plans, sections, etc.	
	Custom design elements	
	Daylighting studies	
	Code analysis	
	Materials board	
	Perspectival materials study	
Construction documents	Large-scale detail drawings	
	Product research/coordination	
	Full set of construction drawings	
	Specifications and schedules	
	High-quality renderings	
Construction administration	CD-set publication	
	Detail sketches	
	E-mail/correspondence	
Documentation and archive	Daily back-up	
	Remote back-up	
	Portfolio production	

Figure 1.1 *Typical design tasks by phase*

Each phase has specific steps that are documented and presented. Most of the individual steps are meant to develop the project carefully, avoiding mistakes or oversights that would be more difficult to change as the project grows in complexity and detail (Figure 1.1).

Many of these tasks haven't changed since the heyday of the École des Beaux Arts. The most important feature to consider is that, regardless of the media used to produce the project, slow and deliberate progress usually makes for the richest and most well-developed designs. Electronic media can make certain steps much easier and quicker (e.g., generating a perspective), while others (such as sketching alternatives for a floor plan) can be more complex.

Students should be encouraged to make last-minute physical touch-ups to printed presentation drawings. This encourages them to check their work, which is a great habit to get into. Also, certain details are lost in the printing process, or are hard to re-create through modeling and manipulation. Knowing that, students won't waste time on the computer, but instead take ten minutes with a white pencil creating shiny highlights and reflections before hanging a printed board.

Project Scope

There is a spectrum of project sizes and scopes. In an educational setting, projects rarely get beyond the design-development phase, and students don't benefit from repeated instances of the same project from which to copy filing schemes, project templates, and components. That said, they will hopefully get exposure at least once to different-sized projects with different scopes. It is likely that the more complex the project, the more jumping around from one program to another will be needed to complete it. Figure 1.2 shows major steps involved in producing projects with different scales and scopes, broken apart to show when a change in software program typically occurs. There's no way to avoid the need to move from one program to another—the key to efficient workflow is to carefully choose when and how to make the move.

Even small projects require many steps and the use of several programs to analyze, model, present, and archive. More complex projects have more jumping around, but the process must still be consistent and deliberate. A design project isn't complete until it's been documented, backed up, and included in the portfolio.

The simplest projects have programs like designing a piece of furniture or casework, a kiosk, or single-room study. These are clearly meant for modeling in a 3D sketching program.

Even a small project is likely to use multiple pieces of software—depending on how much research is involved and what sort of presentation is made (Figure 1.3). Students can display work entirely on the computer or entirely with a physical model, but either way, some accommodation must be made for inclusion in the portfolio.

A medium-size project would have more than one room, and perhaps some complex furnishing or other consideration (Figure 1.4). Examples might be a small restaurant or retail renovation, an office layout, or an auditorium or lobby.

In this case, the software chosen may depend on the overall scope of the project: If the project stops at schematics, it can be completed entirely

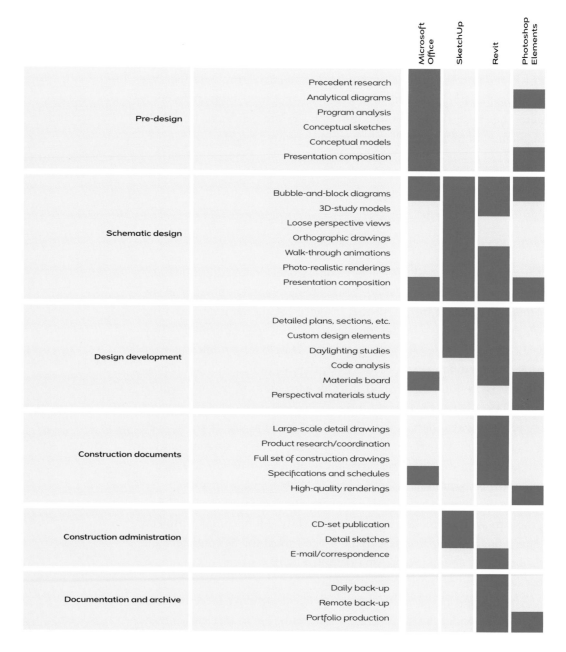

Figure 1.2 *Diagrammatic workflow across phases of design for different-size projects*

in SketchUp. If construction documents are needed, however, Revit is probably the best choice.

A large project would have multiple stories, with significant interior development throughout (Figure 1.5). This would, of course, need the most powerful tool: Revit.

Of course, even a large project might call for quick, simple studies of various elements, or the design of custom elements like furniture or skylights. The main model would be best to produce in Revit, but the studies

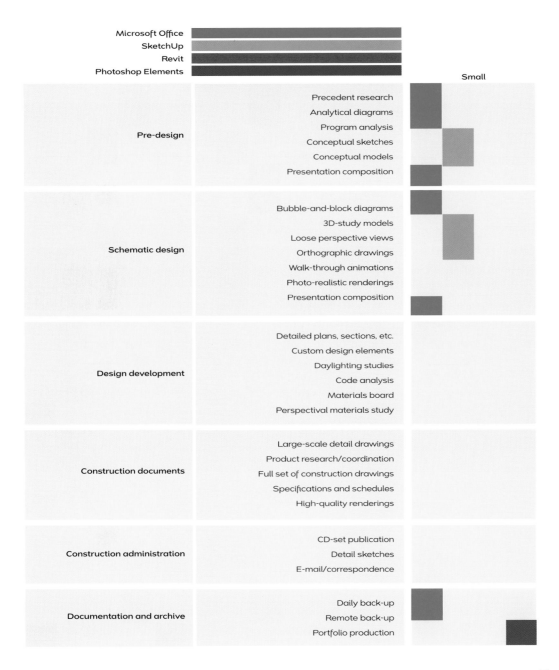

Figure 1.3 *Workflow for a small sketch project*

would be done more comfortably when exported to SketchUp. Elements could be re-imported to Revit for incorporation into the main project. This size project often requires a powerful computer, especially for rendering operations. Students have gotten in the habit of camping out in the labs—rendering overnight on one machine and working on other parts of their projects on their personal computers. Students must learn *how to learn* to use computers. The goal, after all, is not to become a computer operator with a narrow set of skills. The goal is to be a good designer.

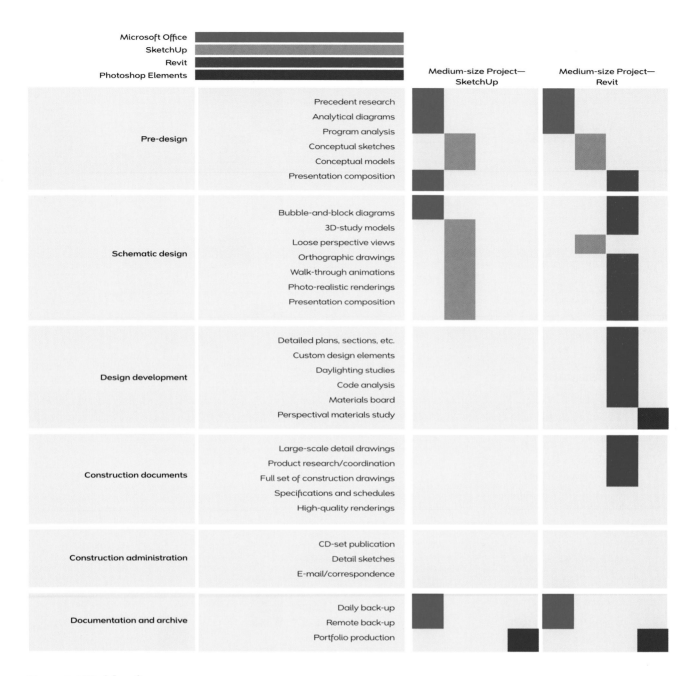

Figure 1.4 *Workflow for a medium-size project with narrow and wide scopes*

Starting a New Project

The best way to learn efficient workflow is to track a design project from the very beginning to completion. It's best to start with a relatively small project—the renovation of a commercial space in Arlington, Massachusetts, to have a café. We'll follow this project from initial predesign research through schematic design, and finally produce a high-quality, materials-based, photo-realistic rendering.

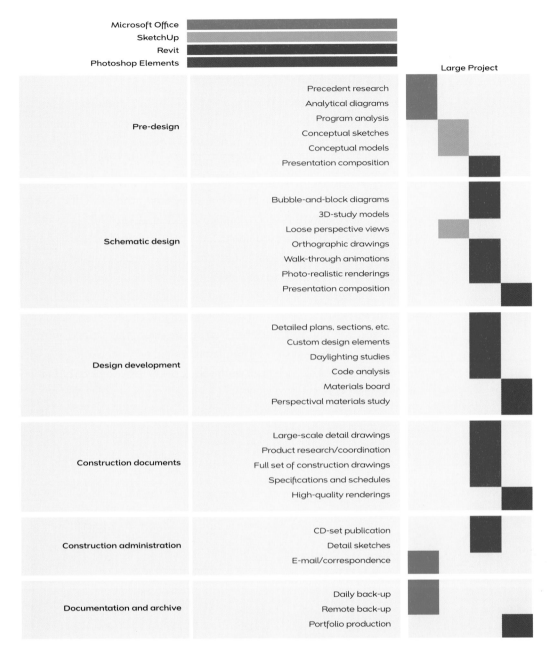

Microsoft Office
SketchUp
Revit
Photoshop Elements

Large Project

Pre-design

Precedent research
Analytical diagrams
Program analysis
Conceptual sketches
Conceptual models
Presentation composition

Schematic design

Bubble-and-block diagrams
3D-study models
Loose perspective views
Orthographic drawings
Walk-through animations
Photo-realistic renderings
Presentation composition

Design development

Detailed plans, sections, etc.
Custom design elements
Daylighting studies
Code analysis
Materials board
Perspectival materials study

Construction documents

Large-scale detail drawings
Product research/coordination
Full set of construction drawings
Specifications and schedules
High-quality renderings

Construction administration

CD-set publication
Detail sketches
E-mail/correspondence

Documentation and archive

Daily back-up
Remote back-up
Portfolio production

Figure 1.5 *Workflow for a large project with complete professional scope*

Project brief: Two chocolatières want to create a café for enjoying high-quality chocolate beverages and pastries. They consider the creation of fine chocolates an art, and would like to share the process with their patrons by having the work area visible from the main part of the shop.

Learning goals and outcomes: After completing this project, the student should be familiar with smooth workflow in a small renovation project.

Background thoughts: What role does chocolate play in our culture and in other cultures? Why do some people love it so much? How are fine chocolates produced—are there any special environmental conditions or opportunities?

Constraints: The project must comply with state and local codes, including accessibility regulations for a retail service counter and restaurant seating. The kitchen must accommodate chocolate-making machinery with required clearances and configuration. Temperature and moisture in the kitchen must be controlled differently than in serving areas.

Process: Predesign research will be done using the MS Office Suite, ending in a presentation of concepts, project analysis, and a precedent study. Schematics will be modeled in SketchUp and presented using Layout, which comes from Google SketchUp also. Finally, renderings will be produced using a plug-in from RPS Systems called IRender nXt.

Site: A single-story storefront infill building located in Arlington, Massachusetts.

The façade in Figure 1.6 is a brick structure covered in stucco, with an aluminum storefront system. The plan is roughly 60' deep and 25' wide. Note that there is a service door in the back of the plan, and two double-hung windows.

Figure 1.6 *Photo and building plan*

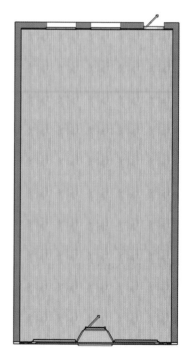

TABLE 1.1 CHOCOLATE CAFÉ BUILDING PROGRAM

Program Area	Approx Area	Comments
Service counter	230 GSF	Service counter with seating for eight; back counter for sink, microwave, hot chocolate and coffee machinery; cash register area
Food display	35 GSF	Display case for pastries and chocolates (approx. six LF)
Package displays	35 GSF	Package displays on shelves or in an electronically lit case
Seating	350 GSF	Table and/or café seating for 14
Kitchen	150 GSF	Kitchen with tempering machine, enrobing machine, cooling table, mobile rack storage, dry storage, wrapping area, fridge/freezer; 40 LF clear counter area; double commercial sink; kitchen either visible from or open to main part of cafe
Stairs	50 GSF	To basement storage area
Garbage	25 GSF	Garbage area away from food, by back door
Toilet room (♀)	50 GSF	Fully accessible
Toilet room (♂)	50 GSF	Fully accessible
Mechanical room	25 GSF	
Circulation	250 GSF	
Total programmed space:	**1,250 GSF**	
Existing net floor area:	*1,250 GSF*	

Creating an Electronic Home for Your Project

MS Windows uses **Folders**, aka **Directories**, to organize files on your computer. The one you're probably already using as a default dumping ground for new and downloaded files is called My Documents. Within that folder, you may already have additional folders called My Music, My Pictures, and probably 500 word processing documents with meaningful names you made up that make sense to you. Each folder can have more folders inside them, and this creates a directory structure or hierarchy. Keeping all of your files organized is a matter of creating a logical organization for your folder structure, than being disciplined about always saving files somewhere that makes sense.

I use Windows Explorer to set up my file structure. Double-click on My Documents on your desktop (or select it in the Start menu) to open the program. For file management, I divide the screen into two panes by

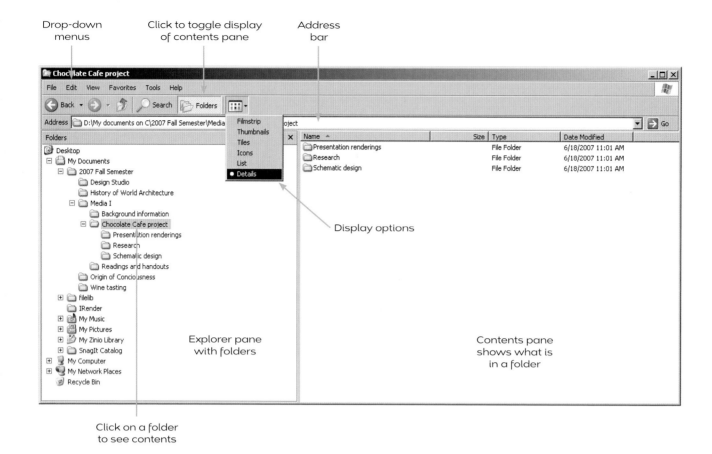

Figure 1.7 *Windows Explorer* folder structure

clicking on the **Folders** button. This makes it easy to drag files from one folder to another. Click the little **+** signs to open subfolders in the left pane, and click on a folder to see its contents in the right pane. Choose **File>New>Folder** from the drop-down menu to add a new folder inside the one you're currently viewing. You'll be prompted right away to rename the folder—call it something clever like *Fall Semester*. In the same way, you can make a new subfolder for the class you're in, and a sub-subfolder for this particular project, the Chocolate Café (Figure 1.7).

You can drag existing documents into the new folder and drag folders all over the place from one folder to the next. I prefer to create a chronological hierarchy of folders—all of my work is stored in My Documents, in a folder named *School*. I've created a new subfolder for every semester, and within those, subfolders for each class. Any time you need to save a file, you should carefully consider where it belongs—that will make it easier to find it later on.

An alternative method for creating subfolders is to right-click on the contents pane of Windows Explorer and select **New>Folder** from the context-sensitive menu.

Day-to-Day Backup

There are two types of backups I use, one for quick copies of a few files and the other for a comprehensive backup. The simpler one is a temporary, day-to-day copy of my current project folder on a USB thumb drive. This process creates a mirror of the folder, which Windows compares to the original and then updates files to match each other (Figure 1.8).

CREATING A BACKUP ON A USB DRIVE

1. Insert a USB drive into your computer.
2. Launch Windows Explorer if it doesn't come up automatically.
3. Click the **Folders** button to display two panes.
4. Click on the USB drive letter in the left pane to reveal its contents.
5. Right-click on the right pane and choose **New>Briefcase** from the context-sensitive menu.
6. In the left pane, click on your folder for this class to reveal its contents.
7. Click and drag the Chocolate Café folder into the briefcase.
8. Download the building program Excel spreadsheet from the On-line Resources for this course (*Chocolate Cafe architectural program. xls*) and save it in the Background folder.
9. Click on the USB drive letter in the left pane.
10. In the right pane, right-click on the briefcase and choose **Update All**.
11. Windows will compare the original file tree on your computer with the one on the USB drive, and hopefully find that you've added a file.
12. Click **Update** to update the USB drive mirror copy.

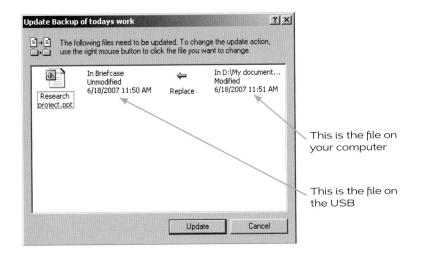

This is the file on your computer

This is the file on the USB

MAGIC TRICK

Several keystrokes can help you build and modify your selections in Windows Explorer, and these are consistent throughout most of our software: Hold down **SHIFT** *while clicking to choose a contiguous group;* **CTRL** *while clicking in the contents pane allows selection of non-adjacent files; using* **CTRL** *while dragging makes a copy of the original file(s) or folder(s). Finally, holding down* **ALT** *while clicking and dragging makes a shortcut to your file or folder—a link back to the original file. This is particularly handy if you're working on a large project where all you do for eight hours a day five days a week is work on one file—place the shortcut on your desktop for quick access.*

MAGIC TRICK

If you're in the middle of dragging a file or folder from the contents pane into a folder on the right and realize that you forgot to open up the file tree, just mouse over the folder you want to open—it will open up all by itself in a few seconds.

Figure 1.8 *The* **Update** *prompt*

Of course, this system works only if you remember to update your briefcase periodically. It takes Windows Explorer a long time to compare more than a handful of files, so it's not great as a backup for your entire system. You'll also need enough space on the USB drive for these files, which is tricky if you've got lots of big models and their backups. This system can also work on USB-connected external hard drives, and those devices often come with their own software for quickly synchronizing large numbers of files.

Long-Term Backup

Why not call it permanent backup? Mainly because no single method and/or media is foolproof—even CDs and external hard drives can fail. It's a good idea to make a weekly copy of your entire data drive onto a removable hard drive or disk. There are many software packages that come with removable hard drives, so I'm not going to cover them. The most stable storage device is a DVD, which can be sent in the mail to some distant, safe location. Second best is an external hard drive, which can be used over and over again.

To back up on a CD or DVD, plunk a blank disk into your drive. Windows will prompt you to **Open a Writable CD folder using Windows**

Figure 1.9 *Drive Properties* and the *Tools* tab

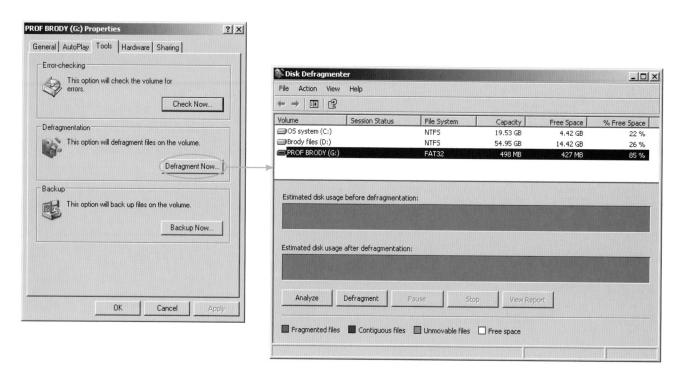

Explorer. Click **OK**. You can drag any file or folder right into the folder from another open window, or from Windows Explorer, or by clicking the folder button and browsing as usual. The file structure within the disk can be the same as on your hard drive, or whatever you choose. Right-click on the icon and choose **Write the files to CD** to finish the process.

These CDs are copies of your original files and are best stored somewhere different from your computer. A good idea is to swap with a friend, or leave them at home during a vacation.

Defragment if needed, and check your other drives while you're at it (Figure 1.9). If your drive does fail anyway, reformatting will bring it back to life, but all data will be lost.

Online Resources

- *Chocolate Cafe architectural program.xls*, which is an Excel spreadsheet
- *Site photo 1.JPG* and *Site photo 2.JPG*
- Example of a Windows Explorer folder structure

Term Project Assignments

- Create file structure for the Café project on your computer.
- Set up a briefcase on your external drive to back up the folders for this project.
- Create a long-term backup of all your files and folders on a CD or DVD, and leave it with a friend.

Exercises and Further Study

- Open and organize all existing files on your computer into a logical tree of folders.
- Back up your files onto a CD or other removable media.
- Defragment all drives and removable media.
- Sign up for an online file-storage service and back up your files there.

MAGIC TRICK

Every drive prefers its own flavor of disk: Some are + or −; some say "R" (can only be written to once), while others are "RW"—which means they can be written to many times and erased. Make sure that you know what's in your computer before you buy a spool of 400 disks.

UNDER THE HOOD

*If any of your drives are slowing down, you can defragment them, which helps them run more smoothly. From the Windows Start menu, choose **Programs> Accessories>System Tools> Disk Defragmenter**. Select the drive in the list displayed and choose **Analyze**—Windows will examine it to see how broken up your files are.*

2

Research Projects

LEARNING GOALS

- Understand interoperability within the MS Office Suite
- Learn to develop presentations with MS PowerPoint
- Skills to create quick, simple drawings within a presentation file

A good design has a strong foundation in research, to help the designer understand the unique opportunities and constraints of a project. This is typically done during the predesign phase. In an educational setting, assignments can be done by teams or individually, and presented to the class so that all may benefit from the research and analysis.

The following topics are most typical, and are what we'll study for the Chocolate Café project:

- **Visual concepts**: usually a collection of visual non-architectural inspirations
- **Partí:** a word or phrase that captures the initial spirit the designer would like to follow
- **Program chart**: lists spaces, requirements, and square footage
- **General building codes**: may include chapter references, Web links, and images where available
- **Accessibility regulations**: with both the most relevant chapter references and images where available
- **Project constraints**: including equipment research and design standards

- **Precedent**: analysis of a similar project, using images, concepts, plans, and analysis drawings

All the software needed for these assignments, and indeed all that we'll cover in this book, are organized in a very similar way, so try to look for those shared elements and configurations as we proceed.

Software Similarities

Most software is similar in the way it's laid out. There's a work area where all the action happens, a series of drop-down menus up top, and some sort of standard toolbar at the top. Often there are toolbars below that for program-specific operations, and sometimes toolbars pop up when you've selected something, to give you more options.

All of these programs also have many, many tools and settings, only a few of which are shown here (Figure 2.1). To see other toolbars, you can usually look under View from the drop-down menu, or right-click on an existing toolbar.

Many programs also now have interactive help (under the Help drop-down menu), which guides you through the steps of different operations.

Standard tools such as Open and Print look the same from one program to the next

MS Office groups related commands on palettes of a sort

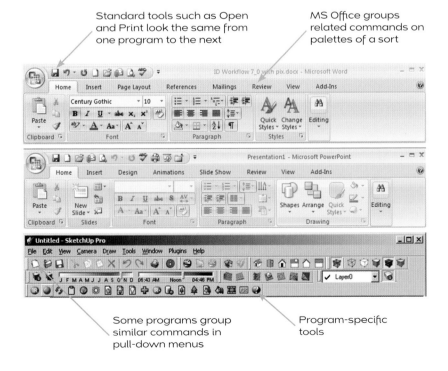

Figure 2.1 *Menus and toolbar areas from MS Word, PowerPoint, and SketchUp*

Some programs group similar commands in pull-down menus

Program-specific tools

In SketchUp, there is the *Instructor*, found under the Window drop-down menu. These are often so good that you could do without this book. Well, not quite—but these and Web-based tutorials have the advantage of constant updates to match advances and demonstrations that can't be offered in book format.

Keyboard Shortcuts

Most of these programs also use the same keyboard shortcuts, which are keystroke combinations (sometimes called accelerator keys): **CTRL+Z** (undo–my personal favorite), **CTRL+Y** (redo), **CTRL+C** (copy), **CTRL+ X** (cut), **CTRL+V** (paste), **CTRL+ P** (print), **CTRL+ A** (select all), **CTRL+ HOME** (top of document), **F1** (help), and **F7** (spell-check). Double-clicking on a word selects the word; triple-clicking selects the line of text. Program-specific tasks also get special keyboard shortcuts, such as **CTRL+ M** in PowerPoint for a new slide.

Any time you execute the same command over and over and over again, it's a good idea to learn the keyboard shortcut for that command. Most programs allow you to customize shortcuts, tailoring them perfectly to your habits for increased efficiency. In Word, click the Office button, then choose Word Options, as shown in Figure 2.3. Then select Customize, and you'll see a list of commands and their shortcuts. You can also add or remove buttons from toolbars and from the top of the application window.

If you're an obsessive typist, just hit the **ALT** key once, and you'll see a tiny letter pop up next to each of the tools and drop-down menus. If you type the letter next to the desired tool, it'll open up that toolbar, where you'll see letters once again for each of the tools available. This two-stroke approach allows you to access almost any tool in any MS Office program.

Figure 2.2 *Tool tips with shortcut keys*

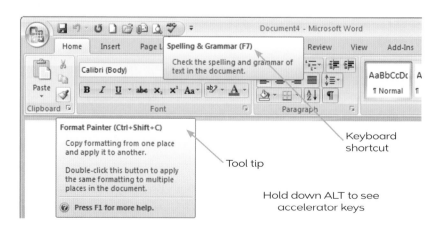

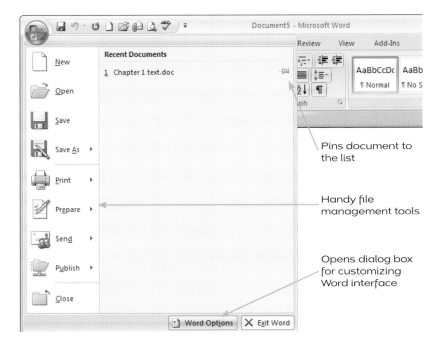

Figure 2.3 *MS Office drop-down menu*

Presentation Setup

PowerPoint is a good all-purpose tool for compiling different types of information formats (words, pictures, spreadsheets, charts, and so forth) in an intuitive way. There are some handy tools for helping compose content within each slide. In this chapter we'll just collect words, images, and charts from various sources and prepare them in PowerPoint.

Here are some guidelines for sheet orientation and background:

- **On a monitor:** Standard slide size and orientation are fine; dark colors work well, as the screen is its own light source. This method, as opposed to printing, is more environmentally friendly, as no trees will be harmed in the production of your show.
- **On a projector:** Standard slide size and orientation are fine; black background is very effective.
- **Printed handout:** Standard slide size and orientation are fine; avoid dark colors.
- **Printed boards:** Set layout to final printed size and orientation; avoid dark colors.

If you'll be printing large boards and presenting on a screen, it's best to start with the full-size sheet—it will make no difference when projected on a screen. As shown in Figure 2.4, you can choose a preset page size or type in a custom one.

BIG PICTURE

The first decision to make is how you'd like to present your project: projected presentations vs. monitor vs. e-mail vs. physical boards. Once you've decided that, you can choose page size and orientation. If you change your mind about page proportion after laying out your slide, PowerPoint will change the proportion of your inserted images, text boxes, and charts. In general, PowerPoint is ideal when there is a variety of objects you need to combine: images, charts, sounds, movies—all will fit happily together in a slide show.

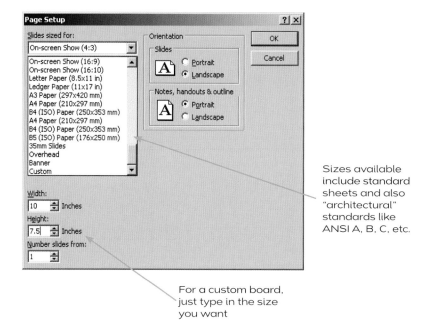

Figure 2.4 *PowerPoint Page Setup for a printed landscape board*

Sizes available include standard sheets and also "architectural" standards like ANSI A, B, C, etc.

For a custom board, just type in the size you want

The biggest problems occur with images and backgrounds. Pictures can usually be dragged from the Internet directly into a PowerPoint slide, but lower resolutions are most common. Resist the temptation to make the image much larger on your board—it will just look more pixilated. Dark, swirly backgrounds look great on your monitor and when using a projector, but will generally turn your paper into a sopping mess of ink.

Organizing Internet Research

There's nothing better than surfing the Internet for inspirational images, articles, and related information at the start of a project, so call up your favorite search engine and let your mind wander. Often there are projects with a similar program, size, or location to the one you're working on, or a magazine or newspaper article related to the building or program. This related information can give insight and depth to your understanding of the project, and make for a richer, more meaningful design. It's a good idea to keep track of all those sites, even if you don't end up with any usable information or images. As with all electronic work, organization is critical to finding what you need when you need it, and surfing for pictures is no different. In both Internet Explorer and Firefox, **CTRL+D** adds a bookmark. Use bookmarks to save interesting pages, and, if you've got millions, use folders to organize them.

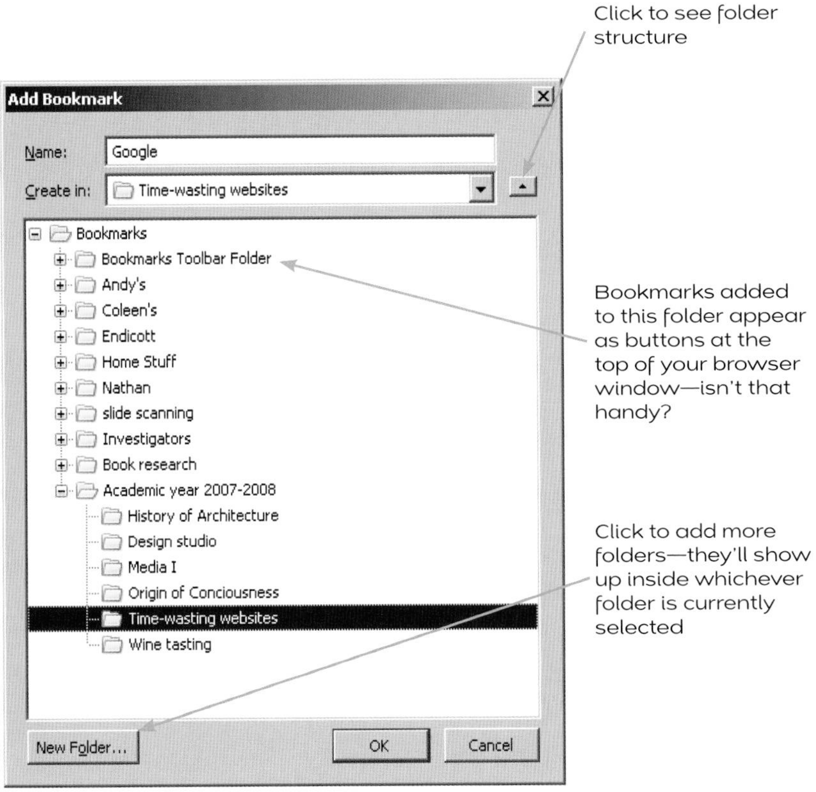

Figure 2.5 *Finding a place for the new bookmark*

Click to see folder structure

Bookmarks added to this folder appear as buttons at the top of your browser window—isn't that handy?

Click to add more folders—they'll show up inside whichever folder is currently selected

To give some order to the hundreds you've already collected, you can create a directory structure to house everything (Figure 2.5). Choose **Bookmarks>Organize Bookmarks...** Once again, it's a good idea to use a folder structure similar to the one you're using to organize your files on your hard drive. Right-click on the list and choose **Sort by name** to alphabetize a given folder. Choose **File>Export...** to save to an independent file, which can be shared, backed up, and imported into another browser. This extra bit of organization will make it easier to find stuff later on, and hopefully make the backup process more automatic.

Collecting Images

We all prefer to do our research online, typing random thoughts into search engines to see what pictures or Web sites come up. This gives us plenty of results, but they are usually way too small for a printed board. Most search engines have preferences to filter for only the largest file sizes. Choose **Large images** from the drop-down list at the top of the page to sort the search results by pixel dimension (Figure 2.6).

UNDER THE HOOD

Many browsers have useful plug-ins for storing bookmarks. Firefox has Xmarks, which is free. Load it and register, and it will synchronize the bookmarks on your computer. Now you can go to another computer, log in to Xmarks, and load all those bookmarks in an instant.

Figure 2.6 *Advanced image search options using Google*

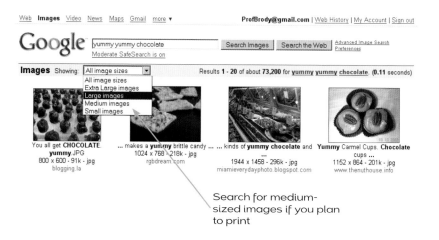

Search for medium-sized images if you plan to print

*That didn't work, did it? Sometimes images refuse to be dragged around. You can always try to right-click on the image in your Internet browser and choose **Copy Image** from the context-sensitive menu. Then, in your PowerPoint file, type **CTRL+V** to paste in the image. If that doesn't work, right-click on the image, choose **Save Image As...** from the context-sensitive menu, and save the image in your project folder.*

Because we may want to print this board, you'll want to choose a large image size to avoid **pixilation**. Once you've found an image you'd like to save, click through until you've found the biggest size possible. Sometimes the image will be so big that your browser won't display all of it, or display a little icon indicating it can be enlarged. Click and drag the image onto your PowerPoint slide to add it to the presentation.

If you plan to collect many images, this would be a good time to create a new subfolder to house them all. From the Save As dialog box, there's a button to create a new folder.

Layout is sharper when objects are consistently aligned with each other and the sheet

Figure 2.7 *Grids and Guides menu*

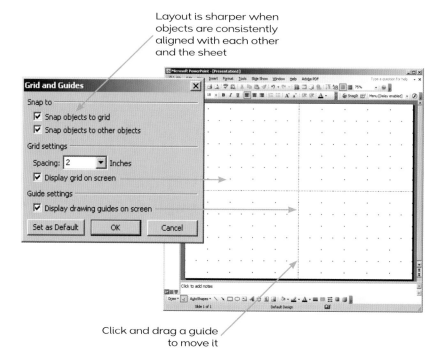

Click and drag a guide to move it

To help align your inspirational images, PowerPoint can display a graph of evenly spaced dots to help you graphically organize and align different objects. Right-click on your layout and choose **Grids and Guides** from the context-sensitive menu.

As shown in Figure 2.7, you can set grid spacing and whether or not objects snap to it. The grid can be distracting, but layouts with multiple elements require that you snap objects to the grid and to each other. The Guide Lines make it easier to center images and other elements vertically and horizontally, which is handy if you have just a few things you need to assemble. We'll do more precise formatting in the next chapter. All of your drawings and presentations will look better when everything is neat and orderly.

A PowerPoint file can be used as a scrapbook of sorts, to collect images, Web sites, text, and other documentation. Give yourself a decent page size, like 11×17, so that you won't have to shrink images to fit.

The Visual Concepts Board

Now that you have the image placed on your board, you can just click and drag it to move it around. Clicking once on the image reveals a series of **Grips**—special handles that allow rapid resizing and rotation (Figure 2.8).

The picture-editing tab pops up when you select the image and allows all sorts of basic editing tasks. Images can also be cropped and given a border using the options on the Picture tab that shows up when you select the image. As shown in Figure 2.9, there are many options for in-place picture modifications and styling.

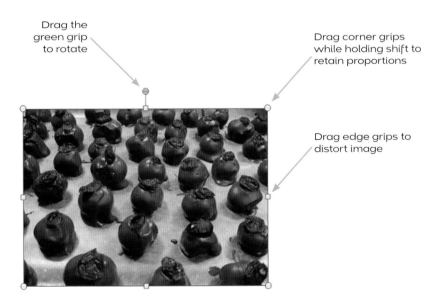

Drag the green grip to rotate

Drag corner grips while holding shift to retain proportions

Drag edge grips to distort image

Figure 2.8 *Image with active grips*

Figure 2.9 *The Picture editing tab*

Basic image adjustments, including the essential Reset tool

Ready-made styles composed of different borders, drop shadows, and other goodies

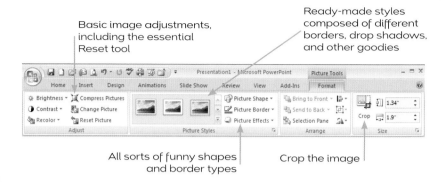

All sorts of funny shapes and border types

Crop the image

LOOK OUT!

If your slide is set up to print a big sheet, but you are using low-resolution images from the Internet, they will appear small in your layout. Don't resize them, as they will just become pixilated when you print, even if they look fine on the screen. If you must have a larger version of a small image, fast-forward to Chapter 4, "Complex Studies with Photoshop Elements," for a possible solution—upsampling.

Adjust brightness and contrast to achieve a washout effect, which is particularly good for background images on the visual concepts board. Other tools are great for oddly shaped borders and simple recoloration. The **Set Transparent Color** tool (under the Recolor grouping) is also handy for eliminating the white background around many images.

Finally, never use copyrighted material without permission, and always indicate when images procured in this way are not your own. This is

Figure 2.10 *Collected, formatted, and arranged images for the ideas board (Courtesy Ann Loh)*

particularly important for materials from print-based journals and periodicals, where you'll need the date and volume number. This board can help set the tone for a project, as shown in Figure 2.10.

The Partí Board

A partí board is meant to be a verbal metaphor for your project. It can be a single word or a mission statement. For this type of board, there may not be more than one or two images, and the words become more important. Thus, the design of the text itself becomes more important to creating a powerful graphic impact. Use the Text Boxes that come with each slide to place the text describing your big idea. To change its appearance, double-click on its edge to bring up the Drawing Tools tab. Here you'll find the usual formatting options, as well as fill color and border options.

INSERTING WORD ART

Word art can be frivolous, or used judiciously in a few cases. It's fun, but it can look cheesy if not done with care and taste. Since this board is all about words, though, sometimes a little extra formatting can achieve the strong impact you may be looking for. See Figure 2.11 for standard style options.

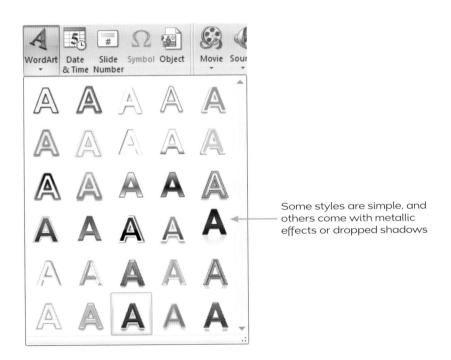

Figure 2.11 *The WordArt dialog box*

Some styles are simple, and others come with metallic effects or dropped shadows

1. Click on the **Insert** tab.
2. Click on the **WordArt** button.
3. Click on the style you'd like.
4. Type out the text in the text box created.
5. Click outside the box to finish.
6. Click inside the box again to edit.
7. Click and drag the dashed bounding box to move.

Nicely formatted text on a simple background can comprise a high-impact metaphors board, but only if clutter (in the form of extra images and unnecessary words) is kept to a minimum.

Program Summary Board

Even in school, an architectural program can contain a long list of spaces, recommended areas, and descriptions of needed equipment, adjacencies, and other considerations. These are easiest to organize in the spreadsheet program Microsoft Excel. As shown in Figure 2.12, the Excel interface contains an ever-expandable grid of cells, each capable of containing either

Figure 2.12 *The Excel interface*

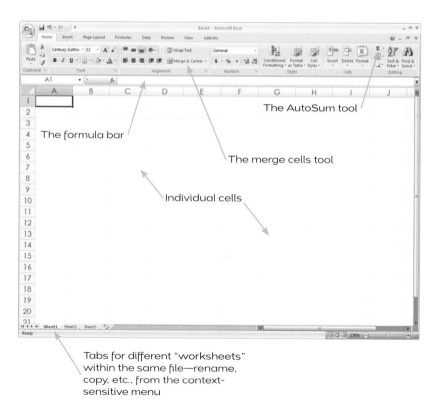

The AutoSum tool

The merge cells tool

The formula bar

Individual cells

Tabs for different "worksheets" within the same file—rename, copy, etc., from the context-sensitive menu

text or numbers. It's particularly handy for adding up numbers, applying a formula, or formatting charts or diagrams. This is the magic tool that your instructors use to make the programmed space perfectly match the available gross floor area, or that your cost estimator uses to show you why your project is 40 percent over budget.

Click inside a cell and begin typing—the words or numbers will show up both in the cell and on the formula bar at the top of the work area. Keep an eye on that formula bar, as things like instructions to add up a column of numbers or multiply different cells are hidden up there—the main grid only displays the results. Font and text size can be set cell by cell, or by clicking and dragging across a whole region. Then choose from the formatting toolbar at the top of the window. And be sure to save the document in a folder with all of your other predesign work, using an easy-to-understand name like *Chocolate Program.*

One of the things Excel excels at is doing math, and it will perform calculations based on the values in cells, updating as you monkey around with the values. So, as you study a building program, you might decide that one space or another needs a different amount of area. Change those individual numbers and Excel will update both the sum and any other formula that uses them, such as percentage values for circulation. To add up a column of numbers, click in the cell where you'd like the number to appear and click on the **AutoSum** button. Excel will display a region that it plans to add up—which you can change by clicking and dragging the little black grips (Figure 2.13).

Since we'll be doing bubble diagrams next, we can have Excel calculate the radius of the circle we'll need for each programmed space. The area of a circle equals *pi* times the square of the radius. Well, we already know the area, so solving backward gives us the formula: radius = $\sqrt{(\text{area}/\text{pi})}$.

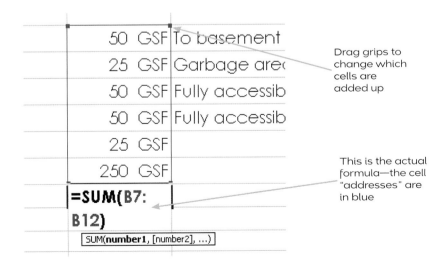

Figure 2.13 *Adding up a column of numbers using AutoSum*

Drag grips to change which cells are added up

This is the actual formula—the cell "addresses" are in blue

We can put this into Excel, using a reference to the cell with the programmed area in it, so that the radius will update if the area changes. The formula can then be copied, so that the same calculation is applied to each programmed space.

CREATING A FORMULA IN EXCEL

1. Click in the cell next to the first item area.
2. Type **=SQRT(** (yes, exactly as written—it stands for square root).
3. Click in the cell with the area in it—you'll see the address (the column letter followed by the row number) show up in the formula bar.
4. Type **/3.14) [ENTER]** to complete the formula, and Excel will calculate the radius to about ten decimal places (Figure 2.14).
5. Click on the cell with the radius again.
6. Choose **Format>Cells...** from the drop-down menu (or type **CTRL+1**).

Figure 2.14 *The formula bar with the finished formula*

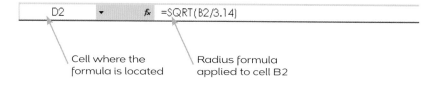

Figure 2.15 *Format Cells dialog box*

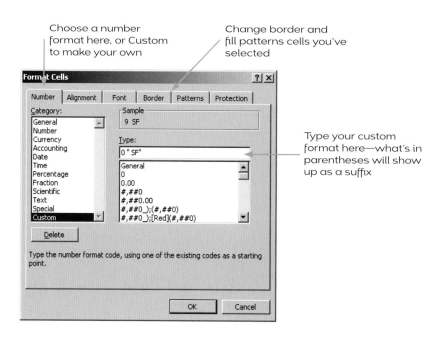

7. As shown in Figure 2.15, on the Number tab, choose the Custom category at the very bottom.

8. Type **0 "SF"** to have the cell contents rounded to the nearest integer (or 0.0 if you want a more precise number) followed by SF. Click **OK**.

9. Click on the cell with the formula.

10. Click and drag on the tiny black box that shows up in the lower-right corner of the cell (it's another form of grip) to copy the formula down as far as you drag.

11. Select all the cells with the formulas in them.

12. Right-click on them and choose **Format Cells…** from the context-sensitive menu.

13. Make the cells **Bold** and a larger font size and click **OK**.

14. Select the cells with the room names and areas.

15. Click on the **Insert** tab.

16. Choose a 3D pie chart, as shown in Figure 2.16 (or whatever type of chart floats your boat, really).

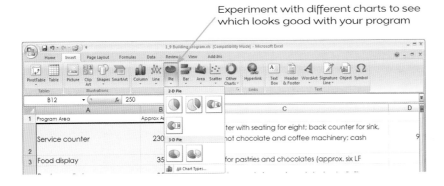

Experiment with different charts to see which looks good with your program

Figure 2.16 *Chart format options*

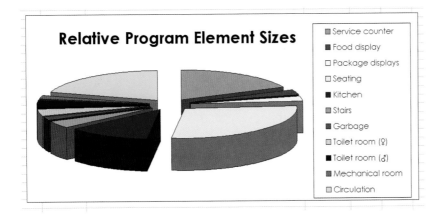

Figure 2.17 *The inserted chart*

17. The chart becomes an object in the current workbook.
18. Click and drag the chart and key to move them around.
19. Drag individual slices to move around.
20. As with most other objects, there are plenty of editing options in the context-sensitive menu.

You can copy this chart into your slide in PowerPoint to give a more graphically interesting representation of the space-planning requirements (Figure 2.17). You can also tweak the pie chart to have different labels or titles, or choose a different style altogether—have fun. This should get you that A you were hoping for.

Building Codes

Here you'll be dealing with both graphic and text information. Most local and state building codes are available online, so once again we'll be turning to the Internet.

It's most valuable to set up a list of the chapters you think will be relevant. It's also handy to retain the original link so you can quickly return to it as questions and issues arise during the design process. In Massachusetts, where this project is located, the building code is online (www.mass.gov), which makes our jobs a little easier. First go to the index page that

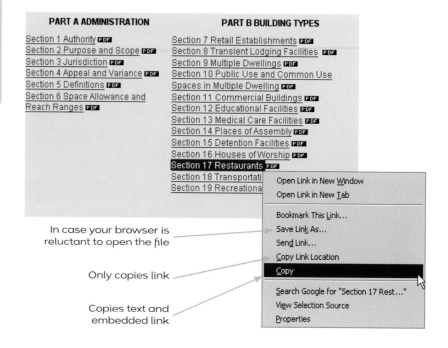

Figure 2.18 *Copying a hyperlink*

Figure 2.19 *Inserting in a hyperlink*

Bookmarks can be placed inside a
long document for quick navigation

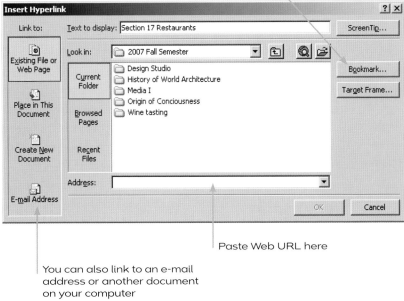

Paste Web URL here

You can also link to an e-mail
address or another document
on your computer

lists and links to all the chapters, which is what we want to copy. With any hyperlink, you can often select both the text and the link at the same time in the Web page. Copy the link, as shown in Figure 2.18, and paste them into your presentation. Be sure to check the link to see if it still works.

As with many things in the computer world, it doesn't always work using the first technique. You can also highlight the URL in your browser and copy and paste it into your file. To be a little fancy, select a piece of text in your document first. Then type **CTRL+K** to bring up the **Insert Hyperlink** dialog box (Figure 2.19).

Type **CTRL+V** to paste in the link. You can also link to "bookmarks" within your own presentation, or to other files somewhere on your computer or a network. You should end up with a list of chapters, and perhaps some diagrams. These might be illustrations of how a compartmentalized egress system works, the meaning of a dead-end corridor, or the required separation of exits.

UNDER THE HOOD

Links embedded in PowerPoint slides will only work in presentation mode. Otherwise, you'll have to hold down **CTRL** *while clicking them to see the Web site.*

Accessibility Regulations

Accessibility regulations often have a huge impact on interior planning and layout. ADA guide books usually have very descriptive diagrams that you can use to present the main concept. In Massachusetts, accessibility regulations are built into state regulations and are also available online. The same process applies here as with the previous example: Find the relevant parts of whichever regulations are in effect, and reference the appropriate chapters.

Many of these regulations will not be needed until you actually start laying out the spaces and their content. But there are some restrictions that should be considered from the earliest planning stage. Nothing beats an image to describe the clearances around a service counter or heights of tables. If the document is a PDF, which is most common, you can copy and paste pertinent diagrams and text into a single summary document, or create a board for presentation. To copy a selected region to the clipboard, use the **Tools>Select & Zoom>Snapshot Tool** in Acrobat Reader. Click and drag around whichever part of the document you'd like to copy and the selection is placed on the clipboard. Then use **CTRL+V** to paste into your file.

Give the image a border, and adjust coloration if needed. Do you like the way a particular image is formatted? Hold down **SHIFT** and click on each picture, one by one, or draw a window around them all to select. Then choose **Format** tab—any border style you apply will affect all selected images. As with any published and copyrighted source, you'll need to provide the proper citation on your board.

Project-Specific Constraints

Most design projects are meant to be built eventually, and more often than not, for other humans. Thus, there are likely to be plenty of constraints relating to equipment and how it's used. And while this doesn't always have a big impact on space planning, for some projects (like a bowling alley), solving equipment considerations constitutes most of the design problem. The process is similar for research on any special requirements or constraints you might need to factor in. The reference book *Interior Graphic Standards* (Kruse & McGowan, 2003) often has guidelines for different project types, and that information is great to have before starting design. In our case, there is some specialized equipment that we need to be aware of for making chocolate. As with many things, the best place to find documentation is online. Study the chocolate-making process and what sort of equipment is needed.

In our case, we find that the two pieces of equipment that will cause the most trouble are the tempering machine and the enrobing machine. These devices are not huge, but they do need clearances, and there needs to be a very heavy cooling table at the end of the enrobing machine to cool the candy. Also, we need the pictures of equipment in order to be able to draw them. Collect images from the Internet as before. See the **Online Resources** for links to chocolate-related Web sites.

Precedent Studies

Unless you're working on a new moon base station, there are probably some examples of the project type already designed and built. Precedent studies give designers an opportunity to learn from these past efforts, to serve as either positive examples of good solutions or as a warning of the pitfalls ahead.

Precedent studies can be elaborate or simple, depending on how close in size, scope, or program the precedent is to the one you're working on. If it's just a source of inspiration for concept or materials, some salient images and materials swatches will do. But if you're looking in detail at the space planning, some analytical diagrams are handy for understanding the project. A circulation diagram of the plan is a good place to start.

DRAWING A CIRCULATION DIAGRAM

1. Insert the plan (from a scan, the Internet, a PDF file, or other source).
2. Double-click on the image to bring up the picture formatting tab.
3. Click on the **Crop** tool.
4. Click and drag on the black bars to crop away unwanted parts of the image (Figure 2.20).
5. Click **Insert>Shapes**.

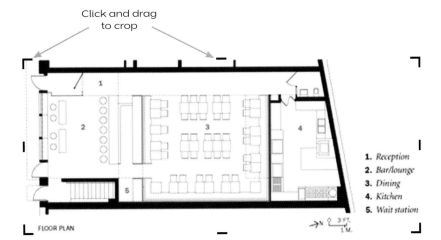

Click and drag to crop

1. Reception
2. Bar/lounge
3. Dining
4. Kitchen
5. Wait station

FLOOR PLAN

Figure 2.20 *Cropping tools*

Figure 2.21 *Shape formatting options*

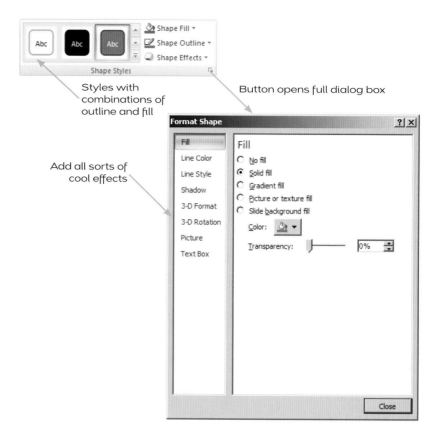

Styles with combinations of outline and fill

Button opens full dialog box

Add all sorts of cool effects

6. Select a rectangle.
7. Click and drag to draw a box.
8. Double-click on the box to bring up the format drawing tools tab (Figure 2.21).
9. Change the color, and remove the outer line if you'd like.
10. Drag the transparency slider until the plan is visible.
11. Add boxes with different colors for vertical circulation.
12. Add arrows for egress doors or other features.
13. Place labels with text boxes.

Figure 2.22 *The finished diagram*

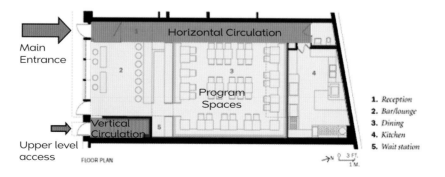

14. Type **CTRL+A** to select all the elements drawn.
15. Right-click on the objects and choose **Grouping>Group** from the context-sensitive menu.

In just a few minutes, this technique can produce an easy-to-read diagram, as show in Figure 2.22. Program distribution diagrams can be made the same way, and should include a key to the different spaces.

Daylighting Diagram

A simple daylighting diagram can be made in the same fashion, but this time using gradients to indicate how light levels drop off as you get farther from the windows. Draw a rectangle or other shapes for a given space. Right-click on the edge of the rectangle and choose **Format Picture** from the context-sensitive menu. Then, under **Fill Color**, choose **Fill Effects** (Figure 2.23).

This brings up another dialog where you can apply a gradient to abstractly represent daylighting. This type of diagram is great for a quick plan or section study, and gives a simplified understanding of the basic design principles at work in a given precedent (Figure 2.24).

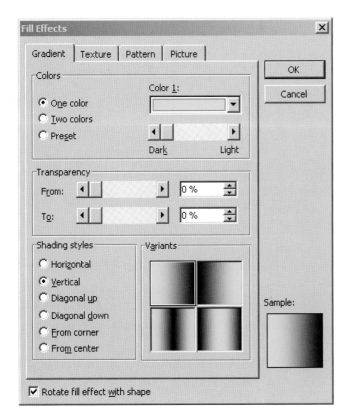

Figure 2.23 *Accessing the* **Fill Effects** *menu*

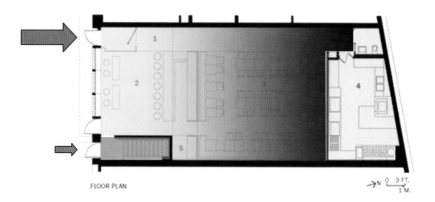

Figure 2.24 *The finished daylighting diagram*

FLOOR PLAN

There are other diagram types that can be used to study different aspects of a design. Geometry and proportional studies are very revealing about the characteristics of a space. HVAC, electrical distribution, and structural diagrams all study how a particular project functions. Specific design elements, such as flooring transitions or exit sign locations, can be diagrammed to study certain aspects of a design.

All of these boards—Ideas, Concepts, Codes, and so forth—need to be strung together to make a solid research presentation.

Designing the Presentation

So now you know technically how to assemble a variety of image and information types. Deciding how the presentation will look has a big impact on the impression your viewers will get of your project. There are a few different kinds of presentations: electronically presented, physically presented, or a stand-alone. For each, you'll need to consider the design of each board and of the overall presentation sequence. There are also some techniques to engage your viewers and hopefully sustain their interest.

For individual slides, you should ask yourself a few questions: Are they well composed? Is there a good balance between graphics and text? Composition is a design preference, of course, but a board can seem crowded, or may lack focus. There are different graphic organization schemes that you can use: Some divide the board into thirds, use axial or bilateral symmetry, or emphasize diagonal relationships between elements. You'll also want to apply consistent border styles to images, text boxes, charts, and other features. Space images evenly from each other and from the edge of the sheet, or use some other alignment scheme (a grid is recommended).

Avoid too many text animations and boldly colored backgrounds—especially if you plan to print. Consistency makes a presentation easy to digest and easy to remember later—which could mean scoring points in an evaluation or winning an account from a client.

You'll want to evaluate if the presentation is interesting and of an appropriate length. Too much text puts your audience to sleep. Treat your slides as brief outlines of what you plan to say, and while you are in front of an audience, be sure that you point to parts of plans or other drawings with a pointing device or the cursor. Finally, does the last slide sum up your ideas for the project? Does it stimulate questions? Good images to leave up are your visual concepts board (just make a copy of the slide and drag it to the end), a concept sketch, or a model.

Making the Presentation

It's not only what you say that matters, but how you say it. That is why it's very important to rehearse—nothing is more painful than to listen to someone stumbling to describe their ideas or rambling on without a clear point. For a design presentation, you've got 15–20 minutes before your audience will start checking their e-mail or composing laundry lists, so you'll need to boil things down quickly and clearly. Powerful, simple images of your designs communicate design intention better than many small, complex images that each need to be explained in great depth (or need a magnifying glass to see). Help yourself by keeping words on your slides to an absolute minimum. That keeps you from reading off the screen, and keeps your audience focused on your speaking.

Another pitfall is talking to the screen—look forward and make eye contact with your audience as much as possible. If they are looking interested and nodding in agreement, you're probably getting your ideas across. If they are scratching their heads and have furrowed brows, you might want to take a break from the script to allow questions. It's fine to turn on the lights or skip over some content if people are falling asleep. Finally, be enthusiastic to hear comments on your projects—brutal public whippings in the design critique are a relic of the twentieth-century architectural education that we're better off without.

Handouts

Printing handouts is sometimes good for note taking and for any mostly verbal subject. You can also print multiple slides to a PDF, which is a

Figure 2.25 *Printing handouts*

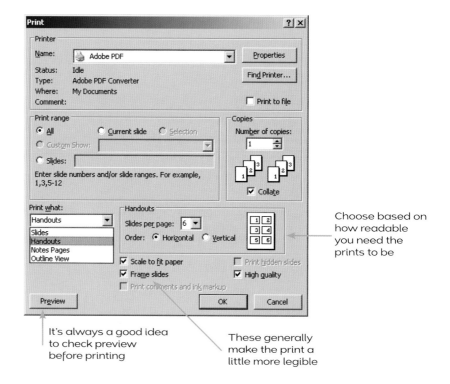

Choose based on how readable you need the prints to be

It's always a good idea to check preview before printing

These generally make the print a little more legible

quick way to get a reduced copy of your presentation onto one sheet. Type **CTRL+P** to call up the print menu (Figure 2.25).

You'll have to decide how many slides to include on a sheet—three leaves plenty of space for notes, but six or even nine can be fine when you have very little on each individual slide. For whole boards, choose Slides instead of Handouts from the **Print What:** drop-down list. Choose to print all or just a range of slides. You can also add a frame around each slide, which is nice when you don't have a strong background. Scaling to fit paper is also helpful when printing single boards—make sure you know how close your printer can print to the borders. Handouts are valuable during your presentation if there's going to be a large group.

For some instructors (and always in a professional setting), you'll have a job book with all the documentation, research, and background materials for a project. Handouts of all these boards, along with the research on equipment and other elements of the project, would normally be included.

Online Resources

- *Chocolate bookmarks.html*, which is all the exported bookmarks from my favorite browser.

- The research project used in the text, Figure *2_10 ideas board example.tif.*
- *Keyboard shortcuts.docx*, a list of MS Office keyboard shortcuts.

Term Project Assignments

- Research and collect images, words, Web sites, and so forth, for the following predesign boards:
  - ▼ Visual Concepts Board
  - ▼ Partí Board
  - ▼ Program Analysis Board
  - ▼ Building Codes Board
  - ▼ Accessibility Regulations Board
  - ▼ Project Constraints Board
  - ▼ Precedent study
    - Images
    - Concept(s)
    - Program distribution diagram
    - Circulation diagram
    - Daylighting diagram

Exercises and Further Study

- Collect image files for the partí of a recent project.
- Field visit to a chocolatière or chocolate café.
- Create a program chart in Excel for another project.
- Create a general code analysis for another project.
- Set up Excel to calculate the *diameter* of bubbles needed for programmed area.
- Export your Internet favorites to a file for easy backup, or sign up for an online synchronization service.
- Back up all your files to removable media.

3

Bubble Diagrams and Presentation Design

BIG PICTURE

A good presentation has certain basic characteristics, regardless of how it's presented: Carefully composed individual slides (or boards), consistent graphic impact from slide to slide (or board to board), even pacing (so everyone can follow how the project developed), and a final summary slide (or board) to stimulate discussion.

LEARNING GOALS

- Build skills to create simple, effective diagrams in PowerPoint
- Understand conversion to different electronic file formats
- Add multimedia content to presentations

Bubble diagrams can be developed quickly and simply using drawing features within PowerPoint. You can set automatic timings, or record them (and a narration) during a rehearsal. Animations and sound clips can be inserted and set to play automatically. Slide design and layout can be controlled globally using the Master Slide.

Bubble Diagrams

Each slide can be configured with a preset layout, and for a bubble diagram, all we really need is a banner title. Each space in the architectural program needs a bubble to represent it. In PowerPoint, circles are not drawn to scale easily, so the diagram will have to be roughly proportional. Lines can be drawn to express different relationships between programmatic elements, and a legend made up to represent things like direct connection between spaces, separation, or alignment. There are several graphic effects that can be applied, such as drop shadow, to give the objects some depth and make the diagram more interesting.

1. Open a new PowerPoint presentation.
2. Right-click on the slide and choose **Slide Layout**.
3. Click on the layout with just the title only, to give us plenty of area for drawing (Figure 3.1).
4. Click **Insert>Shapes**.
5. Select an **Oval**, then click and drag to draw an oval.
6. Hold down **SHIFT** to lock the proportions into a circle.
7. Double-click on the circle to display the Format Object dialog box (Figure 3.2).
8. Apply a standard style to the shape.
9. For fancier effects, right-click on the bubble and choose **Format Shape** (Figure 3.3). You can change all sorts of graphic characteristics here.
10. On the **Insert** tab, click on the **Text Box** button.
11. Draw the text box.
12. Type in "Seating."
13. Select the text box. Hold down **SHIFT** and click on the circle to select it, too.
14. Right-click on the selection and choose **Grouping>Group**.
15. Click and drag on the group while holding down **CTRL** to make a copy.
16. Right-click on the new bubble and ungroup it.
17. Double-click on the new bubble to edit it.
18. Change the color.

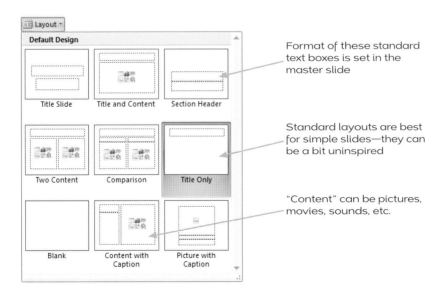

Format of these standard text boxes is set in the master slide

Standard layouts are best for simple slides—they can be a bit uninspired

"Content" can be pictures, movies, sounds, etc.

Figure 3.1 *PowerPoint slide basic layout options*

Figure 3.2 *The **Format Shape** dialog box for a bubble*

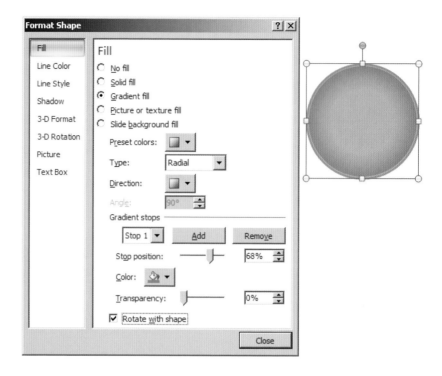

Figure 3.3 *The **Format Shape** dialog box for a line*

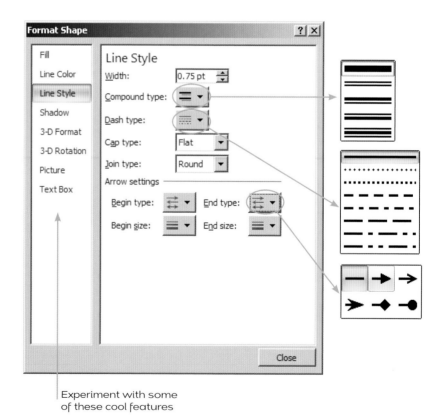

Experiment with some of these cool features

19. Double-click on the new text box and change the label on the circle.
20. Add a star shape for the sun location and label it *South*.
21. Draw a new line shape.
22. Right-click on the line and choose **Format Shape** (this has more options than the main Drawing tab).
23. Change the line weight and color to make it a heavy line, representing separation.
24. Continue to add bubbles and lines—format as needed to indicate different relationships (Figure 3.4).

This may not be the most precise method for creating a bubble diagram, but it beats cutting circles out of colored paper. There are additional features and effects you can add, such as 3D effects, drop shadows, ready-made color schemes, and animated graphics. Explore in the menus, or right-click on objects to see what options are in their **Properties**.

It's also possible to add a legend if needed, and add shaded areas underneath semi-opaque objects. To change the layering, right-click on an object and choose an option from the **Order** subset shown in the context-sensitive menu.

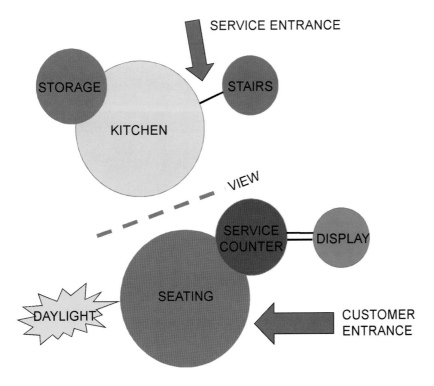

Figure 3.4 *The finished diagram*

Presentation Composition

Now that everything has been assembled, it's time to compose the whole presentation. There are many standard slide designs available in Power-Point, or you can customize using the Master Slide. Extras like music, movies, and narration can be added easily. You can even set up the presentation to advance automatically, with effects (like a fade in or fade out) and varying transition times between each slide.

First you'll want to make it easy to move around your presentation. Switching to Slide Sorter view allows you to move around one or more slides, and also makes it easy to paste in slides from another presentation (Figure 3.5).

Double-click on a slide to view it in the Normal view. There are also viewing modes that help if you plan to create handouts or notes for yourself. Normal view shows icons for slides in a stack on the left, and one slide enlarged. The Slide Sorter shows icons for all slides, which is great for organizing the whole presentation. You can also preview how a slide will look during a presentation.

Figure 3.5 *Formatting sidebar menus*

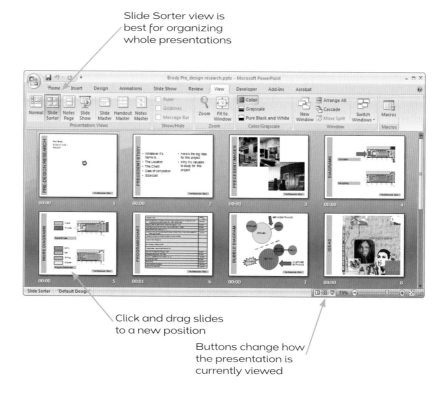

Slide Sorter view is best for organizing whole presentations

Click and drag slides to a new position

Buttons change how the presentation is currently viewed

Graphic Layout

PowerPoint has some ready-made styles that you can use to quickly give your presentation more interest. On the **Design** tab, find **Themes** and click on the lower down arrow to pop out your options. Each theme combines background graphics, font settings, and color schemes that are relatively well composed, if a bit corporate-looking. Just click on one to change all slides (or hover over a style to see a preview of it). Being designers, we often want to customize the presentation background. For that you'll need to make changes to the Master Slide. Click **View> Slide Master** and edit away (Figure 3.6).

You'll see a standard slide layout, with text boxes for the headings, footer elements, and main body text in outline format. Most of the slide layouts use these pieces in different arrangements. You can change colors, fonts, background color, and transition effects globally here. You

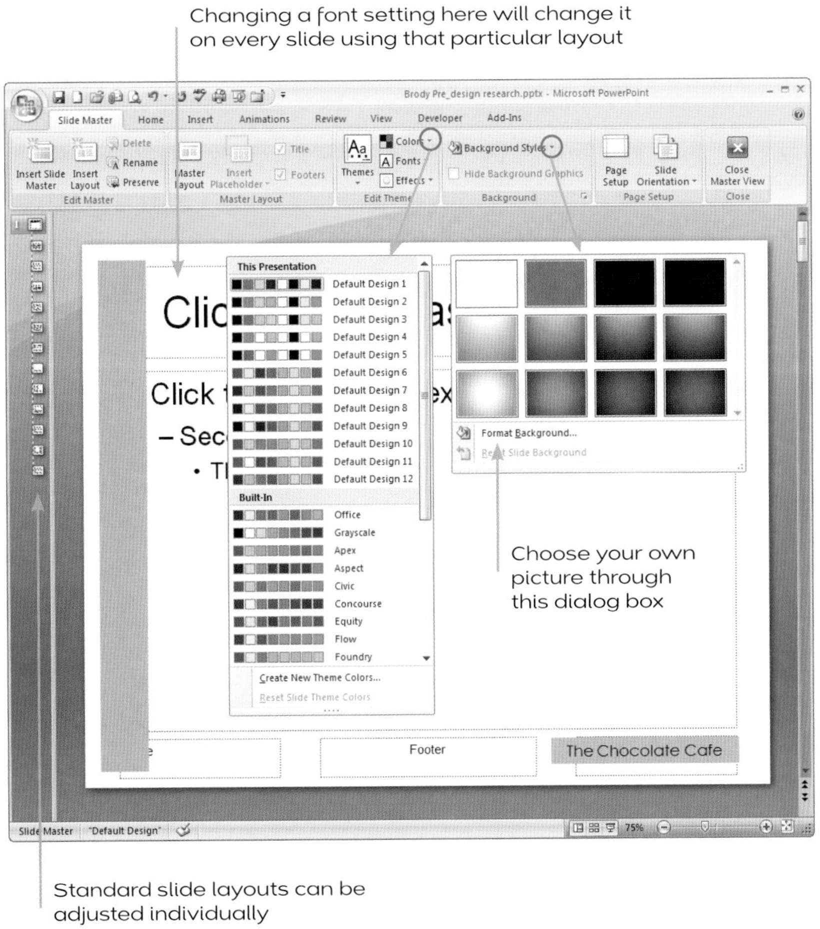

Changing a font setting here will change it on every slide using that particular layout

Choose your own picture through this dialog box

Standard slide layouts can be adjusted individually

Figure 3.6 *Formatting the Master Slide*

can also insert image files as a background, but be sure to wash it out so that text and other elements are not eclipsed or obscured.

Adding Other Content

All sorts of peculiar things can be copied and pasted into a PowerPoint slide. The simplest things are elements of other MS Office documents, like the program chart. Open the Excel document and click and drag over the cells you'd like to copy. Type **CTRL+C** to copy, and, in the Power-Point slide, type **CTRL+V** to paste the cells.

Your chart will retain the formatting from Excel, so set it up the way you like there first. It can be edited from within Word by clicking on a cell or cells, but changes will not be reflected in the original Excel document. Objects from many other programs can be copied and pasted into your presentation, too, but many will not remain operable like the chart. Click on the **Insert** tab to get inspiration for various types of insertable content.

Be forewarned that many "objects" will display unpredictably. An example is content from AutoCAD, which can be pasted in but will reopen in the original program if you double-click on it.

INSERTING A MOVIE FILE

An easy file type to add is an animation, although it has a few more steps. Some of the basic slide layouts are configured for different media, so that's an easy way to start. We can insert our daylighting study, and then a music clip to run during the whole show.

1. Type **CTRL+M** to make a new slide.
2. Right-click on the slide and choose **Layout>Title and Content** to format the slide to accept various media.

Figure 3.7 *Insertable media content icons and what they indicate*

3. Click on the little film reel to open the **Insert Media Clip** dialog box (Figure 3.7).
4. Browse to find your animation file and click **OK.**
5. When prompted for how you want the movie to behave in your slide show, choose either **Automatically** or **When Clicked.**
6. Return to the first slide in your show.
7. Click on the **Insert** tab.
8. Click on the **Music File** button, and browse to find a song you'd like to play during your show.
9. Click on the **Animation** tab.
10. Select the music clip icon and choose the **Custom Animation** tool.
11. To play during the whole slide show, choose **With Previous** from the drop-down menu.
12. Repeat the custom animation settings for the movie clip as well, so the music doesn't cut out.

You can also give the movie window graphic effects such as a border or a drop shadow, or make it play full screen. In fact, you can even animate objects on screen like circles and lines. Select them and click on the custom animation button. As you can see from Figure 3.8, there are a large number of possible animations. Don't go overboard here, as too many effects can be distracting.

You can draw an arc for the sun image to follow, and put it next to your floor plan. Not particularly fancy, but much faster than exporting a movie file. Animation schemes more complex than this, however, are best accomplished with movie-editing software (Figure 3.9).

Click the **Options** button, and be sure to **Include True Type fonts,** just in case. Click **OK,** then save the presentation to a folder.

LOOK OUT!

*So you've copied your studio project onto a USB drive to make a final presentation, and when the movie slide comes up, nothing happens—no animation, no music. This is because large media files (as well as weird fonts) remain on your computer. To make sure you get everything in your project, choose **Office icon> Publish>Package for CD.** This will create a folder (either on your computer or a CD) with all animations, music, narration, and fonts used in your presentation. You can even include a PowerPoint viewer, for people who don't have Power-Point on their computer (Figure 3.9).*

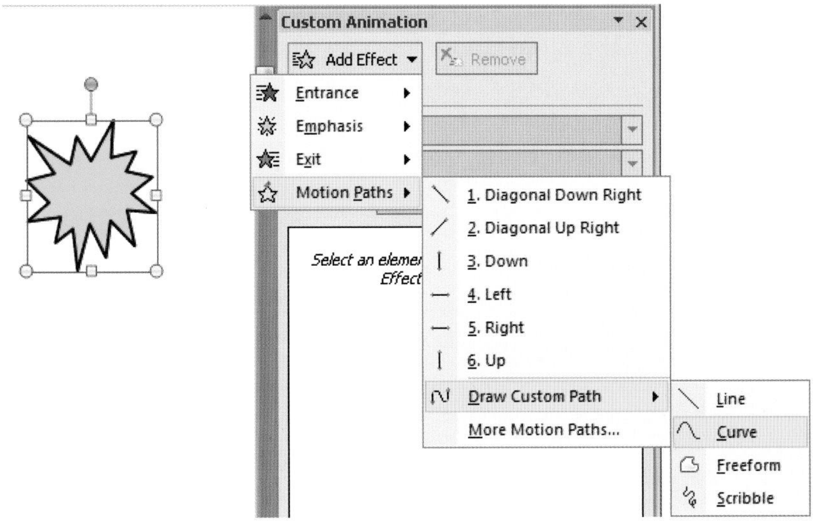

Figure 3.8 *Adding an effect to an object*

Only include the viewer if you're
not sure the computer you're
sending to has PowerPoint

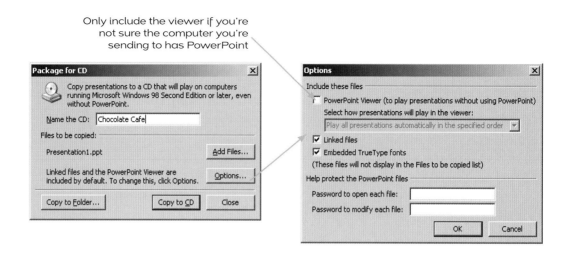

Figure 3.9 *Package*
for CD options

Automated Shows

Every once in a while, you run across someone who gets a tiny bit nervous giving a presentation. Setting up automatic timings forces you to practice your presentation and thus be more familiar with what you plan to say. One way to avoid getting flustered is to set your show up to run automatically. You can set PowerPoint to record the timings of your slide show as you practice a run-through. First switch to the **Slide Show** tab (Figure 3.10).

It's best to talk through your presentation out loud, as this simulates exactly how long you're likely to take. Of course, you could also just record the whole narration. That way you wouldn't have to talk at all, but just play the show and hide behind the podium. Rather than delete forever slides that are still rough drafts at the time of the presentation, hide slides that don't work smoothly in the flow of your project. Select the slide and, on the **Slide Show** tab, click **Hide Slide**.

Figure 3.10 *The Slide*
Show tab

Change resolution to maximize
slides for a specific monitor,
projector, or for printing

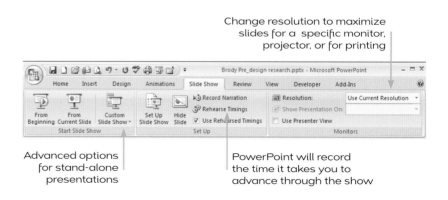

Advanced options
for stand-alone
presentations

PowerPoint will record
the time it takes you to
advance through the show

Online Resources

- *Bubble diagram example.pptx,* from the chapter illustration.
- *Pre_design research presentation.pptx*

Term Project Assignments

- Draw a bubble diagram.
- Assemble your predesign presentation, which includes:
  - ▼ Visual Concepts Board
  - ▼ Partí Board
  - ▼ Program Chart and Bubble Diagram
  - ▼ General Building Codes Board
  - ▼ Accessibility Regulations Board
  - ▼ Project Constraints Board
  - ▼ Precedent Study Board
- Format slide show for screen presentation.
- Change the font globally to your personal favorite.
- Print handouts for your presentation.

Exercises and Further Study

- Draw bubble diagrams in PowerPoint for a current project.
- Create an animation of a sun icon, tracing its path around your plan in PowerPoint.
- Critique your past presentations: Are the individual slides well composed? Is there a good balance between graphics and text? Is the overall presentation interesting and of an appropriate length? Is the last slide a good one for stimulating questions, or does it sum up your ideas for the project?
- Have someone else present your project. Can they understand enough about what you're trying to communicate from just your graphics and small amount of text to figure out what to say?

4

Complex Studies with Photoshop Elements

LEARNING GOALS

- Understand electronic image resolution and dimension
- Develop skills in selecting, editing, and filtering images
- Understand the graphic elements that make up a perspectival image
- Judge effective board composition

Sometimes our own projects or a precedent we may be studying would benefit from a more graphically intensive analysis. This can involve drawing more complex diagrams, similar to those done in Chapter 2. More sophisticated techniques can, in effect, reverse the design process, picking apart a graphic into its constituent parts. For that, we need Photoshop Elements.

In this chapter we'll study a design precedent—the recent renovation of the Yale Museum of Art by Louis I. Kahn. We'll draw both plan diagrams and a perspectival analysis in Photoshop Elements, then compose a presentation board. There are a number of different tasks this handy program can do—when you first start the program, you'll be prompted at the Welcome screen for which of those features you'd like to use. For now, let's just choose **Edit.**

Introduction to Photoshop Elements

Photoshop Elements can be used to draw pieces of different diagrams and to compose the whole presentation board. It offers much greater control of graphic elements than PowerPoint, although it's less flexible about the types of content you can include. Only two-dimensional images can be used by the program, so perspectival views must be composed prior to import. It organizes drawings using layers, which should be familiar to SketchUp and AutoCAD users. Each can contain pictures, parts of pictures, shapes, text, and "adjustments" (for brightness or coloration, for example) to the layers below (Figure 4.1).

The drawing interface of Photoshop Elements is similar to SketchUp and Revit, with a tool area, drop-down menus, a standard set of tools below that, and an **Options** toolbar, which becomes active when you select a tool. There is also a series of palettes on the right side of the screen, to organize the composition and speed up the most common operations.

By default, there are two palettes open—**Layers** and **Artwork and Effects**. Different palettes can be opened or closed from the **Window** drop-down menu, including a tutorial (**How To**) and a sequential list of all commands you've executed in your project (**Undo History**). These can be minimized by clicking the little arrow in the upper right of the palette. Most palettes have a variety of tool buttons, drop-down lists,

MAGIC TRICK

To save space, Photoshop Elements hides similar commands underneath one another in a stack. You'll see a little black triangle in the lower right of a tool that has more than one option hidden underneath. Also, whichever tool you used last will be on top, and will be the one activated by the keyboard shortcut assigned to that tool group.

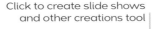

Click to create slide shows and other creations tool

Figure 4.1 *The Photoshop Elements interface*

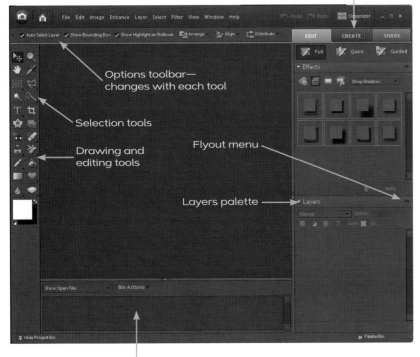

Options toolbar— changes with each tool

Selection tools

Drawing and editing tools

Flyout menu

Layers palette

Photo bin—shows icons of all open files

and sometimes a little **fly-out arrow** indicating more options underneath. Click on the arrow for more advanced options, such as complex ways to manipulate and combine layers.

Photoshop Elements layers are opaque or semi-transparent, and so will mask the layers below them in the list of layers. This is quite different from SketchUp and AutoCAD, where a layer is either on or off. Putting drawing elements on different layers allows very precise control, since any editing command or operation applies only to the current layer (which is highlighted in blue in the palette). New adjustment layers can be created that control properties like brightness, contrast, and hue, and apply only to the layer below them in the list. Special clipping masks can be used to selectively reveal parts of a layer below.

Upping the Resolution

We're going to make a 24 × 36 board with a series of diagrams and perspectival analysis drawings on it, so we'll need images that are at least 5 to 6 inches wide. Sometimes the best image you can come by is relatively low resolution, however, which means it'll be tiny on the board. To complicate matters, there's a subtle difference between image size and resolution, which we'll touch on more in Chapter 15. For now, it will suffice to know that electronic documents are measured in the number of pixels per inch (PPI) they contain, which is slightly different from the dots per inch (DPI) of printers or the megapixels of digital cameras.

If your images are from a PDF file, you can open it using Photoshop. You'll be prompted for which page you'd like to import (there can be many in a PDF) and which resolution (220 PPI is a good average resolution), and let the size be whatever it is in the PDF itself. If the original PDF had a decent resolution, you'll have a nice image to work with.

If your image is from some sketchy Internet source, you'll have to increase the image size by a process called **resampling**. That process makes the image bigger (more pixels per inch), but there's a downside: Photoshop Elements will be forced to make a best estimate for how to fill in all the missing pixels, which can cause blurriness. Choose **Image> Resize>Image Size...** from the drop-down menu (Figure 4.2).

The bicubic option for resampling will probably give the most consistent results. Note that sometimes the results will look pixilated due to the way the re-sampling works—every image will behave differently. You can now tell your mom you've up-sampled all by yourself. Save the file as a Photoshop Document (.PSD), the native file format of Photoshop Elements.

UNDER THE HOOD

JPEG is the most common file type you'll see, and it's what most cameras use. It compresses the original image, however, so not every pixel from a scan or drawing that you see on the screen will be retained in the electronic file. Lossless formats are better, such as TIFF and BMP. PDF is a scalable file format that saves some information as mathematical equations—vectors—which take up much less space than raster-based images. You can then choose a resolution when importing your document. You can get special software to convert a document of any format to a PDF.

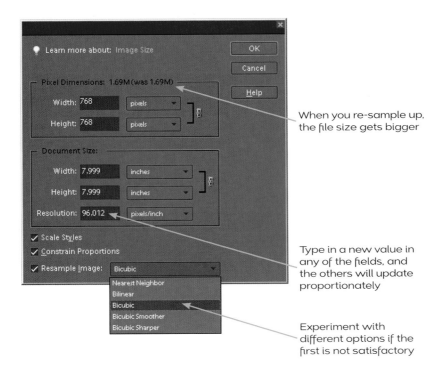

Figure 4.2 *Resizing and resampling an image*

When you re-sample up, the file size gets bigger

Type in a new value in any of the fields, and the others will update proportionately

Experiment with different options if the first is not satisfactory

Drawing Diagrams

Just as in PowerPoint, simple colored shapes and gradients can be used to draw diagrams in Photoshop Elements. The **Paint Bucket** tool allows replacing any colored area (either contiguous with where you clicked, or all similar areas). Colored shapes can be combined in various ways, and simple layer effects can be applied to finish up the drawing.

Let's take a look at an interesting precedent—the renovation of the Yale Museum of Art, originally designed by Louis I. Kahn. We can use plans that are in a PDF file—which were from a scan of a magazine article—to produce circulation and daylighting diagrams. This file format gives you a little flexibility about resolution, and is also convenient if you have multiple images to import.

We'll remove the grayish background (a remnant of the scanned image) before drawing shapes to represent the elements of the circulation pattern. Finally, layer effects will enhance the different shapes for greater clarity. There are three parts to any circulation system: horizontal components, vertical components, and the point of entry / exit. You'll want to choose distinct colors for each, and provide a key nearby to explain their meanings.

BIG PICTURE

The best diagrams address only one particular aspect of a project, such as circulation or daylighting. There are many other ways to study a project. You could look at building geometry and proportions, public and private organization, mechanical distribution, site orientation, structural systems, or airflow. More abstract diagrams might look at metaphorical relationships, such as a project's position within the urban fabric or historical context.

1. Call up Photoshop Elements and choose **Edit** from the welcome screen (choose "Start up with editor" to skip this screen in the future).
2. Click the **Open** button and browse to select your PDF file.
3. Choose the page you'd like to import and set the resolution to 220.
4. Click **OK** to import.
5. Click on the **Rectangular Marquee** selection tool (Figure 4.3).
6. Draw a rectangle around just the area of the page you'd like to keep.
7. Choose **Image>Crop** from the drop-down menu.
8. Click the green **Commit** button at the bottom of the selection to complete the operation.
9. Click on the **Magic Wand** tool (Figure 4.4).
10. Uncheck **Contiguous** on the options bar.

Figure 4.3 *Selection tools*

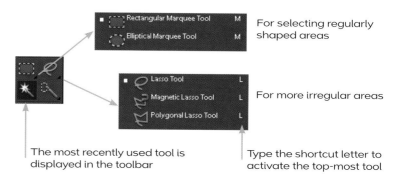

Figure 4.4 *Magic Wand*
options

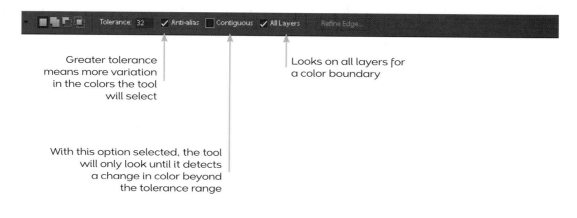

The Magic Wand selects pixels that match the ones
you just clicked on, within the tolerance setting

Figure 4.5 *All the gray*
selected

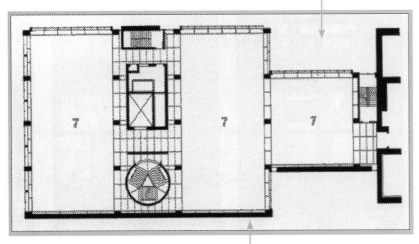

Dashed lines surrounding the
selected areas are referred to
as marching ants

11. Click inside a room somewhere in the plan—all the gray in the drawing should be highlighted (Figure 4.5).

12. Hit the **Delete** button to remove the gray area.

13. Repeat the process to remove the red numbers on the plan, if you have them.

14. Click on the **Rectangle** tool. See Figure 4.6 for the various options.

15. Click once on your screen to start the rectangle, and again to complete it.

16. New objects get painted with the current Foreground color. To change it, click on the **Color** field (see Figure 4.7) on the **Options** toolbar.

Other shapes
are available

Pick a color,
any color

Figure 4.6 Rectangle
options

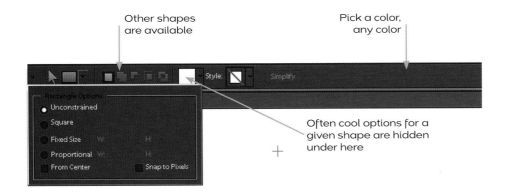

Often cool options for a
given shape are hidden
under here

Figure 4.7 *The color picker*

Drag the circle to change saturation

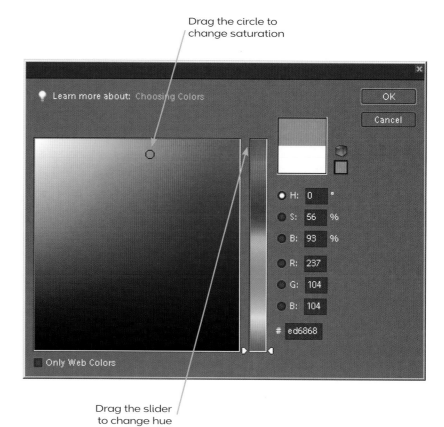

Drag the slider to change hue

17. Use the **Select** tool (hey—looks the same as SketchUp!) to grab the rectangle. Click and drag to move it around, or nudge with the arrow keys (Figure 4.8).
18. Hold down **ALT** while clicking and dragging to make a copy.
19. Use the grips to change the width and height (Figure 4.9).
20. Click **Commit Transform** on the Options toolbar if you've re-sized the shape.
21. Click and drag on the **Rectangle** tool until you see the **Custom Shape** tool.
22. Click to start drawing a custom shape.

Figure 4.8 *Select command options*

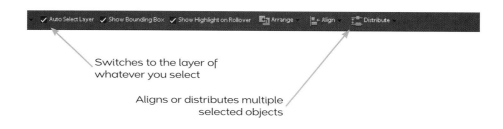

Switches to the layer of whatever you select

Aligns or distributes multiple selected objects

Figure 4.9 *Modifying a rectangle*

Transformation grips—drag to change the size and shape of the selection

Move cursor just beyond any corner to see the rotate icon—drag as desired

Drag to move the selection

23. Click again to define the other end of the line segment.
24. Hold down **SHIFT** and then click to force drawing on the ortho-graphic grid.
25. To draw lines, click on the **Pencil** tool. There are plenty of pencil options, as shown in Figure 4.10.

Figure 4.10 *The **Pencil** tool options*

Appearance of line thickness will vary based on resolution of the file

Can be set now, or changed by layer later

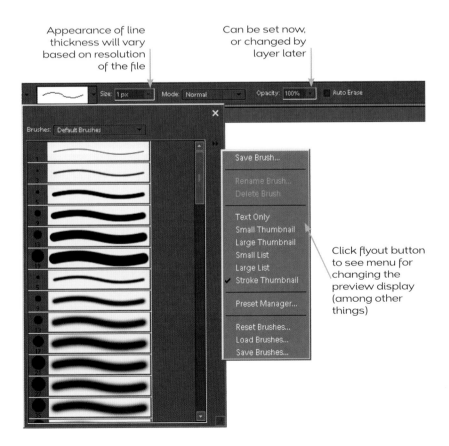

Click flyout button to see menu for changing the preview display (among other things)

Figure 4.11 *Text options*

Standard text
formatting settings

Create warped text

Change text orientation

26. Click once to start and again to finish.
27. Hold down shift to lock in orthogonal drawing.
28. Draw individual lines as needed.
29. Choose an arrow you like, as well as a foreground color. Click once to start the arrow, and again to finish.
30. Draw another to represent the secondary egress out the back of the project. Select and modify with grips as with the rectangle.
31. Click on the **Text** tool. See Figure 4.11 for options.
32. Choose a text font, size, and color.
33. Click on the drawing to place the text base point.
34. Type away to your heart's content.
35. Click the **Commit any Current Edits** button on the Options toolbar to complete it.
36. Click **Save** to complete the diagram (Figure 4.12).

Simple shapes and bold graphics will make the diagram most effective, even if it ignores some of the less significant parts of the plan. As discussed in Chapter 3, there are all sorts of diagrams that can be useful in understanding a design precedent or your own work. Experiment with different types of analytical drawings to see which might be appropriate for the design aesthetic of the project you're studying or working on.

Figure 4.12 *The plan diagram*

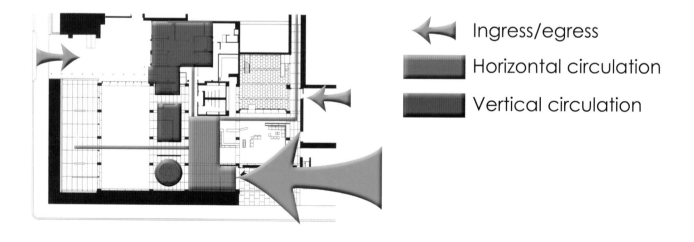

Ingress/egress

Horizontal circulation

Vertical circulation

Layer Styles

Each of these new shapes has its own layer in the document—take a look at the Layers menu to see them listed. Turn them off one by one by poking the little Eye next to their layer. Hold down **SHIFT** or **CTRL** to select more than one. You can control their opacity this way, and there are other handy options in the **More** fly-out menu (Figure 4.13).

Each layer can have effects applied to it to make the drawing more interesting. The **Styles and Effects Palette** has **Layer Effects** on top by default. These are additive, meaning you can have more than one at a time. They can also be removed, so have fun. There are plenty of different styles available from the drop-down list and more can be found on the Internet.

Click and drag a layer effect onto one of the text layers—different pieces of the drawing will become highlighted as you mouse over them. Release the button to apply the effect (Figure 4.14).

When you save the drawing, it's best to keep it in Photoshop Elements (.PSD) format, as this retains the layer structure, applied filters, and the

LOOK OUT!

To apply some filters, effects, and layer styles to a text or shape layer, Photoshop Elements will prompt you to "flatten" the layer. This means it will convert it from an easily edited type of object (based on vectors) to one based on pixels (a raster image), like a photo. This means you won't be able to edit it using grips or the text tool later on, but instead will have to use one of the selection tools.

Figure 4.13 *The **Layers** palette*

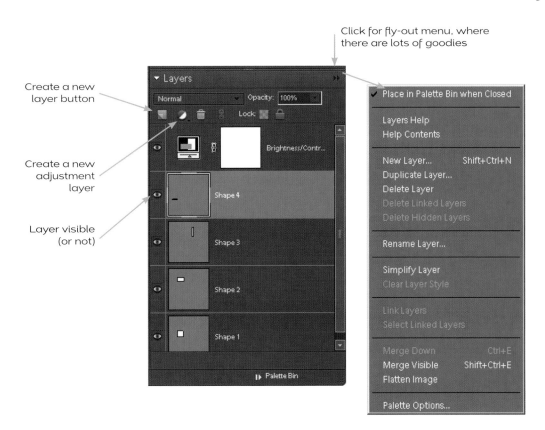

Click for fly-out menu, where there are lots of goodies

Create a new layer button

Create a new adjustment layer

Layer visible (or not)

Figure 4.14 *The Effects*
palette

Filters modify contents
of a layer

Effects menu

Photographic effects menu

Layer styles preview—drag
onto objects in the drawing
area to apply

Choose a layer style

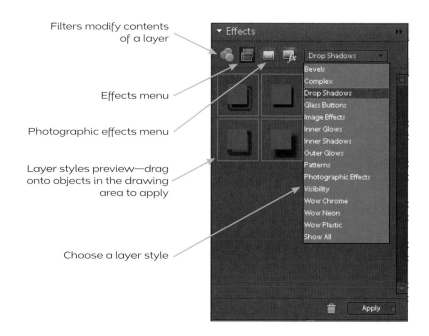

editing history. To save the diagram for insertion into a PowerPoint presentation, choose **File>Save As...** Be sure to choose JPEG format, which is a nice balance between file size and image quality—this automatically makes a copy. I usually save it at the highest-quality level. If the image is already a little blurry, use the TIFF file format, which is higher quality.

Daylighting Diagram

Other plan diagrams can use the same PSD file. All the layers created for this first diagram can be merged into one, although this will make it impossible to edit individual pieces later on. If you think you'll want to go back and edit your previous diagram (which you probably will), save this drawing, then save a copy to work on.

To draw a daylighting diagram, we need to turn off the layers from the circulation diagram. We'll draw gradients over the floor plan to represent daylight penetration into the project. These are rectangular selections on new layers, and we'll make the gradient change from yellow to black.

A DAYLIGHTING DIAGRAM

1. Select all the layers except the Background in the Layers palette.
2. From the **More** fly-out menu, choose **Merge Layers**—this will scrunch the diagram onto one layer.

3. Right-click on the layer in the Layers Palette and choose **Rename**.
4. Call it *Circulation Diagram,* or something clever like that.
5. Poke the little Eye layer to turn the layer off, so you have just the blank plan showing.
6. Click on the **New Layer** button in the Layers Palette to create a layer for the gradient.
7. Click the **Rectangular Marquee** tool to select an area for the gradient to go in (this can be any selected area, by the way).
8. Draw a rectangle along the south interior side of the plan, at about the depth that the sun penetrates (2.5× the height of the window is the official formula).
9. Click on the **Foreground Color** and choose a yellow.
10. Click on the **Background Color** and choose white.
11. Click the **Gradient** tool.
12. To start the gradient, click once by the front wall.
13. Hold down the **Shift** key to lock the cursor to the orthogonal grid as you sketch the gradient direction.
14. Click again farther into the plan—Photoshop Elements will draw the gradient in the shape you've specified.
15. Change the layer opacity to about 70%, so you can see the plan below.
16. You can redraw the gradient if you don't like the way it looks—just click and drag a new path.
17. Click on the **New Layer** button in the Layers Palette.
18. Use the Rectangular Marquee tool to select the rear part of the plan.
19. Set the **Foreground Color** to black.
20. Click at the back (top) of the plan.
21. Hold down the **SHIFT** key to lock in the orthogonal grid, then click in the front of the plan to draw the gradient.
22. Select the black gradient layer in the Layers palette.
23. Change the opacity to 75% to blend it in more.
24. Save the final diagram (Figure 4.15).

Obviously, there's not a whole lot of direct daylighting in a museum—and the diagram should represent that constrained nature somehow. You can add text and export using the same methods as with the circulation diagram. There are plenty of other ways to draw diagrams, including using lines and other shapes.

That was fun, wasn't it? You can also draw diagrams to study program distribution (Figure 4.16), proportion, or whatever is appropriate for the project you're working on. Keep the same plan underlay, but turn off layers for the last diagram.

Other possibilities include geometric proportions, public vs. private areas, mechanical distribution, structural elements, and on and on.

> **MAGIC TRICK**
>
> *The Background layer is normally locked and unavailable for editing. To modify it, choose **Layer from Background** from the context-sensitive menu.*

Figure 4.15 *The finished diagram*

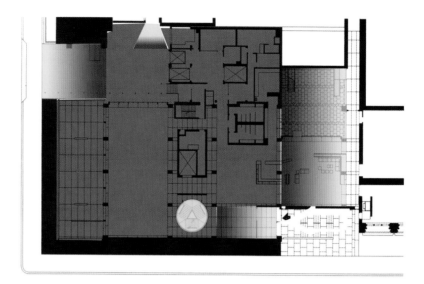

Figure 4.16 *A program distribution diagram*

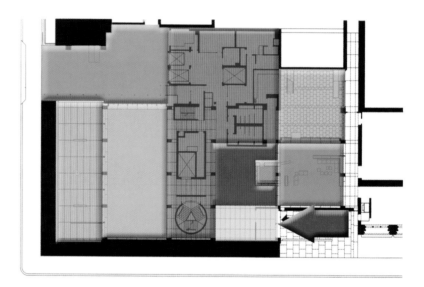

Perspectival Precedent Study

Perspectival views of a precedent (or of your own project) can be picked apart and studied with a variety of graphic filters. This can reveal interesting relationships and compositional techniques not readily visible by just looking at a picture.

A variety of selection tools are needed, usually in combination, and all these areas can be named and saved for later retrieval. Materials and colors can be sampled directly from the image, and filters applied to simplify the drawing into more of a diagrammatic representation. Finally, verbal information can be added and a convincing board created.

Creating and Saving Selections

Open an image from your precedent study that you'd like to examine in great detail. It should be one of the nicest views you can find, and it's important to have a good electronic image size for this project (Figure 4.17), or it will be hard to print well.

The idea of this diagram is to identify areas that have a distinct material or color. The image is then repainted using a sample from each of the areas, resulting in a much simpler view of the project. It's more efficient to go through and save all the areas that have different materials all at once—they can be retrieved and painted later on.

STEPS FOR CREATING AND SAVING SELECTIONS

1. Open the highest-resolution image you can find of your precedent.
2. Using the **Magic Wand** tool, select all of the wall.

Figure 4.17 *Perspective view of a typical gallery area, courtesy of* Architectural Record

Engineers modified the mechanical system above the central bay, which has a conventional flat slab.

3. Choose **Select>Save Selection…** from the drop-down menu.
4. Name it *Gray walls* or something clever like that.
5. To deselect, type **CTRL+D.**
6. To select the floor, use the **Magic Wand** again, but uncheck the **Contiguous** button—this would make the tool select every area in the whole image that has a similar color profile.
7. Hold down **SHIFT** to add in any areas that are missed.
8. Hold down **ALT** to remove any areas that don't belong.
9. Click on the **Polygonal Lasso** tool.
10. Click at each endpoint of the side of the wall.
11. When you get back to the point where you started, a tiny little circle will appear next to your cursor. Click to complete the loop (Figure 4.18).
12. Click and drag on the tiny little triangle in the corner of the Lassos tool to reveal the Magnetic Lasso tool (Figure 4.19).
13. Click along the edge of the wall to start the tool, then move your cursor along the entire edge.

Figure 4.18 *Area selected with the **Polygonal Lasso***

Smooths edges
of selection

Controls how distinct a
color difference will be
recognized by the cursor

Figure 4.19 *Magnetic Lasso* options

14. Continue to save areas as you go until you've gotten all areas of the project. Simplify as needed—you won't need every scrap of area that's different for an effective diagram.
15. **Save As**, and be sure to use the .PSD file format.

These selections will remain as part of the drawing, even if you change the size or location of the original image that they were based on. Selections can be retrieved for use on any layer, and will make this and other diagrams much faster to produce.

Color Study

The goal of this study is to analyze the color scheme in the project, while ignoring the effect of lighting, texture, and other distractions. Different materials are replaced with solid areas of color. Match colors of the photo through sampling, or select from a color wheel. Producing this perspectival color diagram is pretty easy with all these saved areas. Be sure to paint onto a new layer so the original is not lost.

PERSPECTIVAL COLOR DIAGRAM

1. Open up your image again.
2. Click on the Foreground color—a color wheel will pop up where you can click on a color and hue.
3. To select a color directly from the image, move your cursor away from the box and over the drawing—it should change to look like an eyedropper. Click on an area of the floor—the color selection should match the area you clicked on.
4. If the pixel you happened to click on wasn't a decent middle tone, try sampling again.
5. Click on the **New Layer** button in the Layers Palette.
6. Name the new layer *Color Diagram,* or something clever like that.

7. Click on the new layer you just created to make it current—it will have a little paintbrush icon.
8. Choose **Select>Retrieve Selection** from the drop-down menu.
9. Choose the area named Flooring.
10. Dump paint in the area—it should look like the color you just sampled.
11. Sample a new area—one of the walls, for example.
12. Retrieve that selection using the drop-down menu.
13. Paint it again, and continue until the image is a patchwork.
14. If any areas are missing, you can always sample and dump paint in them if needed—the paint bucket has the same option for Contiguous and Sample All Layers.

It may look a little funny, but this type of drawing is informative about the basic color palette the designer was using (Figure 4.20). It's often easy to be distracted by patterns and lighting, and your sampling techniques should adjust for that.

Figure 4.20 *The finished diagram*

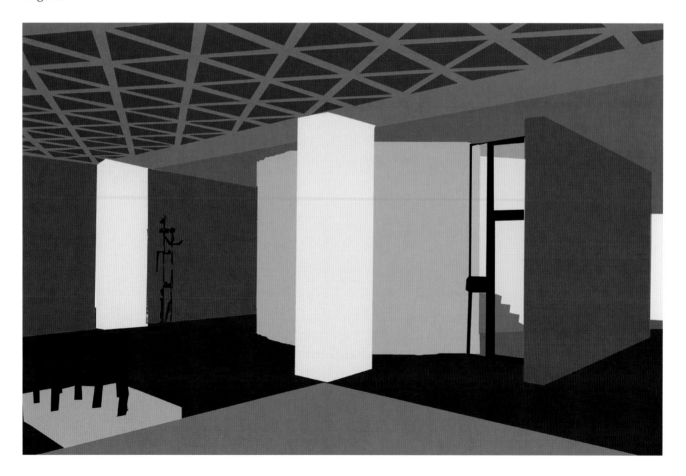

The World in Black and White

The goal with this diagram is to study the textures used in your project, as if it was drawn in monochrome using only a heavy medium like charcoal or pastels. This is a very easy diagram to produce, as it uses a ready-made filter, but you'll need to change to black and white first. Open up the original unaltered image and choose **Image>Mode>Grayscale** from the drop-down menu. Right-click on the Background layer (the one with the original image on it) and choose **Create Layer**—this allows you to make changes. Call it *Black and White Sketch,* or something clever like that. Now choose **Filter>Filter Gallery...** (Figure 4.21).

Browse through the Sketch folder for the **Chalk & Charcoal** filter. This turns the image into a black and white sketch, just like that. Of course, it doesn't always look all that great or really prove particularly interesting. There are other filters in this group that have similar effects. Click **Undo**, and try them to see if the results improve. This view tends to emphasize textures on different surfaces, while completely ignoring color—similar to a shaded design sketch.

Click on an icon to
preview its effect

Figure 4.21 *The filter gallery*

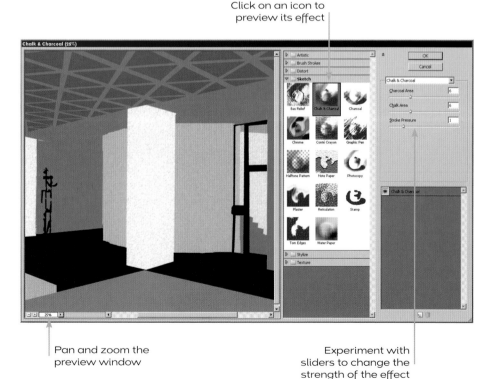

Pan and zoom the
preview window

Experiment with
sliders to change the
strength of the effect

The World in Lines

Continuing backward in the design process, we arrive at what is often the starting point for a design: the sketch drawing. This is also a very easy diagram to create. **Choose File>Save As...** and make a flattened copy (where all the layers have been merged) of your color diagram. Open this new drawing up and choose **File>Mode>Grayscale** to convert the image to black and white. Finally, choose **Filter>Stylize>Find Edges** (Figure 4.22).

And just like that, you have a line drawing. If the lines are a bit thin, type **CTRL+F** to reexecute the last filter. These two black and white images are revealing in that they tend to look at the compositional structure of the view—both spatially and in terms of light and dark.

Gradient Study

Similar to the color diagram created previously, this study uses gradients to study light distribution across the space-defining elements—walls, floors, soffits, and so forth. This will use both the black and white lines of the previous diagram and the saved selections.

Figure 4.22 *The sketch version of the precedent*

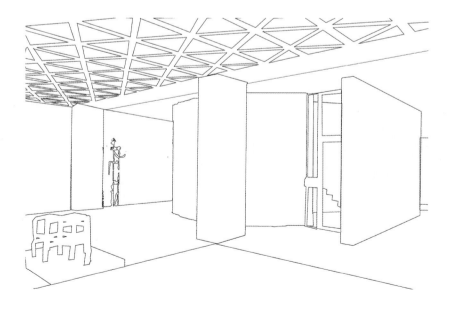

1. Right-click on the Black and White layer and choose **Duplicate Layer**.
2. Poke the eye of the other diagram layers to turn them off.
3. Leave the background image on to refer to, but be sure your current layer is the black and white copy.
4. Lower the Opacity to 60% so you can see the background layer below.
5. Make sure your foreground color is gray and the background color is white.
6. Choose **Select>Retrieve Selection** from the drop-down menu and choose Gray wall.
7. Click on the **Gradient** tool (Figure 4.23).
8. Choose a profile that matches the wall surface.
9. Click and drag from the dark side to the light side, and a gradient will appear within the selection.
10. Click and drag again if it's not exactly right.
11. Hold down **SHIFT** to lock in the orthographic directions.
12. Continue with the other areas until you've finished.
13. Turn off the background layer to see what you've got.
14. Lower the opacity to make the diagram appear less . . . diagrammatic (Figure 4.24).

For most parts of the diagram above, the main source of light, wherever it is, can be identified and a simplified gradient created. Some surfaces will have several light sources, so the several gradients would have to be combined. Like the other diagrams, this is just another way of studying the precedent, making you consider how light plays across the different surfaces of the space.

Figure 4.23 *Gradient tool options*

Choose the direction for the gradient

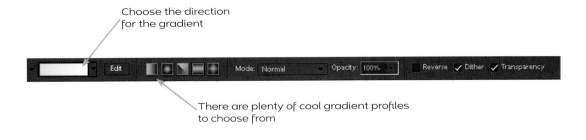

There are plenty of cool gradient profiles to choose from

Figure 4.24 *The lighting study of the precedent*

Board Composition

Let's set up a 24 × 36 board for printing, with our diagrams and other sketches, and information about the project. We'll use a high resolution so that there will be no loss of detail in our final print. This will lead to a very large file size, however, so if your computer is short on processor power or RAM, be sure to keep all other programs closed while working in Photoshop.

BOARD LAYOUT IN PHOTOSHOP ELEMENTS

1. Start Photoshop Elements.
2. Choose **Start from Scratch** from the Start-up menu (or, if the program is already running, **File>New>Blank File**) (Figure 4.25).
3. Under the **View** drop-down menu, choose **Rulers and Grids** for convenience of layout.

4. Choose **Edit>Preferences>Grid** to set spacing to an inch or so (Figure 4.26).
5. Click **OK**—but where's the grid? Choose **View>Grid** to display the grid.

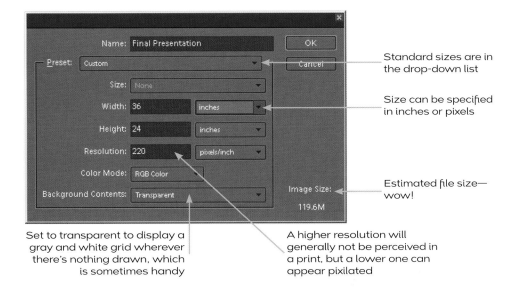

Standard sizes are in the drop-down list

Size can be specified in inches or pixels

Estimated file size— wow!

Set to transparent to display a gray and white grid wherever there's nothing drawn, which is sometimes handy

A higher resolution will generally not be perceived in a print, but a lower one can appear pixilated

Figure 4.25 *The New File dialog box with settings for a blank presentation*

This will make a line every inch

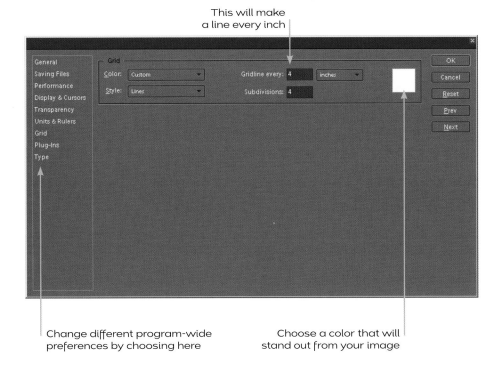

Figure 4.26 *Preferences for the reference grid*

Change different program-wide preferences by choosing here

Choose a color that will stand out from your image

6. Click **Save** and place your drawing in an appropriate folder.
7. Choose **File>Place…** from the drop-down menu.
8. Browse to find your finished perspectival composition and choose it.
9. Click to place on your board—note that it takes up only a portion of the board.
10. Click the **Commit Transform** button (or hit **RETURN**) to insert.
11. Add the two diagrams (and any other images or drawings pertinent to your design).
12. Click on the **Text** tool.
13. Click on the drawing to place the text and start typing.
14. Click the **Commit any Current Edits** button to finish.
15. To change existing text, click on the text tool.
16. Click on the text block and insert cursor. Type some text.

Figure 4.27 *The board area with inserted diagrams*

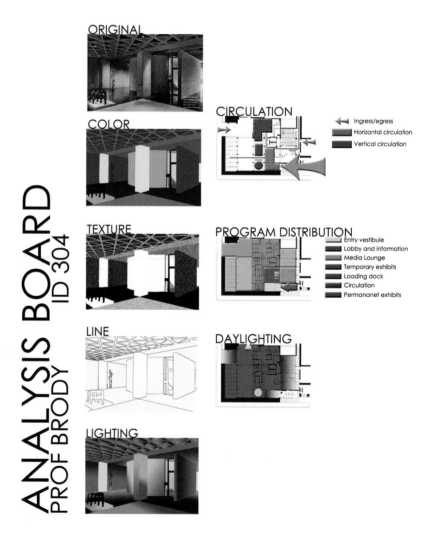

17. **CTRL+A** selects all the text within the block for easy changes.
18. Use the Modify tool to move or rotate (hold down shift to snap to the nearest 90°).
19. Add the floor plan.
20. Add some perspectives with various styles or rendering applied.
21. Use **Layer Styles** for borders where desired.
22. Test-print on plain paper.
23. Add filter such as Speckle to entire board, to blend together the final composition (Figure 4.27).
24. Make final full-size print on high-quality paper.

You can add more studies of additional perspective images and create an interesting analysis board—there are several examples available on-line. So what about the scale of these drawings? Well, once you leave the precise vector world of our 3D modeling programs, it becomes harder to control the scale of image files we commonly deal with. The easiest solution is to include a graphic scale with plans, sections, and elevations, and literally measure the plan image. Scale it until it's at the correct size for whatever scale you're using. Thus, a 40'-wide plan at ¼" = 1'–0" should be 40/4", or 10" wide on the printed sheet. Use the grids and guides when resizing the image, and always hold down **SHIFT** to lock the proportions.

As with single drawings, screen calibration with the printer and the chosen paper will have impacts on the quality of the final product. Nothing beats a test print on the final paper using the same printer.

Online Resources

- *Yale art museum article.pdf*, from *Architectural Record*
- Photoshop file used to create one of the diagrams, *Perspective color diagram.psd*
- Examples of student work from this assignment, *Analysis Board Examples.pptx*

Term Project Assignments

- Complete precedent study, with verbal description, plan, and perspectival diagrams.
- Describe how the analysis will aid your design project.

Exercises and Further Study

- Create plan diagrams for a current design project.
- Dissect a perspectival view of a current design project.
- Lay out a materials board using samples from manufacturers' Web sites for print on a 24 × 36 sheet.
- Switch finished designs with a classmate and lay out their board for them.
- Choose random shapes or configurations for boards, such as circular or very long and short. Try to make the design presentation work with that shape.

Unit 2

Schematic Design in SketchUp

5

Simple Modeling

LEARNING GOALS

- Understand the structure of SketchUp models
- Understand basic workflow in SketchUp
- Acquire basic modeling skills, including drawing and extruding different shapes
- Understand inserting and creating components
- Understand creating and saving views

The three best things about Google SketchUp are: (1) it's quick, (2) it's quick, and (3) it's quick! Simple 3D models are created in an intuitive interface, for such projects as furniture-layout options, single-room studies, or custom-designed architectural elements and furniture. Repeated elements like furniture and lighting can be glued together into miniature drawings called components, making them easy to copy, edit globally, and share with other SketchUp users. Views of the model can be rendered photo-realistically from right within the SketchUp interface. Best of all, there are lots of free components, textures, and whole models available free.

SketchUp is not a good tool for detailed construction drawings. In fact, even a simple thing like modeling wall thicknesses can be a headache, as components like windows and doors won't "break" more than one face at a time. There are workarounds for these situations, but complex multispace, multilevel projects are better to model in Revit. Composing sheets of scaled model views, however, is very easy with **Layout**,

> **BIG PICTURE**
>
> *Models are developed by drawing and manipulating faces, which are formed by coplanar edge lines. These can be lines, arcs, and the like. Drawing tools will look familiar to users of AutoCAD and Revit, and, like those programs, all drawing is at 1:1 scale. Faces are extruded using the **Push/Pull** tool, or by moving around individual edges or points in three dimensions. You can draw on any face with any tool, and objects are sticky—anything they touch will be dragged along when you move them, warping the whole model, if you're not careful.*

a bundled program from Google designed to work with SketchUp models. A single room can be modeled accurately and in great detail using
SketchUp—we'll use the kitchen space from the Chocolate Café program. This chapter introduces the basic concepts of 3D modeling and
outlines good work habits. We'll model the existing conditions for the
Café project and do a simple equipment study for the kitchen.

SketchUp Overview

As in other drawing and modeling programs, most of the action happens
in the drawing area. I tend to have all of my toolbars visible when the
program starts up—this helps me remember what the different drawings and editing options are. A list of available toolbars can be found
under the **View>Toolbars** drop-down menu. Moving around a 3D
model is easiest with a scroll-wheel mouse. Roll the wheel to zoom in
and out, and click and drag the wheel to orbit, which rotates the model
around a central point. You can also click and drag the scroll wheel and
the left mouse button at the same time to pan—try not to get your fin-
gers tangled up (Figure 5.1).

Commands are available either as buttons, in the drop-down menus,
or through keyboard shortcuts. Have SketchUp's Quick Reference Guide

Figure 5.1 *SketchUp
window with the basic
toolbar set*

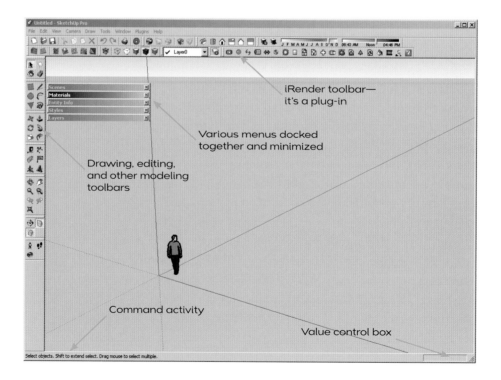

handy (look under the Help menu), or use **Tool Tips** to find the commands as you draw to help remember where everything is. As you draw, keep an eye at the command activity area of the screen for prompts about what you're supposed to do next.

Note that this textbook shows the Pro version of Google SketchUp. The free version is missing some of the export options and other hidden goodies, but it's basically the same program. Files created in one can be opened in the other, and there's the same ability to save a model to Google Earth.

Modeling the Architecture

The first thing you'll want to determine when working in SketchUp is if this will be primarily an interior or exterior project. This is because windows and doors are much more complex to handle if you model both the inside and exterior faces of the perimeter wall. Interior models generally just have the inside faces, while exterior models have just the outside. We will create an interiors model, but build up both faces of the façade wall so the view from the street looks correct. We'll start by drawing simple two-dimensional shapes and then manipulating them into three-dimensional objects.

As you draw any new element, the cursor will "infer" which orthogonal direction it thinks you want to go—red, green, or blue. To lock that inference, forcing a line along one of those axes, hold down **SHIFT** after the inference appears.

The model is built in several steps. First the overall building shape is modeled, including the sidewalk and street in the front. We'll use simple shapes and type dimensions to achieve an accurate representation of the dimensions of the building.

THE BASE MODEL

1. Click on the **Rectangle** tool.
2. Click once to start the rectangle, and again somewhere else to finish it—the exact spot doesn't matter.
3. **Type 25',50'**, then **ENTER**—no need to click anywhere; the dimensions automatically go into the Value Control Box.
4. At this point, you'll have to click and drag your scroll wheel—this will orbit your model so that you can see better in three dimensions.
5. Click on the **Push/Pull** tool.
6. Click on the face of the rectangle—it gets "stuck" to your cursor.

UNDER THE HOOD

Immediately after many commands, you may type in a dimension or other modifier, which allows accuracy and speed. Draw a line, for example, then type 4' and press **ENTER***. Like magic, the line will change to 4'-0" long, no matter how you had drawn it before. There's no need to click anywhere, and the number you're typing shows up in the* **Value Control Box** *at the bottom left of the screen.*

7. Move your cursor up about 15' (follow the dimension in the Value Control Box) and click again to finish.

8. Type in **15'**, then **ENTER** to precisely define the height (Figure 5.2). You may also enter this value before clicking on a second point—saves a whole click!

9. Click the **Rectangle** tool again.

10. Move your mouse over the lower-right corner of the building—you should see a green box and the tool tip for **Endpoint**.

11. Now we'll draw the sidewalk in front. Click on the endpoint to start a rectangle.

12. Draw a small rectangle along the front of the building.

13. Type in **8'**, then **ENTER** to keep the length as drawn, but limit the other dimension to 8 feet (leaving out one of the dimensions but including the comma keeps the sketch for that side but changes the other side).

14. Click the **Push/Pull** command.

15. Click on the sidewalk, then move your cursor down to define the thickness of the sidewalk.

16. Type **6'**, then **ENTER**.

17. Now **Push/Pull** the sidewalk left and right so that it marches past the façade (Figure 5.3).

Now you have the basic volume of the existing conditions. It's important to plan ahead for which parts of the model will be seen from the

Figure 5.2 *The basic shape of the site*

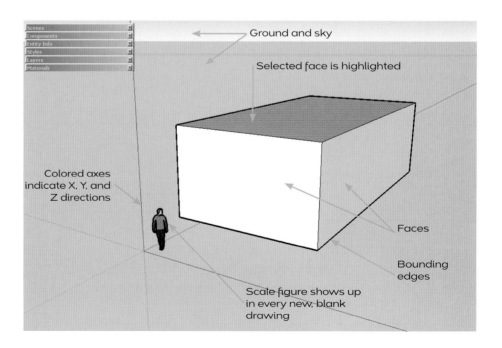

Ground and sky

Selected face is highlighted

Colored axes indicate X, Y, and Z directions

Faces

Bounding edges

Scale figure shows up in every new, blank drawing

84   Unit 2: Schematic Design in SketchUp

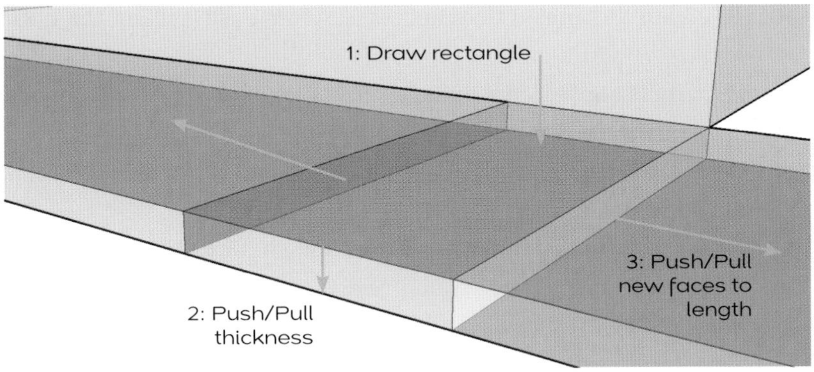

Figure 5.3 *Drawing the sidewalk*

1: Draw rectangle

2: Push/Pull thickness

3: Push/Pull new faces to length

outside of the building and which parts will be seen only from the inside. This is because components, which are used for doors and windows, can only be inserted into one face. The fastest solution is to model only one face for the exterior wall—either interior or exterior, depending on the focus of the project. It's not as critical in this project, where there are no windows in the side walls. Now we'll develop the façade in greater detail. See Figure 5.4 for dimensions.

ADDING ARCHITECTURAL DETAIL

1. Draw the street using your new modeling skills. Start with a rectangle, extrude it down to form the curb thickness, and then extrude the sides.
2. To draw major divisions on the front façade, we'll copy edge lines. Make sure nothing is currently selected and choose the **Move/Copy** command.
3. Hit the **CTRL** key to indicate that you plan to make a copy. You'll see a tiny plus sign next to your cursor.
4. Mouse over the top line of the model, where the front façade meets the roof, until the line turns blue.
5. Click once on the line to start the copy, then move your mouse down.
6. Type **8**, then **ENTER**. SketchUp assumes you mean inches unless you type in the foot symbol.
7. Click **CTRL** again, and then copy that new line down another 3'2".
8. Now copy the vertical lines on both sides in toward the center 24" to define pilasters that go almost all the way to the roof.
9. Define the door opening using additional copies of the new side lines 7'-6" in from the pilasters.

10. To create the angled door recess, start by push/pulling the door back 24".
11. Click the **Select** command and select one of the lines defining the front of the door recess.
12. Hold down **SHIFT** and click on the other line defining the front of the door recess.
13. Click the **Move** command and grab the lines by their endpoints.
14. Move your cursor over the outer edge of the recess and click—the side walls of the recess should be angled (Figure 5.5).
15. Next we'll create the panels on the fascia and pilasters. Use the **Select** tool and click on the center face at the middle of the fascia.
16. Click on the **Offset** tool.
17. Click on one edge of the selected face.
18. Move your mouse toward the center of the face, and type **8**, then **ENTER**.
19. Repeat the process of selection and offset for panels on the fascia and both pilasters.
20. Use the same process to create 3" window frames.
21. Finally, let's give the panels some depth. **Push/Pull** the perimeter of the fascia panel out 2".
22. With the **Push/Pull** tool still active, double-click on one of the pilaster bases—it should pop out the same amount as the last one.
23. **Push/Pull** the perimeter of the pilasters and the strip above and below the fascia out 1" using the same technique.
24. **Push/Pull** the front window glass back into the building 4" and the frames back 2".

Figure 5.4 *Major divisions of the façade*

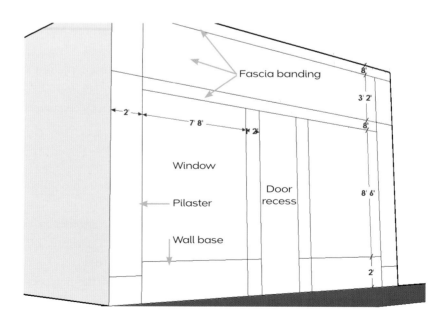

Figure 5.5 *Creating the door recess*

Side wall will angle as you move the edge lines

Hold down SHIFT or CTRL to select more than one line

Grab lines from the endpoint to avoid moving line vertically

25. To build up a parapet, copy the top line of the façade back toward the rear of the building 18".
26. **Push/Pull** up 8".
27. To create a drip edge, click on the **Push/Pull** command.
28. Hold down **CTRL** and click on the top of the parapet—this will copy the top surface during the operation.
29. Type **1**, then **ENTER**.
30. Finally, **Push/Pull** the vertical drip-edge forward 1" to get a decent shadow.

With a minimum of commands and not much time at all, you've modeled a fairly complex building. Of course, there are no wall thicknesses and many of the architectural subtleties are missing. You could continue refining the model by adding flashing around the doors and windows, or sloping the windowsills and pilaster projection. Open up a photo to see all the detail you're missing. Better yet, go to the building site with your computer, so you can measure and electronically model at the same time.

In summary, SketchUp is all about drawing quickly and *somewhat* accurately. Chasing down very precise measurements could lead to frustration—if it's that critical, switch to a slower, more precise modeling program like Revit.

> **LOOK OUT!**
>
> *You'll run into headaches if you try to make changes to the angled walls and windows at the entry recess. The only way to accurately model a situation like this (or a curved façade, for that matter) is to offset the shape in plan—usually from below. Then **Push/Pull** up, and start drawing on the recessed portion. We'll do this later on when we draw the kick space of a curved counter.*

Adding Color and Components

SketchUp organizes Materials and Components into general categories that are pretty self-explanatory, such as solid colors, carpeting, or transparent. You can also use an image file as a material.

ADDING DETAIL TO THE EXISTING CONDITIONS

1. Click on the **Paint Bucket** tool (Figure 5.6).
2. From the Transparent folder, choose a sky-colored paint.
3. Click in the middle of the face to paint the window.
4. From the Solid Colors folder, choose a gray or black.
5. From the Brick folder, choose a Cladding-plaster-rough and dump it on the rest of the façade.
6. To add a door, choose **Window>Components...** (Figure 5.7).
7. Double-click on the Architecture folder and then the Doors folder.
8. Choose **Glass 3-0x7-0 Framed.**
9. Move your mouse over the base of one wall and click to place the door in the outside wall.
10. Place street trees from the Landscape folder.

Figure 5.6 *Paint Bucket*

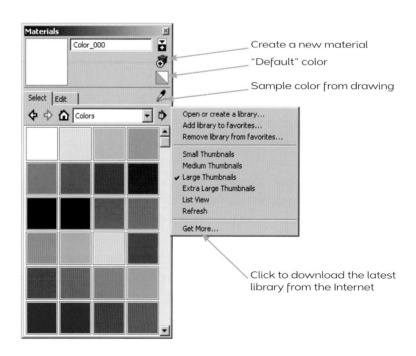

Create a new material

"Default" color

Sample color from drawing

Click to download the latest library from the Internet

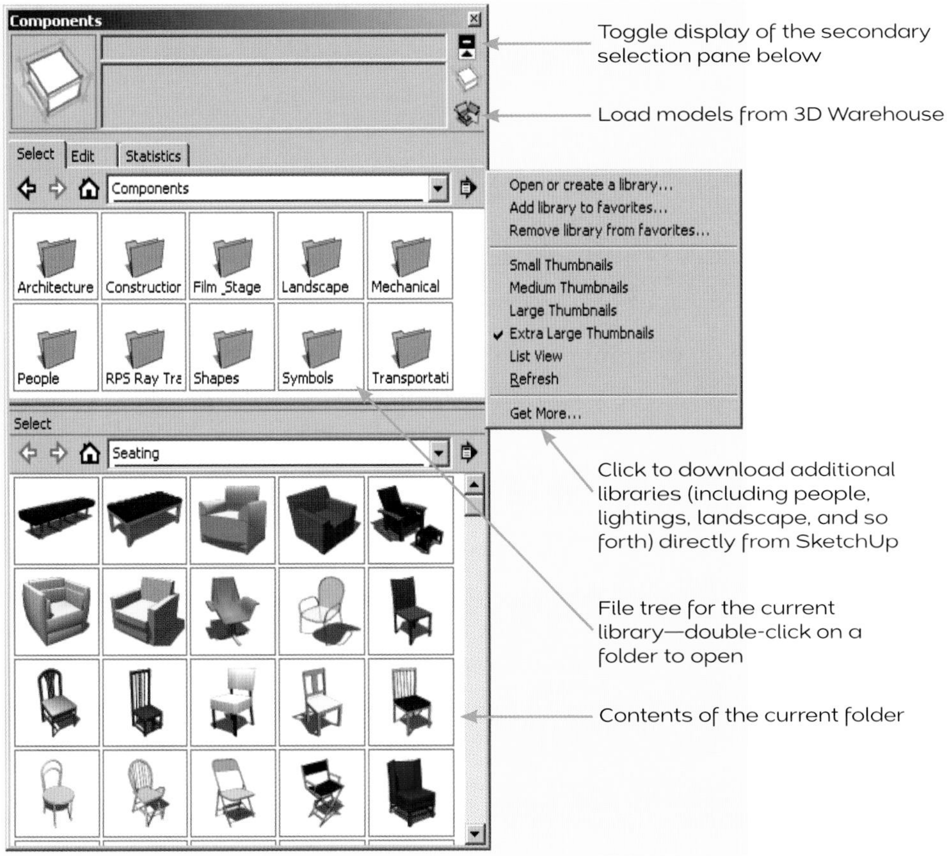

Figure 5.7 *Navigating the* **Components** *menu*

Toggle display of the secondary selection pane below

Load models from 3D Warehouse

Click to download additional libraries (including people, lightings, landscape, and so forth) directly from SketchUp

File tree for the current library—double-click on a folder to open

Contents of the current folder

11. Place a car from the Transportation folder of the Components browser.
12. Orbit the model so you can see the rear wall.
13. Use the **Tape Measure** tool to draw reference lines on the back wall 5'-0" from the floor and another 6'-0" from the east side.
14. Open the Components browser again and choose **In Model** from the drop-down list.
15. Select the glass door and place it at the vertical reference line.
16. Choose **Window_Doublehung_Mullions_23x58_Triple**.
17. Place two windows evenly spaced between the door and the west wall.
18. Paint the rest of the north and south façades brick.

And there you have it—an instant 3D model of the existing conditions. Note that we haven't drawn any wall thicknesses and really won't need to just yet—this model is for an interior study. Models meant for architectural exploration follow more or less the same process, except you're modeling the extents of the built mass rather than the volume of

---

MAGIC TRICK

All entities in SketchUp are either edges or faces, and only faces can be painted with a material. You can paint one side of a face differently from the opposite, however—you'll see two paint chips in the Entity Info dialog box instead of one.

---

interior space. Also, views of architectural models tend to be less distorted because the station point for a perspective can be so much farther away.

These basic tools—drawing and extruding, painting and enhancing with components, zooming and orbiting—allow you to draw just about anything.

Composing Views of the Model

One of the nice things about modeling in 3D is you can easily get a perspective view to show off your design to greatest advantage (and ignore all the stuff you messed up or left out), orbiting and scrolling to just the right composition. Then, unfortunately, a random click and drag of your scroll wheel can ruin the whole thing! Fortunately, you can save the views using **Scenes**, which are easily accessible compilations of view settings (like eye height, section plane activation, field of view, and so forth) and current style.

Most of the properties you'll be concerned with can be controlled with tools on the **Camera** toolbar, including changing the eye height for a seated or standing view and the field of view. Be sure to use Tool Tips or the Quick Reference Chart to find the tools referenced below. Click on the **Zoom** tool and the **Value Control Box** gives the current field of view in degrees. Type **70**, then **ENTER** to widen the angle—this is a fairly distorted perspective, but will show a healthy balance of walls, floor, and ceiling.

Use the **Look Around** and **Orbit** tools to change the focal point. You can also **Walk** forward or backward, or **Pan** one way or another—both of these move the station point that SketchUp is using to generate the perspective. Several of these tools allow you to type in a dimension for the eye height, so consider if your client is Yao Ming (the tallest basketball player in the NBA) or someone shorter.

Saving Scenes for Ready Reference

OK, now let's save a series of views to help us work on the model and evaluate the design. SketchUp records a variety of data about a given view into a scene, including geometric data about camera angle and placement, and also display settings like line characteristics and whether or not a particular section is active. These latter settings are generally controlled using **Styles**, which can be applied to any view and saved as part of a scene. We'll save a few key views and make one of them look like it's hand drawn.

SAVING SCENES

1. From the **Window** drop-down menu, choose **Scenes** to bring up a manager for saving and controlling set views with different properties (Figure 5.8).
2. Orbit your model to compose a decent overview perspective.
3. Click the **Add** button on the Scenes Manager.
4. When SketchUp prompts you to associate a style with this scene, click **Yes**. You'll see a new tab appear at the top of the drawing area.
5. To get inside the model, for now just keep scrolling until you crash through a wall (we'll learn a fancier way later on).
6. Use the **Look Around** tool to change your view (and type in an eye height in the values control box, and press **ENTER**).
7. Use the **Zoom** tool to zoom in or out (and to change the field of view—interiors often need 60–70 degrees).
8. Click **Add** in the Scenes Manager to save that view.
9. Choose **Window>Styles** from the drop-down menu (Figure 5.9).

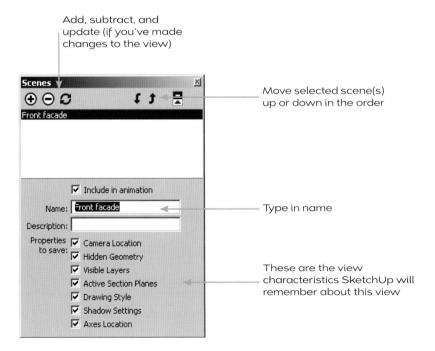

Add, subtract, and update (if you've made changes to the view)

Move selected scene(s) up or down in the order

Type in name

These are the view characteristics SketchUp will remember about this view

Figure 5.8 *The **Scenes Manager***

Figure 5.9 *Editing a style*

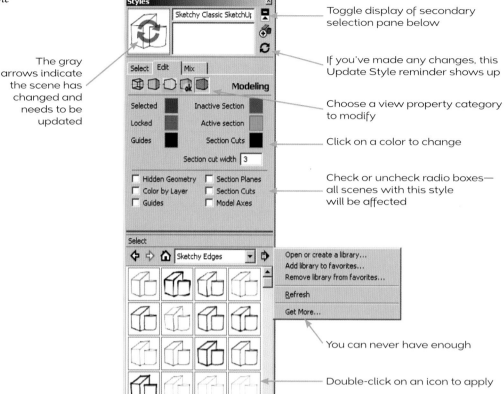

The gray arrows indicate the scene has changed and needs to be updated

Toggle display of secondary selection pane below

If you've made any changes, this Update Style reminder shows up

Choose a view property category to modify

Click on a color to change

Check or uncheck radio boxes— all scenes with this style will be affected

You can never have enough

Double-click on an icon to apply

10. Find a style you like and double-click on it.
11. Save a new scene with that style applied.
12. In the **Scenes** manager, click on the last one you created.
13. In the name field, type "Exterior-Sketchy" or something descriptive like that, and hit **ENTER** to apply the name change.
14. Rename the other scenes to describe them more accurately.

To return to any of these saved scenes, just click on the tabs at the top of the screen. I like to leave all of my managers and browsers on screen (there are quite a few)—just click once on the top bar to minimize. Dragging one bar next to another nestles them together, so you can have them all snuggled at the top of your screen.

These different types of views can help evaluate your project, as sometimes too many colors or too completed a composition will make it hard to contemplate making changes. Thus a more sketchy view, which only hints at most details, is preferable early on in design, where you want clients to feel comfortable giving you feedback (Figure 5.10).

UNDER THE HOOD

A single style can be associated with many scenes. If you make a change and update that style, all those scenes will be affected. If you apply a new style to a given scene that you like even better, just right-click on the scene name at the top of the drawing window and choose **Update***. This will redefine the scene to reflect any view changes you've made.*

Figure 5.10 *Different styles applied to the same view*

Adding Complex Profiles

Another nice touch for your models, and to add some human scale to the interior space, is to draw a crown molding and base. Draw the profile in one of the corners of your space using lines, arcs, and whatnot, and be sure the shape forms a complete closed loop (Figure 5.11).

Click to divide into segments, or type in a number. Now that line is magically broken into equal pieces, and you can use the new snap points to draw in proportionally precise elements.

If you're feeling especially efficient, you can use a CAD file readily available from millwork dealers. Choose **File>Import...** from the drop-down menu. SketchUp can, with varying degrees of success, import all sorts of file types: 3D models like SKP (SketchUp, of course), DWG (AutoCAD), and 3DS (3D Studio Max); and raster images like JPEG, BMP, and TIFF.

Just choose the type you're looking for from the **File of Type** drop-down list. Browse to find your downloaded file and click **OK**. Once in the model, you might have to rotate the lines along one or another axis to position it in your model (Figure 5.12).

> **MAGIC TRICK**
>
> *Often moldings and other profiles are based on simple proportions. Lines can be broken into fractional pieces to assist in snapping. Right-click on one of the edge lines and choose **Divide** from the menu. Type in the number of segments you'd like and hit **ENTER**.*

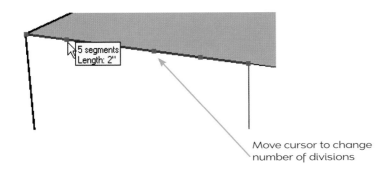

Move cursor to change number of divisions

Figure 5.11 *A divided edge of simple molding*

Figure 5.12 *Getting the detail to fill in*

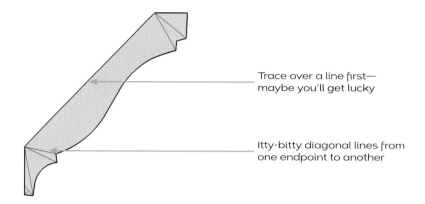

Trace over a line first—
maybe you'll get lucky

Itty-bitty diagonal lines from
one endpoint to another

These diagonals can usually be erased after the shape fills in. Finally, to get your shape to cut the model geometry, you may need to select it and choose **Intersect>With Model** from the context-sensitive menu. Erase any extra lines you had to draw in to make the surface close.

Now choose the **Follow Me** tool—your cursor will change to look just like the **Follow-Me** tool icon. Click in the middle of the profile face to select it as the base for your extrusion. As you move your mouse along the nearest wall, the profile will follow your cursor along the nearest edge (Figure 5.13).

For a continuous cornice, hold down the **ALT** key and move your mouse over the middle of the ceiling. SketchUp will extrude the profile around the entire face, no matter how many ins and outs there are. That'll surely pose a challenge to the best finish carpenter.

Figure 5.13 *Cornice profile and following the* **Follow Me** *tool*

The tool is following
the red axis

Mouse over face (using ALT)
to trace entire perimeter

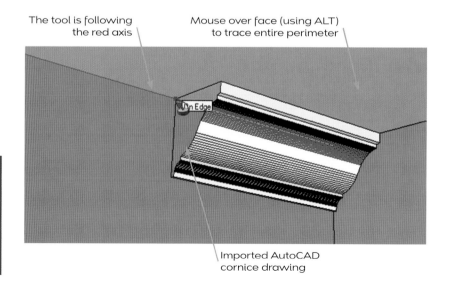

On Edge

Imported AutoCAD
cornice drawing

Drawing with Inferences

SketchUp tries hard to figure out which geometric landmarks in your model will be useful as you model. Just like in AutoCAD and other drafting programs, these are called **snaps**, and there are all sorts (Figure 5.14).

Some objects are line-based locations that the cursor will find. When drawing other objects—rectangles and arcs, for example—there are other snaps that will show up in a variety of colors and line types. If you're not sure what the cursor is telling you, look for the boxed **Tool Tip** that pops up when your mouse pauses over a snap point.

The most powerful contextual inference is when the program tries to guess which direction you want to draw in. Lines can be snapped to align with one of the three axes—green, red, and blue (vertical). Start a line and then move your mouse around until you see a dotted line the same color as the direction your mouse is heading. You can lock this inference, preventing the line from going in any other direction, by holding down the **SHIFT** key when you see the active inference (Figure 5.15).

Figure 5.14 *A variety of object snaps*

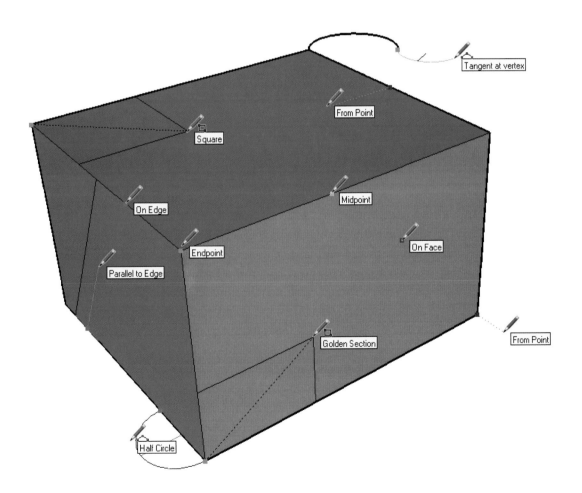

Figure 5.15 *Locked inference for the Green direction*

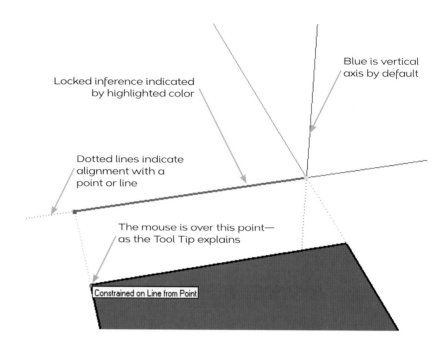

Locked inference indicated by highlighted color

Blue is vertical axis by default

Dotted lines indicate alignment with a point or line

The mouse is over this point— as the Tool Tip explains

Constrained on Line from Point

You can then align the next point with any object by mousing over it and clicking on the appropriate snap tips. You can even get the cursor to draw lines parallel to an edge that's not on the orthogonal grid. Start a line, then mouse over the angled edge. When you move your mouse over, it usually finds a cyan-colored Parallel inference.

Modeling the Kitchen

Adding components and changing their materials is one of the most enjoyable things you can do in SketchUp, and it allows you to quickly evaluate design decisions. The simplest of all interior sketch projects involve a design without walls—just a furniture or equipment grouping. Let's ignore room divisions right now and just study the layout of the kitchen in greater detail, using SketchUp to model equipment and evaluate the layout. The first step is to save a view of the kitchen that's convenient for adding equipment. Then we'll start inserting ready-made drawings called **components**.

Components are bundles of lines and faces glued together for convenience, just like the eponymous objects from Revit or AutoCAD blocks. In the classroom setting, why spend too much time working on creating new components for stoves and counters that are perfect in every detail? SketchUp provides a generous number of components right within the

SketchUp interface, as we saw when choosing doors and windows. If you don't see what you're looking for, click on the fly-out button on the Components browser and choose Get More from the menu—this will load a whole bunch of appealing components onto your computer. You can also click on the **Search 3D Warehouse** button and search for models on that gigantic open database.

Add the elements that are typical for a working kitchen into the model: counters, tables, a commercial stove and oven, a refrigerator, cooling racks, a cooling table, and even garbage cans.

MAGIC TRICK

3D Warehouse has many of the building models you see on Google Earth, so you can save a good deal of time downloading a site model wholesale instead of creating it yourself. You can also search formfonts.com for many more goodies, although you have to pay a subscription fee to download.

LAYING OUT THE KITCHEN WITH COMPONENTS

1. Open the **Components** browser and click on the **Appliances** folder.
2. Add components for a table, stove, sink, countertop, and so forth.
3. Click on the **Move/Copy** command.
4. Mouse over the top of stove component until the **Quick Rotate Compass** appears on the surface (Figure 5.16).
5. Click and drag on the protractor to rotate the stove.
6. To avoid the protractor, move your mouse over the bottom of a component until the tool tip at your mouse reads Endpoint.
7. Click once to indicate the base point for the move command.

Figure 5.16 *The* **Instant Rotate** *tool*

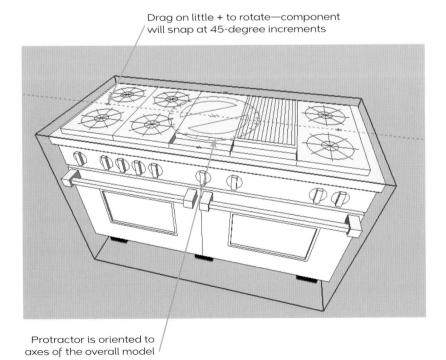

Drag on little + to rotate—component will snap at 45-degree increments

Protractor is oriented to axes of the overall model

8. Click again to plant the object somewhere else.
9. Repeat the last two steps after pressing the **CTRL** key (you'll see a tiny **+** next to your cursor) to make a copy.
10. Type **+3**, then **ENTER** to make three copies—an array based on the original spacing.
11. Type **/3**, then **ENTER** to make three copies—spaced evenly between the original and the first copy.

In this way you can quickly fill up the kitchen with equipment. To edit, say, a base cabinet component, double-click on it. The rest of the model will be grayed out, although you'll still be able to snap to any object you can see. Any changes you make will be reflected in all instances of the component, so beware of stretching or otherwise modifying willy-nilly. Draw locally, think globally. To fill in the end panel of the base and wall cabinets, just use the pencil tool to trace over one edge of the open area—this usually fills it in. If not, you'll have to start drawing diagonal lines, as you did with the AutoCAD molding profile.

Painting components is a little more complex than painting faces, since you can paint the whole component or open it up and paint pieces. Imagine a component for a chair. If you dump paint on the outside of the chair (without opening it for editing), the whole object will display that new material, including the knobs, top, and feet—but only that one instance of the chair. This is because all elements *inside* the component have been painted with the Default color. To change all instances, you must open up the component (the rest of the screen will become gray) and paint pieces however you like. After you close it, all instances will change.

Custom Components

It's always easier to insert and edit ready-made components than it is to draw a new one. If you can find a model that's pretty close, it's still better to modify that one. The exception is when you have something unique or custom—in which case you should create your own. Let's create components for the chocolate tempering and enrobing machines—you'll have to go online to get typical dimensions. Or, better yet, go to a chocolate factory!

From our research, we learned that the enrobing machine is where things like caramels are covered in chocolate. It's fun to watch (as is the tempering machine), and so is placed up front near what will probably be seating in the café. Both machines need plenty of clearance for operators, too, and should be near each other and the cooling table.

1. Move to a blank portion of your model.
2. Draw a rectangle on the ground.
3. Type **30,96**, then **ENTER.**
4. **Push/Pull** up 42".
5. Paint stainless steel.
6. Click on the **Modify** command.
7. Click and drag from the left to the right, completely surrounding the shape—this selects it.
8. Right-click on the selection and choose **Create Component** (Figure 5.17).
9. Be sure to click the **Replace Selection with Component** button.
10. Name it something clever like *Enrobing Machine* and click **OK.**
11. Repeat for the tempering machine, which is about 3' in diameter and 5' tall.
12. Move, copy, and rotate all the components until the kitchen is configured efficiently (Figure 5.18).

Experiment with different ways of drawing objects—start with an overall mass and eat away at it with various tools, or build it up as we did here. Efficient modelers will often only draw parts of the model, and mirror or otherwise copy the pieces. This can make painting complex—keep double-clicking on the bit you want to paint until you reach the actual model.

> **LOOK OUT!**
>
> *Moving around objects in your model can be tricky, because SketchUp will snap to any point in three-dimensional space. Use the bottom edge of a component as the base point (you'll see the **Endpoint in Component** tool tip), rather than just clicking and dragging randomly. This prevents chairs and other objects from going under your floor or up into the air. Also, look for the **On Face** tool tip to place an object in the middle of a face.*

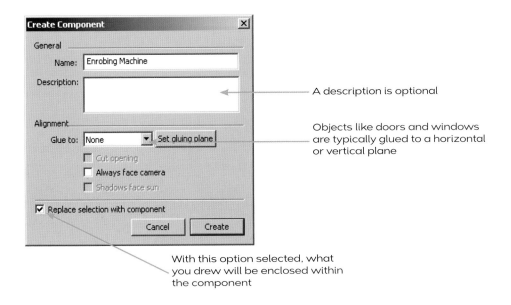

Figure 5.17 *The **Create Component** dialog box*

A description is optional

Objects like doors and windows are typically glued to a horizontal or vertical plane

With this option selected, what you drew will be enclosed within the component

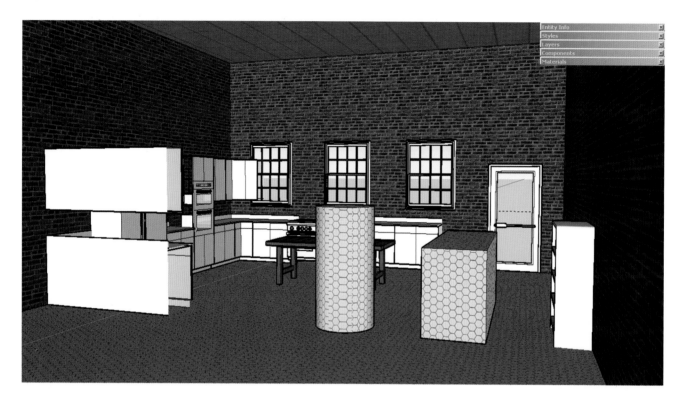

Figure 5.18 *The completed kitchen*

All the components will need to be painted, and each can be edited to look more like the actual equipment. There are other refinements, of course. Using correctly modeled equipment gives us a very good feel for what the kitchen organization should be.

REFINING THE ENROBING MACHINE

The block we used for the enrobing machine was a bit rudimentary—let's edit it to show the enrober and cooling tunnel. This will have to be approximate, as a great deal of time can be burned up making these components perfect. And there's nothing worse than burned chocolate.

1. Double-click on the enrobing machine to edit.
2. Choose **View>Component Edit>Hide Rest of Model** from the drop-down menu.
3. Click the **Rectangle** tool.
4. Click on the bottom edge of the long side of the block about a third of the way along.

5. Type **,28**, then **ENTER** (that's right, no first number) to make the rectangles 28" high.
6. Draw two more rectangles to make hollows for the legs.
7. Click **Push/Pull.**
8. Click on the face of one of the rectangles.
9. Mouse over the rear corner of the block and click when the tool tip indicates Endpoint to core through to the other side of the block (Figure 5.19).
10. Draw rectangles along the ends and **Push/Pull** through again.
11. Draw lines on the top to define the feed and output trays, and the lowered cooling tunnel, and **Push/Pull** down.
12. If you're feeling detail-oriented, hollow out some more for the actual tunnel and add the metal mesh conveyor belt, on/off switch, and so forth.
13. Triple-click on any face to select the whole kit and caboodle.
14. Click on the **Paint Bucket.**
15. Under the Metals heading, choose *Metal_Corrugated_Shiny.* Paint the selected objects and click outside the dotted black box to close the component (Figure 5.20).

In a studio setting, there's really no need for every single person to generate existing conditions models or certain repeated project elements,

UNDER THE HOOD

*SketchUp, AutoCAD, and Revit have similar conventions about making selections. Clicking and dragging from left to right creates a **Selection Window**, where only drawing elements that fall entirely within the window are selected. Clicking and dragging from the right to the left creates a **Crossing Window**, where all drawing elements that fall entirely within the window or just cross it are selected. To add to the selection set, hold down **SHIFT** (**CTRL** in Revit) and click on a new object—clicking on one you've already selected will remove it from the selection set.*

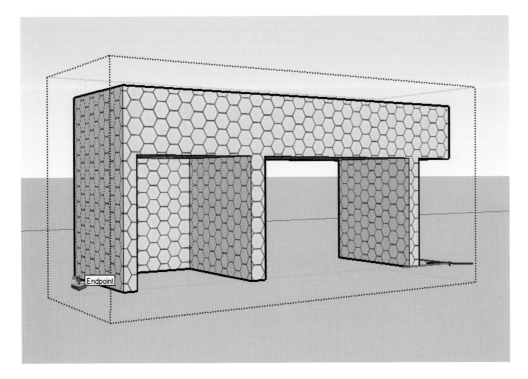

Figure 5.19 *Hollowing the block*

Figure 5.20 *The finished enrobing machine*

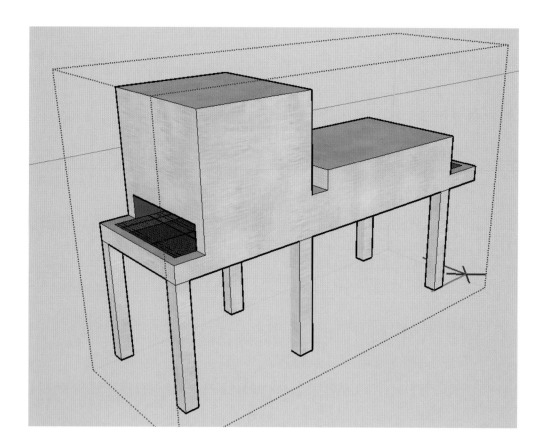

such as the enrobing machine created above. Collaborate—or, better yet, vote to have different people work on these pieces for the whole class, and then share when they're done. To export a component from a model, right-click on it and choose **Save As...** from the menu. This will export only that component as an eponymous file, which can be shared with others.

Slicing the Model for Plans and Sections

Models can be sliced open to peer inside by inserting a **Section Plane**. This is better than hiding walls or layers, since they're easier to include as part of a saved scene. Section planes can be oriented to cut away the top of your project for a plan view, or one side for a section view. One drawing can have many section planes inserted and active at one time, including planes inside components.

Most modeling is done in perspective, but it's nice to have a true plan saved for reference. Insert a section plane and change some of the view settings to produce and save a true orthographic view.

1. Click **Extents** to zoom out of your model.
2. Click the **Section** tool.
3. Mouse over the model to achieve the correct orientation.
4. Hold down **SHIFT** to lock the directional inference.
5. Move your mouse until it's about 3' above the main floor—this is the standard cut height for a floor plan. Click to crop away the upper half of the model (Figure 5.21).
6. Click on the edge of the section plane to select it.
7. Use Move to reposition it higher or lower.
8. Click the **Top View** button on the Views toolbar.
9. Uncheck Perspective from the View drop-down menu.
10. Apply a **Style** if you'd like.
11. Turn on **Daylighting** for shadows—these add depth.
12. Save a scene and name it *True Plan*.

Scenes are not external files—they are views of your model that are saved within SketchUp. When you save one, a little tab appears at the top left of your screen. You can click on that tab at any time to return to that saved view.

MAGIC TRICK

Amaze your friends and impress your family—have two section planes open at the same time. The magic happens because one of the section planes was inserted inside a component while it was open for editing. Close the component and you'll be able to activate one of the other section planes in the drawing (Figure 5.23). Note that you won't see the gray plane of the embedded section.

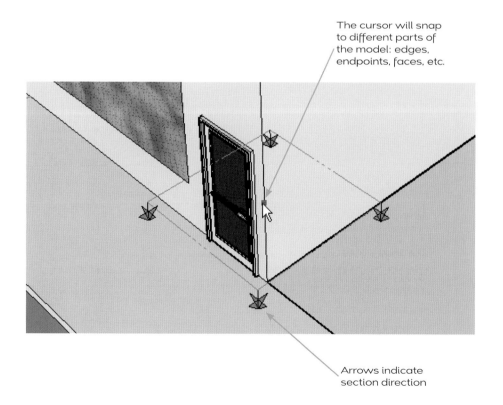

The cursor will snap to different parts of the model: edges, endpoints, faces, etc.

Arrows indicate section direction

Figure 5.21 *The section plane directional inference*

Figure 5.22 *Section planes in the model*

Double-click on a gray section plane to activate it

Double-click on the active section plane to deactivate it

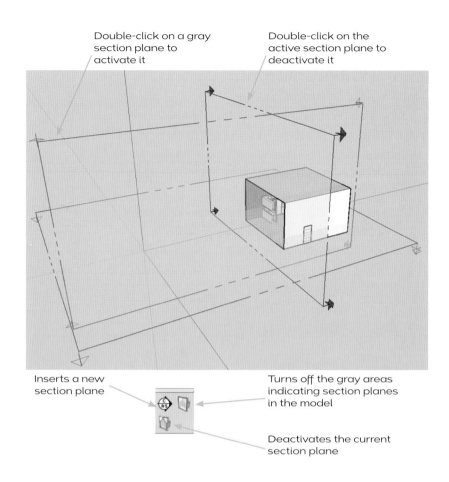

Inserts a new section plane

Turns off the gray areas indicating section planes in the model

Deactivates the current section plane

Figure 5.23 *Two section planes active at once*

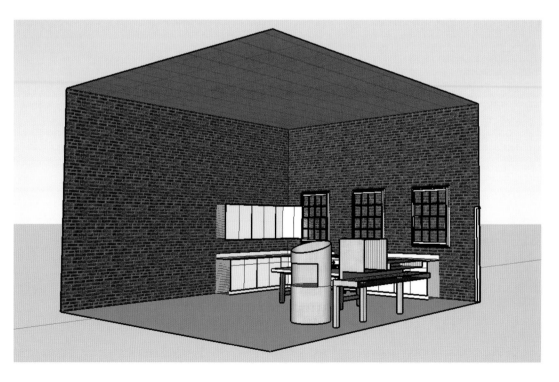

Different sections display as gray planes in your model (Figure 5.22) and can be turned on by double-clicking, or saving them in a scene. Use the **Sections** toolbar to turn off the current section from within a model and to hide those gray planes.

Double-click on whichever section plane you want to activate. Those gray areas are a little annoying, particularly when you're composing perspectives—turn them off, and be sure that the style you're using is updated.

Bug Splat

Sometimes good models go bad and you'll get a **Bug Splat** message—this is how SketchUp keeps track of problems. It often occurs when there's a problem with the geometry somewhere in the model, or the file is just getting a little too big. It's a good idea to restart your computer after this happens, and then call up your model again.

Occasionally these crashes damage the original model, and so you'll need that backup! Now that you've made this cool model, and maybe a walk-through and a daylighting movie, and everyone loves it, it's time to back up your work! SketchUp files have the extension .SKP, but if you happen to look in that directory, you'll also have .SKB files. These are backup files that SketchUp automatically saves, and you should keep them.

Printing

Printing right out of SketchUp is pretty much What You See Is What You Get (**WYSIWYG**), but you have to choose the image size and tiling options. Also, views can only be printed to scale if perspective is turned off and you are in one of the preset views such as Top View; otherwise, the scale options will not be highlighted in the print menu.

PRINTING PERSPECTIVAL AND SCALED VIEWS DIRECTLY FROM SKETCHUP

1. Click on the Scene of a perspective you'd like to print.
2. Type **CTRL+P** to print (Figure 5.24).
3. Click **OK** to print.
4. Click on the True Plan saved scene.
5. Type **CTRL+P**.

Figure 5.24 *The print menu for a perspective drawing*

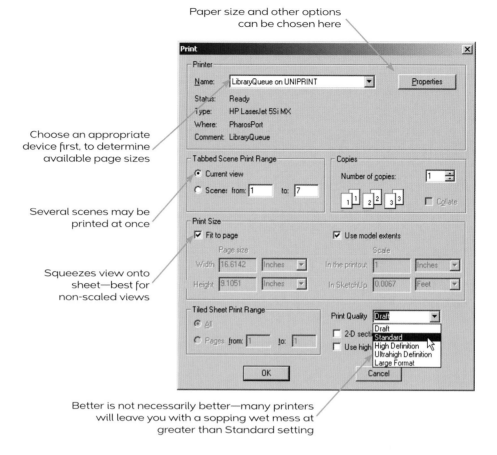

Paper size and other options can be chosen here

Choose an appropriate device first, to determine available page sizes

Several scenes may be printed at once

Squeezes view onto sheet—best for non-scaled views

Better is not necessarily better—many printers will leave you with a sopping wet mess at greater than Standard setting

6. Uncheck the **Fit to Page** radio button (Figure 5.25).
7. For a ¼" = 1'-0" printout, fill out the Scale fields: Type ¼ (inches) for *In the printout* and 1 (foot) for *In SketchUp*.
8. Click on the **Scale** box to update the size of the sheet.
9. Change the scale if it doesn't fit onto the size sheet you were hoping to use, or change the size paper and click **OK** to print.
10. If your test prints look decent, print using a higher-quality setting.

Printed drawings will often look significantly different from what you see on your screen. Your computer monitor is backlit, for one thing, and tends to show only a portion of the drawing anyway. Also, the paper you choose has a huge impact on the behavior of ink: Glossy photo paper will look great, but just a few drawings will use up a whole $40 three-color cartridge in no time. All this adds up to one thing: ***do a test print***. This is especially true if you are only printing a few images for your project, or this is the first time your idea has moved from the electronic world to the real one.

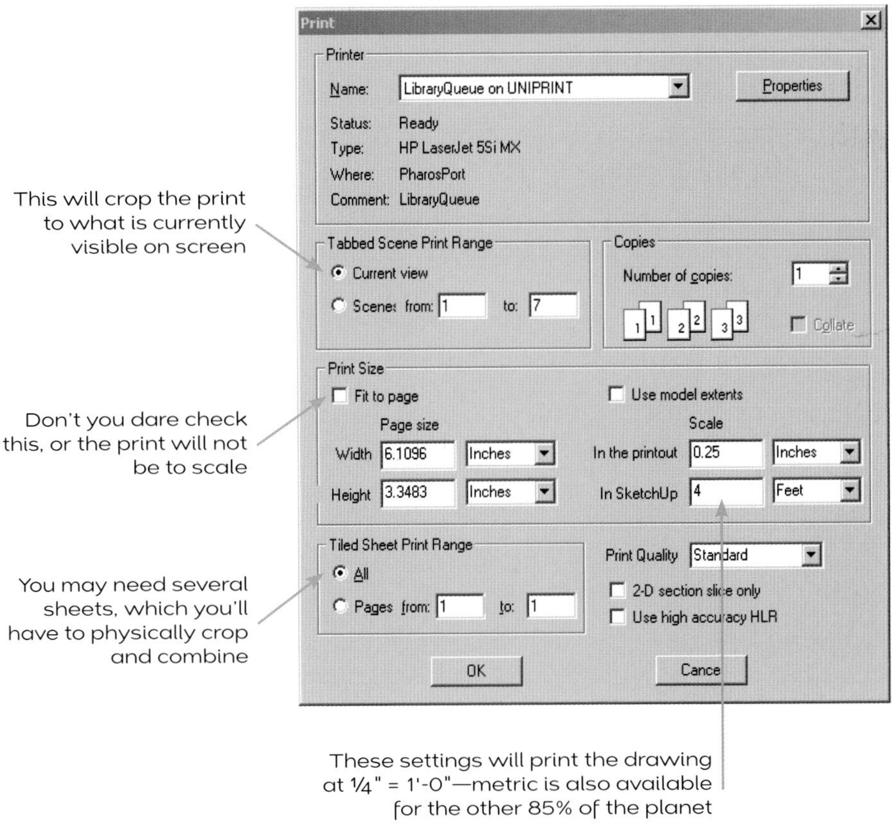

Figure 5.25 *The Print menu for a scaled drawing*

This will crop the print to what is currently visible on screen

Don't you dare check this, or the print will not be to scale

You may need several sheets, which you'll have to physically crop and combine

These settings will print the drawing at ¼" = 1'-0"—metric is also available for the other 85% of the planet

Online Resources

- *Chocolate cafe base model.skp*, which includes existing conditions and saved scenes
- *SketchUp Quick Reference Card.pdf*

Term Project Assignments

- Complete the base model.
- Save interior perspective scenes.
- Save true plan and section scenes.
- Populate and lay out the commercial kitchen with components.

Exercises and Further Study

- For practice with components, model a seating group for ten people without using walls.

- Model the room you're sitting in.
- Draw rooms with complex moldings and trim.
- Create one class charrette for a sales kiosk.
- Create one class design charrette: Design the service counter for the Chocolate Café.
- Create a daylighting study of a single room from a past project.
- Experiment with the **Sandbox** tools, which allow modeling of organic-looking surfaces.

┌─────────┐
│   │
│   6   │
│   │
└─────────┘

Schematic Design for
Small Projects

LEARNING GOALS

- Understand modeling strategy for more complex projects in SketchUp
- Understand appropriate level of detail for a schematic model
- Develop skills at creating, isolating, and controlling complex objects
- Develop skills at creating animations
- Produce sheets of drawings in Layout

SketchUp can model multiroom projects, but especially for interior renovations, this works against some of the best features of the program. Massing models, checking finish schemes quickly, moving around furniture layouts, and creating anything custom are Sketch-Up's strengths. Also, projects where there's a long gap between schematic sketches and full plans, or when you plan to go to AutoCAD rather than Revit, tend to lend themselves to SketchUp. There are distinct strategies for developing a more complex model, which are meant to help keep the model organized and allow for quick, flexible modifications.

The Modeling Process for
Complex Projects in SketchUp

1. Draw existing walls, floors, and ceilings as a group (as we did in the previous chapter).
2. Import bubble diagram from **PowerPoint** if needed.

3. Separate multilevel projects into different groups.
4. Save scenes for easy maneuvering around the project.
5. Draw interior partitions as groups, including the door openings.
6. Populate with furnishings, groupings (like our kitchen layout from the previous chapter), and entourage.
7. Make complex objects like custom casework and ceilings into groups.
8. Use layers to organize elements of your drawing.
9. Render using **iRender nXt**.
10. Create presentation drawings using **Layout**.

We already completed Step 1 in the previous chapter. Now it's time to develop and organize the model to produce more sophisticated drawings and renderings. We will review most of these strategies as we develop the design project.

SketchUp models tend to be very sticky, and this can cause problems as we move forward. Any geometry more complex than, say, an ottoman should be separated from other things using either components or groups. To avoid unintended consequences, the first thing we should do is make the existing conditions into a **Group**. From an interior view, triple-click on any surface—this selects the surface, its edges, and any free geometry that is connected. If any of the kitchen components happen to get selected, hold down **SHIFT** and click on them to remove them from the selection set. Now right-click on the selected items and choose **Create Group**.

MAGIC TRICK

If you have a multilevel project, each level should be its own group, not a repeated component. Groups bind all sorts of objects together for convenience, but they are a one-off deal: Changes to one instance of the group have no effect on any others. Change a component, on the other hand, and you'll change every single instance in your model. So copy the first-floor group vertically, type in the floor-to-floor distance, and there you have it: a multilevel project.

UNDER THE HOOD

Whenever you need to get content from one program into another program, it's almost always a matter of Exporting from one and Importing into another. The trick is to find the right file format, where the information you need can be accessed in the destination software. JPEG and PDF are the most common formats used for graphic information and printing, while DWG is most common for three-dimensional information.

Importing the Bubble Diagram

To insert a bubble diagram from your predesign research project, you'll have to export it as an image from PowerPoint first. SketchUp allows you to insert all sorts of content into a model, including pictures (try dragging in an image straight from a Web page), AutoCAD files, and Autodesk 3D Studio Max models.

INSERTING A BUBBLE DIAGRAM

1. Open the PowerPoint slide with the bubble diagram (Online Resources, Chapter 3, *Bubble diagram example.pptx*).
2. Type **CTRL+A** to select everything in your slide.
3. Right-click on the objects and choose **Save as Picture** (you can also choose Save As from the Office menu and select JPEG to save the whole slide, border, and everything).

4. Give the image a name, and save in your project folder.
5. Choose **JPEG** format from the **Save as type** drop-down list.
6. In SketchUp, choose **File>Import**.
7. Select **JPEG** from the file type drop-down list.
8. Browse for your file, select it, and click **Import.**
9. Click once to plant one corner of the diagram—choose one side of your plan.
10. The other side of the image will follow your cursor, so click on the opposite end of your plan to make it about the right size (Figure 6.1) hold down **SHIFT** to lock the aspect ratio.
11. When you're done tracing the bubble diagram, click on its edge and hit the **DELETE** key.

If you'd like to see the diagram right under the model, paint the floor with glass—this will make it transparent. You could even set the whole model to X-ray view, but I find it a little annoying to draw in that mode. Paint all the walls, floors, ceiling, and equipment with finishes of your choice.

To add goodies like carpets and photographs on the walls, just find one using an image search engine. Then drag in from your browser. The drawing window must be visible below the browser window to make it

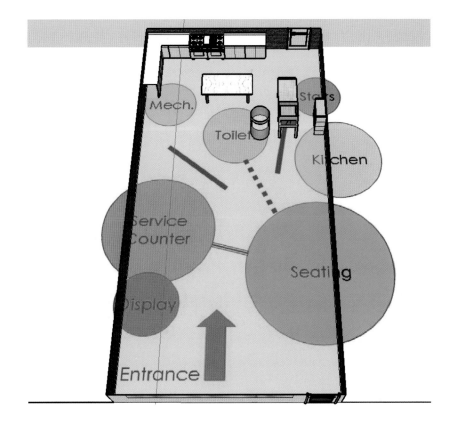

Figure 6.1 *The bubble diagram in the building shell*

work, and not all images will allow it—you'll have to save them to your computer first. Images can be resized using their corner grips, but they can't be cropped or otherwise edited.

Drawing Interior Partitions

With the bubble diagram in your model, it's easier to decide where you'd like to have partitions and other elements. Unlike in the previous chapter, you'll have rooms next to each other, so you'll have to model the thickness of the walls. This presents two problems: First, as you design, you often need to move walls around, and the sticky geometry can wreak havoc. This can be resolved by drawing two faces for the wall and then turning them into a group. The second problem is that components only cut through one face at a time, not two, so your doors will literally open onto a wall. For this you'll need to insert a door frame on the face opposite your door and align it to produce what looks just like a proper opening.

BUILDING AN INTERIOR PARTITION GROUP

1. Draw a rectangle in the middle of the floor roughly where you'd like the partition to go.
2. Type in **,5**, then **ENTER** to make the rectangle 5" wide or 5, **ENTER**, depending on the proportion. (After you draw a rectangle using the cursor, SketchUp allows you to type in the X and Y dimension, and they must be separated by a comma. If you leave out one of the values, it keeps the X or Y value that you drew and changes the other value to what you type in. Thus, in the first example, it retains the drawn X but changes the Y to 5.)
3. Double-click on the rectangle face and choose **Make Group**.
4. Double-click on the group to edit.
5. **Push/Pull** up to the ceiling—click on the **On Face** or **On Edge** cursor tips as you mouse over the ceiling.
6. Click on the saved plan view.
7. Choose **Camera>Perspective** from the drop-down menu.
8. Save another scene called *Overview* or something clever like that.
9. **Push/Pull** to the width of the project if that's what your design calls for.
10. Insert a door into one side of the wall (Figure 6.2).
11. If the wall is hard to see, choose **View>Component Edit>Hide Rest of Model** to get rid of the rest of the model.
12. On the face opposite where your door is, insert another door.

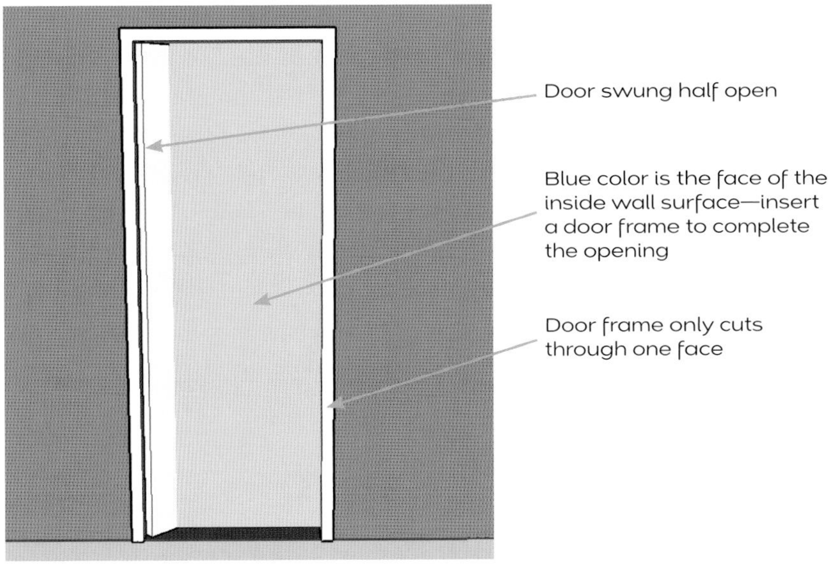

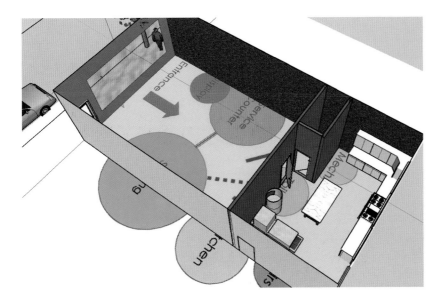

Figure 6.2 *The door to nowhere*

Door swung half open

Blue color is the face of the inside wall surface—insert a door frame to complete the opening

Door frame only cuts through one face

13. Right-click on the new door and choose **Make Unique**.
14. Now edit that new door by double-clicking on it.
15. Delete the door leaf.
16. Click outside the gray dotted bounding box to close the door component.
17. Click outside the gray dotted bounding box to close the wall group.
18. Select the wall with the **Select** tool.
19. Hold down **CTRL** and click and drag on the wall to make a copy.

Figure 6.3 *The plan with a few interior partitions groups on top of the bubble diagram*

After drawing an interior partition with a door, I tend to use a bird's-eye perspective overview (Figure 6.3) to move them around, copy, and rotate them. With the move command activated, mousing over a face of the wall group or component allows click-and-drag select and move at the same time, and also reveals the **Quick Rotate Compass**.

Sometimes the door needs to swing the other way. Rather than insert another component that's facing the right way, right-click on the wall and choose **Flip Along>Green Axis**. This will mirror the group along one of the standard axes. If that was the wrong one, click **Undo** and try the Red or Blue axis instead. Any group and component can be flipped individually like this.

Customizing Your Interface

Once you've become familiar with the basic drawing and editing tasks, you'll find that there are a few commands that you use over and over again. These can be accessed more quickly with keyboard shortcuts.

CREATING KEYBOARD SHORTCUTS

1. Choose **Window>Preferences>Shortcuts** from the drop-down menu (Figure 6.4).
2. Commands are listed by where they occur in the drop-down menus. Choose **View>Component Edit>Hide Rest of Model**.
3. Type **H** in the **Add** box.
4. Click the **+** sign (SketchUp will tell you if it's already used).

Figure 6.4 *The **Shortcuts** dialog box*

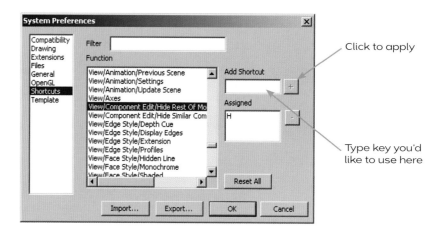

5. Now scroll down to find **Edit>Select.**

6. Since I draw with my left hand, I tend to use keys convenient to my right hand—so I'll use "L" for this common tool. Click the **+** sign to assign the shortcut.

7. If you work on lab computers frequently, click the **Export** button.

8. Browse for a location to save your profile. On a lab computer, click the **Import** button to open the profile (carry it with you on a USB drive).

9. Click **OK** to exit the dialog box.

10. In your model, double-click on a component to edit it.

11. Type **H** to hide the rest of the model.

12. Type **H** again to view the rest of the model.

Organizing the Model with Layers

If you're familiar with AutoCAD, you know about layers and how powerful they are. Any entity in SketchUp can be placed on a layer, and this can be convenient as you draw. Also, using layers helps the interior designer deal with objects imported from AutoCAD and allows objects created in SketchUp to render more easily in Revit.

To make a new layer, open the **Layer Manager** from the **View** drop-down menu. You can make new layers here, set them current, and turn them on or off (Figure 6.5).

Figure 6.5 *The **Layer Manager***

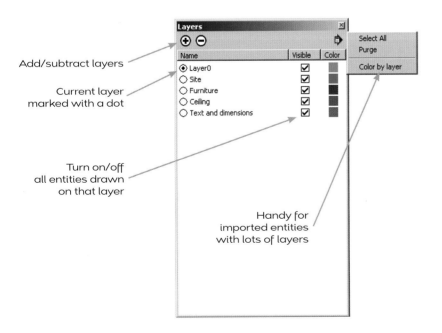

Add/subtract layers

Current layer marked with a dot

Turn on/off all entities drawn on that layer

Handy for imported entities with lots of layers

Right-click on a piece of furniture and choose **Entity Info**—you can
change the layer from within this dialog box. This allows you to turn off
all of your furniture quickly, which is handy if you're trying to move
around doors and windows or draw a chair rail, for example.

Drawing Complex Objects

Sometimes objects that appear complex can be drawn easily using components in a 3D array. A good example is a stair, which is just a series of
repeated treads and risers of exactly the same dimension. Use the geometry of the tread/riser component to make copies with the correct rise
and run. Then edit the component to define nosing and edge profiles,
riser and stringer materials. Overlapping lines can be hidden to smooth
out the view. Nothing is more fun than drawing stairs!

DRAWING STAIRS

1. Click the **Rectangle** tool and draw one off to the side of your
   project.
2. Type in **11, 48**, then **ENTER**.
3. Right-click on the rectangle and choose **Make Component**.
4. Call it *Tread and Riser* or something clever like that.

Figure 6.6 *The copied
single tread/riser
component*

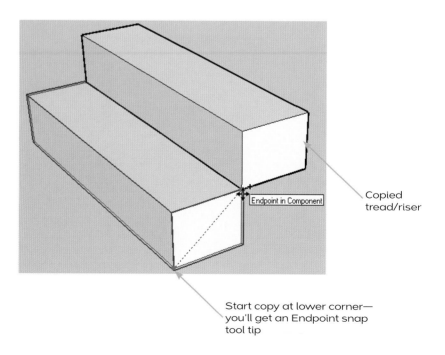

Copied
tread/riser

Endpoint in Component

Start copy at lower corner—
you'll get an Endpoint snap
tool tip

5. Double-click on the tread to edit.
6. Use **Push/Pull** to make it 8.25" high.
7. Close the component.
8. Click on the component to select.
9. Click on the **Move/Copy** command.
10. Hit **CTRL**, then click on the lower left of one side of the tread.
11. You'll see a copy glued to your cursor—click on the upper right of that same side to place the copy (Figure 6.6).
12. Create an array by typing **×14**, then **ENTER**—this makes 14 copies instead of just one.
13. Select all the treads.
14. Choose **Group** from the context-sensitive menu.
15. Select the group and click the **Move** command.
16. Move the stair into your plan and orient correctly.
17. Draw a rectangle for the opening through the floor.
18. Click on the middle of the rectangle to select it, and press **DELETE**.
19. Double-click on the stair group and then on a tread to edit.
20. Draw an arc at the edge of the tread to define the nosing.
21. Use **Push/Pull** to make it the length of the tread.
22. Use **Push/Pull** again to make the side overhang.
23. Paint the riser and side.

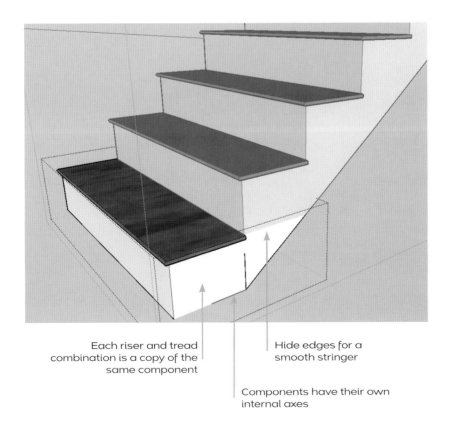

Figure 6.7 *Refinements to the tread/riser*

Each riser and tread combination is a copy of the same component

Hide edges for a smooth stringer

Components have their own internal axes

24. Use the **Line** tool to sketch the stringer.
25. Hold down **SHIFT** while erasing extra lines at the top and bottom of the stringer to hide them (Figure 6.7).
26. Close the component and the group.
27. My stair needs a landing, so I'll divide what I've created so far into two runs. Select the lower eight steps, then click the **Rotate** command.
28. Make sure the compass is indicating a horizontal orientation, and click to place the base of rotation at the corner of the top riser.
29. Click once to define the axis of reference, and then click again to place that axis 90 degrees from the top run of stairs.
30. Move the lower treads to align with the top run.
31. Right-click on the top tread of the lower run and choose **Make Unique**.
32. Use **Push/Pull** to stretch it into a landing. Do the same for the upper landing, if necessary, and just like that, you have a set of stairs (Figure 6.8).

Stairs can be a dramatic part of a design, and this method allows quick studies of different configurations and styles. Save each as a group and compare them side by side.

Figure 6.8 *The finished stair construction*

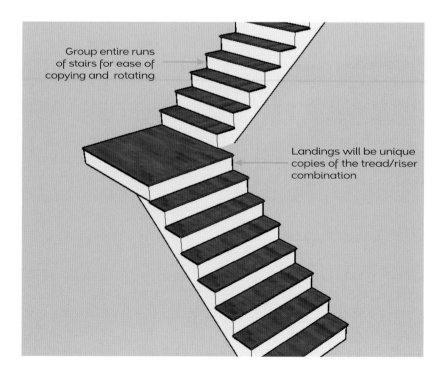

Group entire runs of stairs for ease of copying and rotating

Landings will be unique copies of the tread/riser combination

Drawing Complex Custom Objects

Custom complex objects can be made manipulating the surfaces and edges of simple shapes. Continuous edges or just sections can be offset to create new surface divisions, which can in turn be Push/Pulled to the geometric volumes of a given object.

DRAWING A CURVED SERVICE COUNTER

1. Draw the plan of your counter plan using rectangles, lines, arcs, and squiggles.
2. Draw a line to divide off a handicapped-accessible checkout counter (Figure 6.9).
3. Select all the lines and faces and create a component.
4. Double-click on the component to edit.
5. Push/Pull the main part of the counter to 42" and the accessible portion to 30".
6. Double-click on the top face to select. Click on the **Offset** tool. Click on the edge of the top to start the offset.
7. Move your mouse out away from the main mass to draw the overhang. Type in 2" **ENTER** to define the distance of the overhang.
8. Use Push/Pull again to make the countertop thickness.

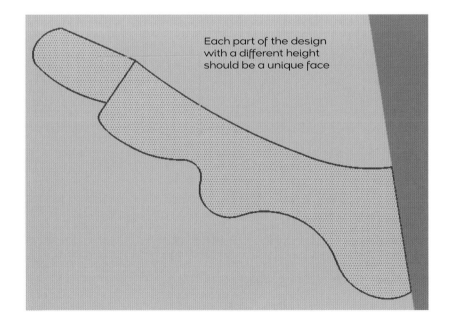

Each part of the design with a different height should be a unique face

Figure 6.9 *The counter profile*

9. Orbit the model so you can see the underside.
10. Select the front-facing arcs, lines, and squiggles on the seating side.
11. Use the **Offset** tool to create a 14" overhang.
12. Repeat the process for the accessible counter.
13. Double-click on the bottom face of what's left of the base cabinet.
14. Click the **Offset** command. Offset in 3".
15. Erase any extra weird squiggles (Figure 6.10), and use **Lines** to clip off pieces where you don't want a kick space, such as against a wall.
16. Push/Pull the outside up 4" for the kick space.
17. For the handicapped section, we'll just have a shallow reveal. Rotate the model to see the underside.
18. Double-click on the bottom to select the face and its edges.
19. While holding **SHIFT**, click on the highlighted face to deselect.
20. Click on the **Move/Copy** to make a copy.
21. While holding down **CTRL**, click once on the base to start the copy.
22. Type **4**, then **ENTER**.
23. Paint the faces whatever materials make you happy.
24. Open the **Layer Manager** and make a new layer called *Countertop*.
25. Rotate your model so that the top of counter can be selected easily.
26. Right-click on the objects and choose **Entity Info**.

Figure 6.10 *Creating an offset for the kick space*

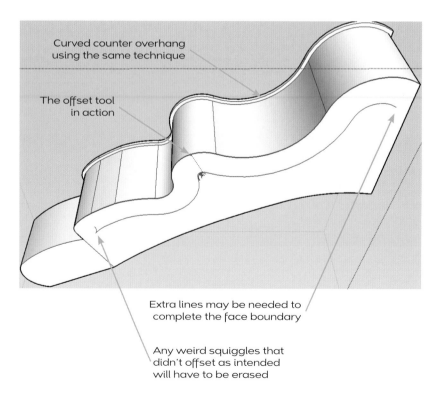

Curved counter overhang using the same technique

The offset tool in action

Extra lines may be needed to complete the face boundary

Any weird squiggles that didn't offset as intended will have to be erased

Figure 6.11 *The finished service counter*

27. From the **Layer** drop-down list, choose Countertop. You can also choose a material here by clicking on the swatch.
28. If you'd like a smoother look to your counter, choose **Soften/ Smooth Edges** from the context-sensitive menu.
29. Use the slider to make the edges look smooth and silky, and click **OK** when done (Figure 6.11).

Curved faces like these have to be modified in plan, as Push/Pull only works on flat (co-planar) surfaces. For major modifications or design options, it's usually easiest to re-draw the whole thing from scratch.

Refining the Plan

As you look at the model in floor plan, you'll probably want to see the exterior wall thickness as a dark hatch pattern. As we saw with the interior partitions, it's a royal pain to model wall thickness. A way to fake it is to draw in the wall thickness on the ground, and paint it with whatever poché color you'd like. Be sure to paint all walls, including interior partitions, so that the poché is consistent. Be sure to delete any overlapping faces (the ones that look like broken glass) and the bubble diagram image, before printing or exporting the plan view.

Other quick modifications include flipping the orientation of doors and other groups and components. SketchUp doesn't have a mirror command, but I can accomplish change by right-clicking on a component and choosing **Flip Along>Component Green Axis** from the context-sensitive menu.

Put a Lid on It

Drawing a ceiling is just like drawing any other custom shape—use a combination of drawing and editing tools to produce the shapes you'd like. Often it's more efficient to make use of shapes already drawn in the model, such as if you want a soffit to match the crazy curves of the counter. Create a group for the main part of the ceiling first. You can select a face from the counter, copy, and then paste it into the ceiling group.

MODELING A CEILING

1. From an interior view, double-click on the existing conditions group.
2. Double-click on the ceiling face to select it and its edges.
3. Type **CTRL+C** to copy the entities to the clipboard.
4. Close the group and choose **Edit>Paste in place** from the drop-down menu. You'll be happy to see a copy of those objects show up right on top of the originals.
5. Right-click on the entities and choose **Make Group** to create the ceiling group.

Figure 6.12 *The finished ceiling and soffit*

6. Open up the countertop group and double-click on the underside, where the irregular profile is most visible. Type **CTRL+C** to copy the selection to the clipboard.

7. Close the counter group and open the ceiling group.

8. Once again, choose **Edit>Paste in place** from the drop-down menu, and move the surface up to the ceiling.

9. From the context-sensitive menu, choose **Intersect>With Model** to ensure that the new geometry breaks the face of the ceiling.

10. **Push/Pull** down the soffit to a pleasing height.

11. Add other soffits with lines, arcs, squiggles, and whatnot.

12. Place all of your lighting before closing the group (Figure 6.12).

Note that you'll have to edit the group to insert light fixtures or to paint surfaces more than one color.

Annotation

Adding room names, notes, and dimensions is pretty easy. SketchUp guesses what you want to annotate and so automatically labels faces and components with their areas or names. Click on a line or two points to add a dimension string.

ANNOTATING THE PLAN

1. Click on the True Plan scene tab at the top of the drawing area.

2. Choose **Window>Layers** from the drop-down menu.

3. Create a new layer called *Text and Dimensions.*

4. Click the round radio button to make that layer current (the box has toggles that turn the layer on and off).

5. Click on the top bar to minimize the dialog box.

6. Click on the **Text** tool, then click on a room in the model.

7. An arrow appears, with a rubber band line to a piece of text. Click to plant the text.

8. Click the **Select** command.

9. Click on the text (or leader line).

10. Right-click on the text and choose **Entity Info** (Figure 6.13).

11. To eliminate the leader line, choose **Hidden** under the **Leader** drop-down list.

12. Click **Change Font...** to choose a font and text size.

13. Click on the top bar of the **Entity Info** dialog box to minimize.

14. Click the **Dimension** button.

MAGIC TRICK

*These dimensions have the annoying habit of moving as you rotate the model, so it's a good idea to place them in a view that you plan to print or export. Or, better yet, add annotation in **Layout**, where you're more sure of the size and shape of the intended output.*

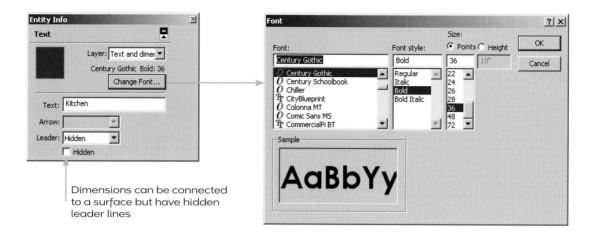

Dimensions can be connected
to a surface but have hidden
leader lines

Figure 6.13 *The **Entity
Info** dialog box for a
dimension string*

15. Click on the edge line at the left side of the plan.
16. A dimension string will attach itself to the cursor. Click to place it.
17. Add a dimension string for the top side as well. Move your mouse over the end of a wall until the endpoint cursor tip appears. Click once, then move your mouse over the end of the next interior partition. Click again to define the dimension.
18. Click to place the dimension (Figure 6.14).
19. Click and drag on the dimension to move it.

Figure 6.14 *The labeled
and dimensioned plan,
with faked wall thickness
and plenty of components*

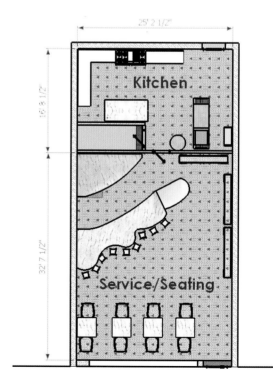

Figure 6.15 *Global annotation settings*

Click to change font, size, and color

Selects all the leaders you've already drawn, so they'll reflect any changes you make

One nice thing about leader lines is that SketchUp automatically types in a guess at what you want to write—either the name of the component or the area of a face. You can set standards globally for the different kinds of annotation. Choose **Window>Model Info...** from the drop-down menu and click on the **Text** group (Figure 6.15).

Be sure to select all the leaders you've already drawn, if you've already drawn any. Then any changes you make will affect all the leaders in your drawing, in addition to the new ones.

You can also change dimension settings and specify a precision for dimensions, on the Units tab. For rough schematics like this, ½" or even 1" is adequate, especially if you're just tracing a plan. For more detailed larger-scale drawings, ⅛" is more like it.

Animated Walkthroughs

Animated walkthroughs are one of the most interesting ways to present your design, and are very easy. The hard work is developing the model with different spaces, materials, and components. SketchUp will play a slide show of your saved scenes with timings you set. This can be exported in a standard movie file format for smoother presentations or for posting online.

LOOK OUT!

*The text will show up in other views, too, so you'll need to turn that layer off in saved scenes. When you do, be sure to right-click on the Scene tab name and choose **Update** from the context-sensitive menu. This saves the new layer configuration to that particular scene. Also, text (and leaders) move as you rotate the model, so be sure to place them in the Scene you plan to use, and the final zoom depth.*

1. View your model from the position you'd like to start in.
2. Save a scene and call it "start of my movie."
3. Use the **Walk** tool to move forward a few feet.
4. Save another scene (I usually don't name these).
5. Walk forward some more and save another scene.
6. Use the **Look Around** tool to view different parts of the space without moving your location within the model.
7. Save another scene.
8. Apply a different **Style**, and save an extra scene of a particular view—it will add interest to your movie.
9. Save 20–30 new scenes (Figure 6.16).
10. Preview your movie by choosing **View>Animation>Play Slide-show.**
11. Change settings to **Transition** (the time between slides) and **Page Delay** (the time the movie lingers on each slide) (Figure 6.17).
12. Export the movie to a file by choosing **File>Export>Animation.**
13. Choose a location for the file that you'll remember, like a folder called *Schematic Design*. Click on the **Options** button at the bottom of the dialog box (Figure 6.18).
14. For a presentation on a computer screen, about 400 pixels wide is fine; for presentation on a projector, about 800 is better.
15. A frame rate of 5 is good for a test; 10 is OK for a presentation or something on YouTube; 15 is very smooth.

Figure 6.16 *Cartoons of scenes for animation*

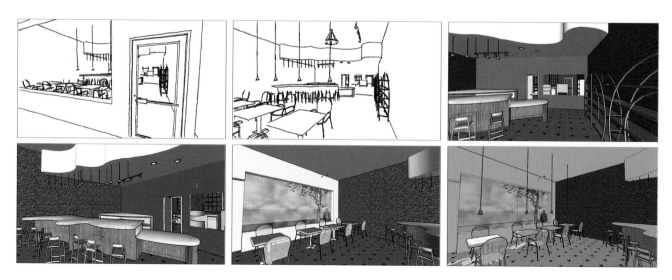

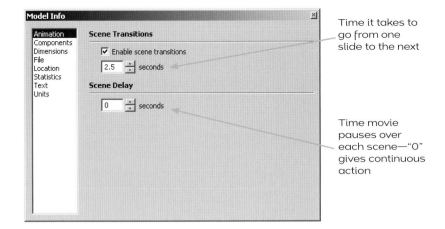

Time it takes to
go from one
slide to the next

Time movie
pauses over
each scene—"0"
gives continuous
action

Figure 6.17 *Slide show settings*

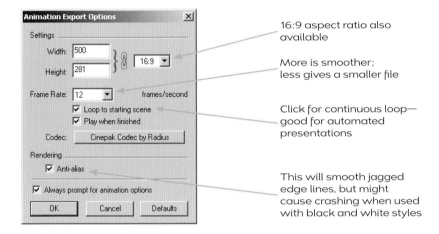

16:9 aspect ratio also
available

More is smoother;
less gives a smaller file

Click for continuous loop—
good for automated
presentations

This will smooth jagged
edge lines, but might
cause crashing when used
with black and white styles

Figure 6.18 *Animation Export Options*

16. Click **OK** twice to export the movie—this can take a few hours, depending on the resolution and frame rate.

These animations can be placed in presentations in PowerPoint or Photoshop Elements to make a splash to illustrate a special feature like daylighting.

Daylighting Studies

Another way to evaluate your project is to examine how well your design adapts for the different daylighting conditions during the day and during different seasons. You need a model with windows to the outside, and a view from the space looking out those windows. Then it's a matter of two saved scenes.

Figure 6.19 *Daylighting settings for the two scenes*

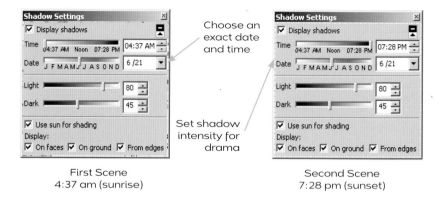

First Scene
4:37 am (sunrise)

Second Scene
7:28 pm (sunset)

Choose an exact date and time

Set shadow intensity for drama

A DAYLIGHTING MOVIE FOR THE SUMMER SOLSTICE

1. Set up an interior view of a model facing south with some windows.
2. Click on the settings button of the **Sun Settings** toolbar and turn on daylighting (Figure 6.19).
3. Set location to where your project is located.
4. Set date to January 1, and the time to dawn. Save a scene.
5. Set time to dusk and save another scene.
6. Under **Animation Settings**, change Transition time to 10 seconds.
7. Play the slide show to see how daylighting tracks across the space during the course of the day.
8. Export to a movie file for a smoother view.

You can use the same process to make a movie for the summer, when lighting conditions will be significantly different. Thus, the effectiveness of window treatments, light shelves, baffles, and other tools can be judged in a quick and effective manner.

Exporting Still Images

If you're doing board presentations or a slide show, you'll need to get still images of a decent quality out of SketchUp. Screen shots are the quickest way—type **CTRL+Prnt Scrn** and whatever's on your screen will be copied to the clipboard. You can paste it into PowerPoint or Photoshop Elements or an e-mail to your mom. The resolution on a screen shot isn't good enough to print, though, so you'll need to go through the export menu to get a higher-quality image.

1. Open your Chocolate Café file (Online Resources for Chapter 6, *Chocolate cafe schematic design.skp*).
2. Choose the plan scene.
3. Turn off daylighting and change the **Face Style** to **Hidden**.
4. Choose **File>Export>2D Graphic…**
5. Browse or create an appropriate file location.
6. Choose **JPEG image file (*JPEG)** from the **Export Type** drop-down list.
7. Click on the **Options** tab.
8. Choose 2,400 pixels wide for a high-quality export—the height will adjust proportionately. Click **OK** twice to export the image.

This size is not entirely random, but it's not an entirely simple to explain resolution, either. For a detailed method for determining the optimal image size, see Understanding Pixels, in Chapter 15.

Design Boards in Layout

Often a small project can be presented using one or two sheets, and consist of plans and perspective drawings. SketchUp's companion software, Layout, makes it easy to compose a presentation using a model, allowing you to work right up until the moment you decide to print your board.

The interface is very similar to SketchUp—zooming, panning, drawing, and intuitive. Import your SketchUp file and you'll have access to all of your saved scenes and styles. Viewports can be set to scale, and the whole sheet given a nice graphic look.

> **LOOK OUT!**
>
> *Larger sheet sizes will become very slow to manipulate unless you have a monster of a computer. The file sizes will also be triple the size of your original SketchUp file.*

1. Call up Layout—it's under the Google SketchUp program group in your Start menu.
2. Choose a blank from the **Getting Started** menu (Figure 6.20)—this will give you a sheet with gridlines.
3. Choose **File>Document Setup.**
4. Click on the **Page** tab to change the sheet size.
5. Set the sheet size to 36" wide, 24" high (that is, of course, if your plotter supports that size sheet). Click **OK** (Figure 6.21).
6. To import your model onto the blank sheet, choose **File>Insert.**

Figure 6.20 *The* ***Getting Started*** *dialog box*

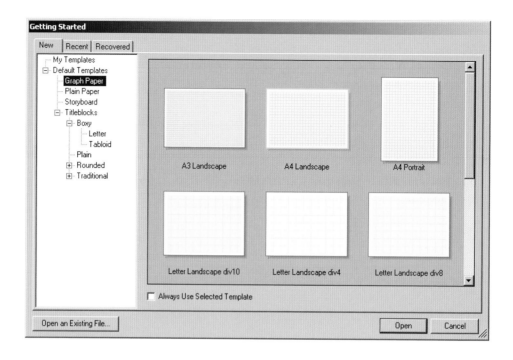

Figure 6.21 *The* ***Layout*** *interface*

Editing and drawing tools

Adds a new sheet and switches between existing sheets

Palette for making changes to a given viewport

Drawing area

Good for help on different options

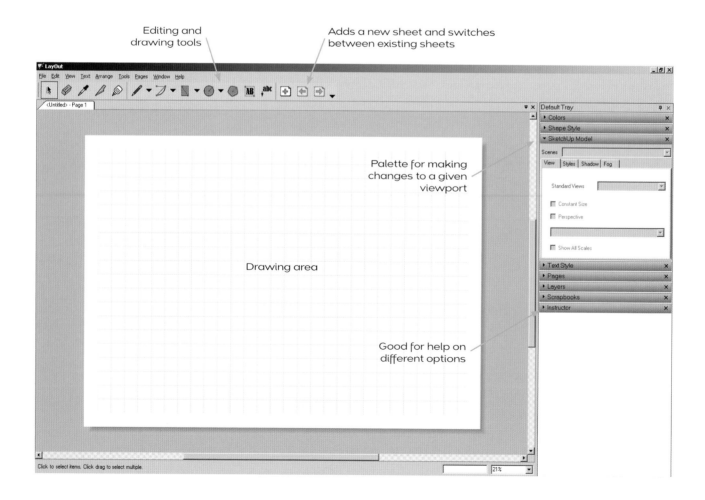

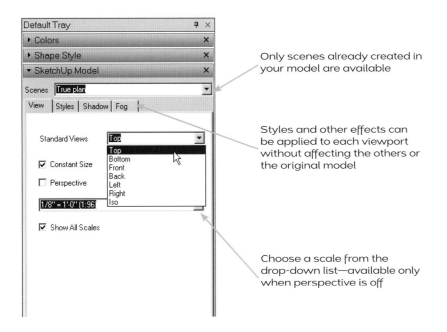

Only scenes already created in your model are available

Styles and other effects can be applied to each viewport without affecting the others or the original model

Choose a scale from the drop-down list—available only when perspective is off

Figure *6.22 SketchUp*
Model menu

7. Browse for your drawing and click **OK**—it comes in as a viewport showing whatever view you had visible last.
8. Click on the **Select** command.
9. Click on the edge of the viewport. Click and drag the edges to change extents of the image vertically or horizontally—the field of view will automatically expand or narrow.
10. Double-click on the viewport to enter it and orbit around the model.
11. To access View commands, right-click on the screen.
12. Click outside the viewport to exit.
13. Hold down **CTRL** and drag on your image to make a copy of the current viewport.
14. From the **SketchUp Model** menu, choose another scene (Figure 6.22).
15. Apply a different Style if desired.
16. Select the viewport and click on the **Move Back** button to control overlaps.
17. Copy the viewport again and apply the **True Plan** scene.
18. Choose a scale from the **SketchUp Model** tab.
19. Copy the viewport again.
20. Set the saved scene to an elevation.
21. Set to scale.
22. Click on the **Text** tool. Click to place a title at one side of the sheet. Type a name for the project. Select the text and choose a font and size that fits.
23. Click the text tool again to add titles for individual drawings.

Figure 6.23 *Overlapping images assembled for final composition*

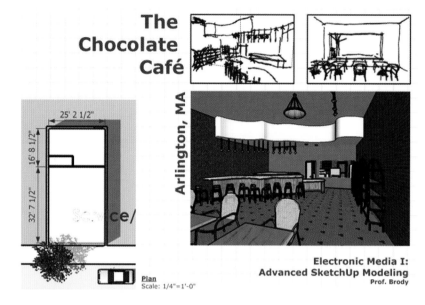

Reflected ceiling plans can also be created here, with a little advance planning. In SketchUp, insert a section plane facing up so that it crops away the bottom of the model. Save a scene with this section plane active and perspective off. Rotate the model to as close to a ceiling plan as you can get. Then, in Layout, apply this scene and then choose Standard Views>Bottom View. *Finally, choose* Flip>Top to bottom *from the context-sensitive menu to orient the same way as the floor plan.*

24. To add more sheets of drawings, click the **Add Sheet** button. Add additional drawings as needed.
25. To present from within Layout, choose **View>Full Screen** (Figure 6.23).
26. To put in a format for sharing, choose **File>Export PDF...**

Viewports can be copied by clicking and dragging while holding down the **CTRL** key. To change overlapping, right-click on the offending entity and click on the **Move Forward** or **Backward** button.

Layout is designed with a simple interface, so most of the view control features from SketchUp are hidden in its context-sensitive menus. In fact, most of the viewport features can be changed here, and you can also open up the model to make editorial changes.

Images can also be inserted to represent materials or to enhance rendered views. Just choose **File>Insert...**, and browse for the image you'd like to add. They'll be sized proportionally to the sheet size and resolution. If you don't plan to print, just leave the page size at 8½" × 11". Be sure to include a graphic scale on all electronic presentations, though, as there is no other reliable way to judge the size of things.

Exporting to AutoCAD

SketchUp is great for quick sketch modeling and even small projects. As soon as you need construction drawings, however, it's probably best to move to AutoCAD, Revit, or some similar program. SketchUp models can be exported as a two-dimensional slice through the model, which makes it much easier to manipulate in AutoCAD. All three-dimensional information can also be exported for use in AutoCAD, or any other program that accepts that file type.

EXPORTING YOUR PLAN AND ENTIRE MODEL TO AUTOCAD

1. Click on the True Plan scene.
2. Choose **File>Export>Section Slice…** and browse to find a handy file location.
3. Click on the **Options** button at the bottom of the dialog box.
4. Be sure to export in a version of AutoCAD that you have—click **Options** to specify.
5. Click **OK**, then **OK** again.
6. To get a 3D AutoCAD file, choose **File>Export>3D Model…**
7. Make sure the **File Type** is AutoCAD drawing.
8. Check the options as before, and click **OK** to export (Figure 6.24).

The section slice will open as a flat 2D AutoCAD drawing. Components generally export as blocks, although multiple instances will each

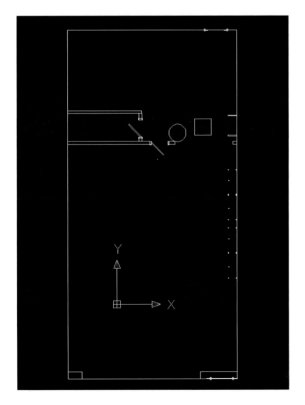

Figure 6.24 *The project as it looks in AutoCAD*

have different block names (bummer!). Also, all hatching and materials are lost. The 3D model will retain face information, which comes in as surfaces. Materials and other behaviors can be assigned per usual. SketchUp used in this way can become a handy solid modeler, and generally much easier to use than the native AutoCAD tools.

Importing from AutoCAD

What if you've got a plan in AutoCAD and you'd like to bring it into SketchUp? If it's already in 3D (basically, lines and other objects have some thickness assigned), then you're all set. Choose **File>Import...** and make sure the **File of Type** drop-down list says CAD Formats. Then browse for your file. You may have to explode nested blocks and other goodies. Alas, any assigned materials will be lost. If there was already content in your model before import, the CAD plan will be grouped. Double-click on it to edit. When imported into an empty model, the plan will be broken down into its constituent lines and arcs.

Unlike the SketchUp model, your section slice is not in 3D, and what's worse, there are no faces filled in, only lines. There are three strategies for generating the 3D model. The first is for simple projects: Use the line tool to trace over the CAD lines, in the hope that they'll fill in. Always use snaps to different points on the existing lines, and look to create closed loops and simple shapes, like triangles. This is the same process we used with the imported molding profile earlier—see Figure 5.12. The results are often inconsistent, however, and you can spend a good deal of time drawing diagonal lines all over the plan trying to get the walls to fill in.

The second method, if you're working in AutoCAD, is to add 3D information before importing into SketchUp. While still in AutoCAD, select all the exterior walls and give them a "thickness" (enter a value in the **Properties** dialog box) based on how tall the ceilings are supposed to be—this will translate into the vertical (blue) direction in SketchUp. To get fancy, you can control the Start- and End-Z values. Set them both the 6'-8" for a door head, for example. The thickness will then be the distance from the door head to the ceiling—3'-4" for a 10' ceiling. The face will show up at the right height in SketchUp. Once imported into SketchUp, these faces will behave properly, so you can insert door and window components, paint, and so forth.

The last method for generating a 3D model involves tracing over the imported CAD plan with rectangles, lines, and arcs. Leave the plan as a group (or group it) and trace over the plan elements. This method is probably a little tedious for complex plans, but it ensures a well-functioning SketchUp model.

Working in Metric

Let's say you live somewhere other than the United States and you need to work in metric measure. If you're working where the metric system is integrating with the products and supply industry, you'll be using "hard" metric. That is, standard sizes and spacing will be rounded for ease. If you're doing a project for the federal government or in Canada, it'll be "soft" metric—that is, you'll use standard building products manufactured to imperial dimensions. So any dimension strings will look a little odd—not nice, rounded numbers.

Within SketchUp, you can change the settings of the model for whichever system and level of precision you prefer. Choose **Window>Model Settings...** This is the place to set all global variables for your drawing, like text and dimensions. Click on the **Units** tab (Figure 6.25).

Of course, you'll have to be familiar with metric sheet sizes and typical scales for different elements. And, of course, perspectives are not scaled. You can also change the units setting in Layout. Choose **File>Document Setup** and click on the **Units** tab.

Note that you can work entirely in Imperial units and switch at the last minute. Hard metric projects require the use of properly sized components, however, so you'll have to consider that when you start the project, not after completing the model. This menu has other goodies for controlling the Layout interface—explore and customize!

Many model-wide settings are grouped here

Units can be set to millimeters, centimeters, or whole meters

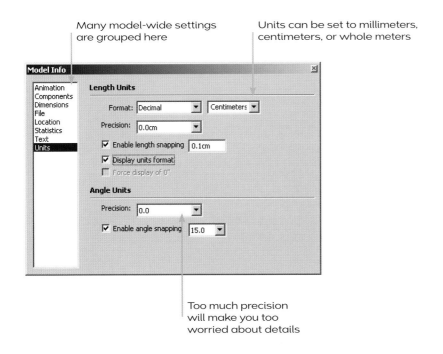

Too much precision will make you too worried about details

Figure 6.25 *SketchUp Model Units settings*

Online Resources

- Base model with interior partitions and furnishings, *Chocolate cafe schematic design.skp*
- Layout file used in the examples, *Chocolate cafe schematic board.layout*
- Graphic scale component for SketchUp (*Graphic scale.skp*)
- SketchUp models exported in 2D and 3D, *Chocolate cafe plan in CAD.dwg* and *Chocolate 3D CAD model.dwg*

Term Project Assignments

- Create a schematic design presentation in Layout that includes:
  - ▼ Plan and reflected ceiling plan at ¼" = 1'-0"
  - ▼ Interior elevations at ¼" = 1'-0"
  - ▼ Graphic scale
  - ▼ Four perspective drawings
  - ▼ Title, name, date

Exercises and Further Study

- Draw a dogleg stair.
- Draw a spiral stair.
- Create an animated walkthrough of a past project.
- Create a title page for your animation and turn it off after the beginning using layers.
- Import a Revit model and apply materials.
- Import a CAD plan, make it three-dimensional, and apply materials.

Unit 3

Schematic Design in Revit

7

Modeling Existing Conditions

- Understand the difference between building Information modeling and sketch modeling
- Understand the structure of Revit models
- Master basic modeling in Revit, including generating walls and floors
- Understand component families and instances

Using Building Information Modeling (BIM) to generate an architectural project provides a more sophisticated set of tools for design and evaluation, but you pay for them with a slower and less flexible start to the process. All of the typical views of a design project, from traditional bubble diagrams and orthographic drawings to schedules and keys, are kept in the same model. This keeps your electronic workflow smooth. You can create a block diagram directly from a bubble diagram, for example, and then generate walls directly from the block diagram. Each phase of these larger projects is more complex than we've seen in the previous chapters, however, and has much more interlinked information.

Revit Overview

In Revit almost all drawing objects are parametric, which is to say they have properties that can be defined and modified, most typically through a menu somewhere, rather than being drawn. A wall is not just a pair of

---

BIG PICTURE

As in SketchUp, in Revit, you develop a single model of your project, which has all the data about materials, dimensions, and performance. Plans, sections, perspectives, and even schedules are just views of that single database, filtered by different criteria. These can include when objects are created and/or demolished, and which phase of construction the current view is meant to represent; thus, views are snapshots of both a place and time within your project.

- *Start using a template.*
- *Draw a bubble diagram using "rooms."*
- *Draw the existing conditions.*
- *Adapt the bubble diagram to make a block diagram.*
- *Draw interior partitions, ceilings, floor openings.*
- *Model complex elements like stairs and railings.*
- *Insert furnishings, fittings, and equipment.*
- *Develop custom objects in SketchUp.*
- *Configure views on sheets, including drawings and schedules.*
- *Render perspectives and export walkthroughs.*

MAGIC TRICK

I like to keep my own personal Revit library folder for downloaded templates, components, materials, and custom families. Locate the folder where you're going to back it up—in My Documents somewhere, or on a special data drive.

lines with some hatching in the middle, but instead a complex object representing a nonbearing structure of metal studs that's sandwiched between two layers of ⅝" drywall. That material, in turn, has display characteristics assigned to it, with rendering properties including color and reflectivity. Light fixtures are defined both in terms of their graphic appearance on the reflected ceiling plan and their light output distribution, which will in turn be the basis for shadows in the rendering process.

From these parametric objects you can quickly generate more complex drawings like detail sections and schedules. Project-wide parameters are stored under the Settings drop-down menu, and, like element parameters, can be modified at any point during the design process. Custom objects like casework will be a bit cumbersome to create within Revit, however, and are best modeled in SketchUp.

To start a new project, call up Revit, and you'll be greeted with a welcome screen listing recently accessed **Projects** and **Families**, along with options for **Browse...** or **New...** for both types of document. Click new for the default template (Figure 7.1). I have provided a template configured for an interior renovation in the Online Resources for this chapter. Save it to your computer, and use for this project.

Revit allows you to keep track of the phases typical of an interior renovation in a sophisticated manner—so demolition plans are generated automatically when you put in new doors, for example. For new projects, just create new exterior walls along with the interior ones, or generate an exterior massing model first.

The main Revit interface looks similar to most drawing programs, with a drawing area surrounded by menus and toolbars. However, there are far more tools available, and they are grouped by function under ribbons at the top of the Revit interface. The **Project Browser** allows you to navigate around different views of the project. What appears on the **Contextual** ribbon varies with the current tool. Editing tools are up top. The **Type Selector** drop-down list becomes active when you select a tool, and depends on which tool is current.

Building Program for a Complex Project

As we saw with SketchUp, the best way to learn new software is to try it out with a real project. Revit is best suited for projects with more complex scope. In this case, let's choose a larger-scale renovation, where we'll have existing conditions, demolition, and a new mezzanine. First, let's talk about the program for the project we'll be doing: a bowling alley (Table 7.1).

Project brief: A small northeastern college has decided to convert an old gym into a bowling alley, for use by students and the general public.

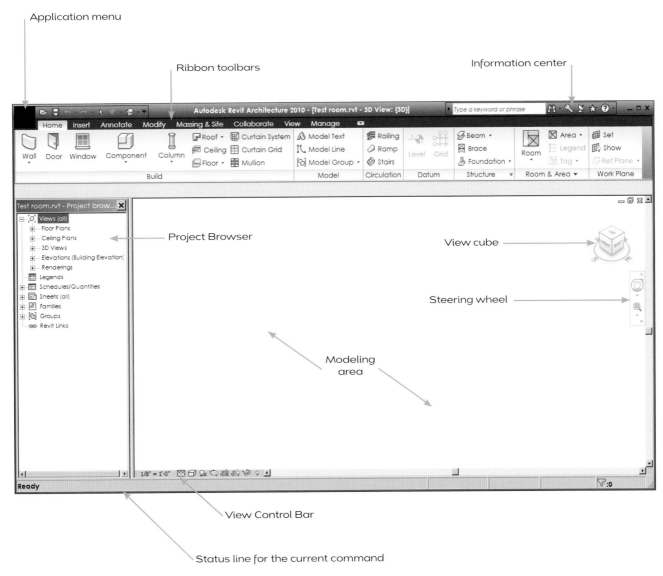

Application menu

Ribbon toolbars

Information center

Project Browser

View cube

Steering wheel

Modeling area

View Control Bar

Status line for the current command

Figure 7.1 *The parts of the Revit interface*

Learning goals and outcomes: After completing this project, the student should be able to produce a large, multilevel project modeled in Revit.

Background thoughts: What images come to mind when you think of a bowling alley? The aesthetic of bowling shoes and shirts have strong associations. What constraints might be involved with this project type?

Site: A concrete block and open-web steel joist gym attached to a sports facility at a small college in Massachusetts (Figure 7.2). The mechanical unit is up on the roof, and feeds the space through two huge supply ducts.

Constraints: Must comply with state and local codes, including all accessibility regulations. Entrance should be from an interior corridor at the current location, at the northwest corner of the plan. This corridor serves

TABLE 7.1   BOWLING ALLEY BUILDING PROGRAM

Program Area	Main Floor	Mezzanine
Bowling Lanes		
14 bowling lanes with ball-return alley and mechanism	7,300 SF	
Lane Seating and Storage		
Scoring desk—1 per lane w/4 seats	400 SF	
Movable table seating for spectators—4 per lane	500 SF	
Storage for seating	200 SF	
Subtotal for program group:	**1,100 SF**	
Service Counter		
Service counter for shoes rental—10 lf	100 SF	
Pro shop kiosk by service counter; balls, towels, shirts, etc.	100 SF	
Shoe storage closet behind front desk—16 lf tiered shelving	50 SF	
Ball storage racks near counter—3 @ 8' long	50 SF	
Subtotal for program group:	**300 SF**	
Food and Beverage Service		
Bar and food service with seating for 10	150 SF	
Drink prep counter behind service counter	100 SF	
Small kitchen w/commercial stove, fridge, freezer, fryer, and micro; 16 lf clear counter area	120 SF	
Food and beverage receiving storage	50 SF	
Spectator seating at tables for 35	450 SF	
Subtotal for program group:	**870 SF**	

the rest of the building complex as well as our site. Seal off all unused door and window openings to other parts of the site, except for upper lounge borrowed lights. Secondary egress door should have an airlock. Consider adjacencies when laying out bubble diagrams, and no areas or adjacencies are set in stone. Stair entrances must separated by at least 70'.

Process: Predesign research is the typical first step and can include precedent studies, code analysis, accessibility research, and looking into the equipment and other architectural considerations. This can be done

TABLE 7.1 (CONTINUED)

Program Area	Main Floor	Mezzanine
Toilets and Services		
Bathrooms (3 ♀ 2 ♂ each)	200 SF	
Janitor's room	30 SF	
Mechanical room	50 SF	
Garbage and bottle empties area away from food	25 SF	
Subtotal for program group:	**305 SF**	
Vertical Circulation		
Main stair (roughly 10 × 20)	400 SF	400 SF
Secondary egress stair (roughly 10 × 20)	400 SF	400 SF
Elevator (roughly 8 × 8)	100 SF	100 SF
Subtotal for program group:	**900 SF**	
Mezzanine		
Multipurpose room with seating for 50; must overlook bowling area; can be glassed in or open		500 SF
Multipurpose room with seating for 50; must overlook bowling area; can be glassed in or open		500 SF
Bathrooms (3 ♀ 2 ♂ each)		200 SF
Office with four desks		400 SF
Break room with view to the south		100 SF
Janitor's room		30 SF
Elevator mechanical room		50 SF
Subtotal for program group:		**1,780 SF**
Subtotal:	**14,250 SF**	**4,460 SF**
Circulation @ 25%	3,563 SF	1,115 SF
Total programmed space:	**17,813 SF**	**5,575 SF**

in PowerPoint (see Chapter 2) or, for more advanced graphic analysis, Photoshop Elements (see Chapter 4). Bubble diagrams, however, will be drawn in Revit this time. These will develop into block diagrams, which in turn will be converted into a building plan. Eventually, the design will be fleshed out with furniture, casework, finishes, lighting, and the like. Construction drawings, schedules, **materials takeoffs**, and photo-realistic renderings will all be produced from the same model.

Figure 7.2 *Plan of the site*

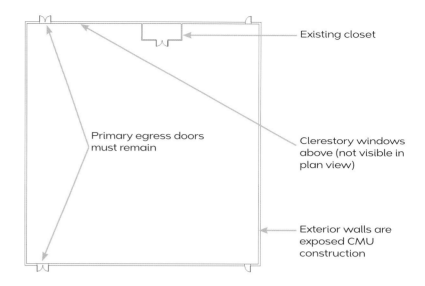

Existing closet

Clerestory windows above (not visible in plan view)

Primary egress doors must remain

Exterior walls are exposed CMU construction

Modeling Overview

Drawing objects in Revit is fairly logical, as the relevant tools are named clearly and the available options appear as each tool is selected. Objects must be created within one of the phases of your project—existing, New Conditions, or a user-defined stage—and they can be "demolished" during those phases as well. All objects are three-dimensional and can be selected and manipulated in any view where they are visible. Most objects are bound to a host or level (such as a light fixture in a ceiling), so when their references are moved during the design process, the objects move, too.

One of the most powerful organizing systems of a Revit project is the phase setup. Every view you project on is a snapshot of a particular part of your project (plan, elevation, perspective, finish schedule) at a particular point in time—for example, views can be set to display current phase with new conditions, the current phase with only existing and demolition, or only existing conditions and nothing new. These are defined by the **View Properties** dialog box for that view, and can be altered later on depending on what you'd like to show (Figure 7.3).

Every view—plans, sections, even schedules—is set to some phase, and objects created in that view will take on that phase. That view will also only display objects created either in the current or previous view. Every view also has a phase filter, which determines which objects will be displayed. A plan set to the New Construction phase and the Show Previous and New filter will only display objects from the Previous and New Construction phases, but not from the Demolished phase. There are often several versions of the same view, but with different phase fil-

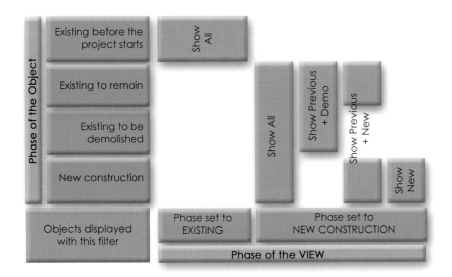

Figure 7.3 *Drawing objects displayed with different current phases and filters*

ters. An example is the main floor plan, where there will be one for existing conditions (phase: Existing conditions; filter: Show All), one for demolition, and another for new construction.

These settings can be applied to any view at any time, and objects must always be drawn on the intended phase for this complex house of cards to keep standing. If an object is in the wrong phase, it can be changed in the **Element Properties** dialog box. You can add more phases. For new and relatively small architectural projects, you really need only the New Construction phases, or perhaps the Existing one, for site work. For more complex projects, however, and certainly for large renovations, you'll often be required to include different construction stages, to accommodate continuous occupation of the building or required sequencing within the construction process.

Drawing the Exterior Walls

The key to managing a Revit project with more than one phase is to realize that anything drawn in a particular view will take on that view's current phase. The most common project type for architects (and certainly interior designers) is a renovation, where you'll have to produce accurate existing conditions drawings, figure out what needs to be demolished, and then show what is going to be new. When a project's phases and filters are set up correctly, modeling is merely a matter of drawing or inserting Revit's parametric objects in the right views. All drawing and editing commands function the same regardless of phase, filter, or even left-handedness.

Of course, none of us is entirely perfect in our work habits, so I've included a Project Template for interior renovations with Chapter 7 Online Resources (*Interior renovation template 2008.rte*), where you'll find ready-made views configured for the different drawing tasks we'll need in order to produce our project. For the rest of the chapters on Revit, I'll assume that you're using that template and will reference views and settings accordingly.

DRAWING THE EXISTING EXTERIOR WALLS OF THE BUILDING

1. Double-click on the **Main Floor Existing** view in the Project Browser to open it up.
2. Click on the **Home** ribbon.
3. Click the **Wall** tool, and you'll see a contextual ribbon of tools pop up (Figure 7.4).
4. Choose **Basic Wall: Exterior—CMU Insulated** from the Type Selector drop-down list.
5. Select **Roof** from the Height drop-down list.
6. Click the **Chain** radio button and click on your screen to start the wall.

Figure 7.4 *The* **Wall** *tool with options*

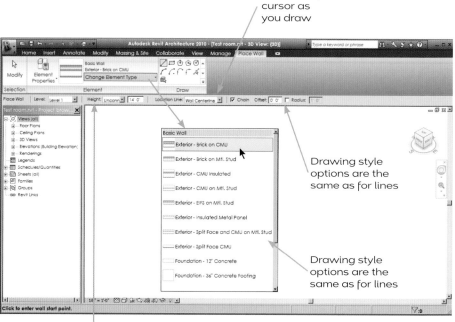

Location of cursor as you draw

Drawing style options are the same as for lines

Drawing style options are the same as for lines

Use a selection window to select windows but not walls

7. Move your mouse to the right, noting the distance in the cursor readout.

8. Type in **120**, then **ENTER** (that's correct, no apostrophe) to make the wall 120'-0" long.

9. Move your mouse down (south) and type **120**, then **ENTER.**

10. Move your mouse to the left until a dashed green alignment indication appears, and click (Figure 7.5).

11. Click on the remaining endpoint of the wall to complete the square plan.

12. To make the foundation wall, choose **Basic Wall: Foundation— 12" Concrete** from the Type Selector drop-down list .

13. On the **Contextual** ribbon, make sure the Level is set to Main Floor and the Depth is set to **T.O.** (top of) **Footing.**

14. Click on the **Select** button on the **Contextual** ribbon.

15. Move your mouse over one of the walls until the dashed green centerline cue is visible.

16. Click on the cue to place the wall—since it's underground, it won't actually be visible in this view.

17. Click on the other three walls to place foundations there.

18. To draw the footing, choose **Basic Wall: Foundation—36" Concrete** from the Type Selector drop-down list.

19. On the **Contextual** ribbon, make sure the Depth is set to **B.O.** (bottom of) **Footing.**

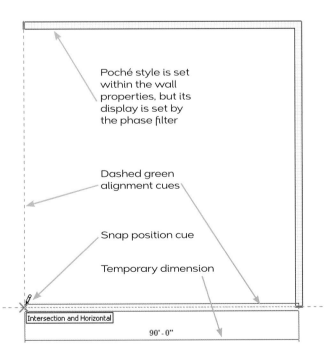

Figure 7.5 *The alignment indication line*

20. Click on the **Select** button on the **Contextual** ribbon. Then select each of the four walls to place the footings.

To edit a wall, select the modify command and then click on the wall. You'll see blue dots at either end of the wall segment. These are grips that allow you to change the length and angle of the wall. You can also type in a new number in the dimension string that appears next to the wall. Dragging an endpoint onto another wall joins them.

It's not uncommon to model elements without actually seeing them—this is another difference from drafting programs. For example, we can draw the footings in plan view, where we can reference the main walls, even though we'll only see them in section view. Check the building sections to see the foundation walls, and be sure to make changes if needed. Also, changes made to an object in one view will be reflected in any of the other views where that object appears, including elevations, perspectives, and schedules.

Modeling Floors

Drawing floors (and many other complex objects, like stairs, railings, and custom ceilings) requires entering a special sketch mode to draw boundaries. This can be sketched with lines, or you can use the Select option to pick existing walls. Properties such as construction type and materials are defined, although they can be edited in the future. Heights and slope can also be defined in this sketch mode.

DRAWING A FLOOR

UNDER THE HOOD

Reference levels organize objects in the model, and also help name views. If you change the name of a level, plans and RCP associated with it will change also—although you can force Revit to name a view independently of the level. If you move a reference level up or down, all of the walls, floors, etc. that are connected to that level will move with it.

1. Choose **Main Floor Plan** from the project browser.
2. Click on the **Home** ribbon.
3. Click on the **Floor** tool.
4. Select walls defining the boundary (Figure 7.6).
5. Click on the **Floor Properties** button (Figure 7.7).
6. Choose **Gym Floor** from the Type drop-down list.
7. Click **OK**.
8. Click **Finish Sketch** to complete the floor.

Let me level with you about floors: A level is not a floor, although floors make reference to a level. If you change the offset distance in the **Element Properties** dialog box, the floor will move up and down relative to its reference level.

Figure 7.6 *The floor boundary*

Dark line indicates boundary

Flippers switch line from the inside of the wall (most typical) to the outside

Boundary lines can be edited with their grips

Figure 7.7 *The Floor Properties dialog box*

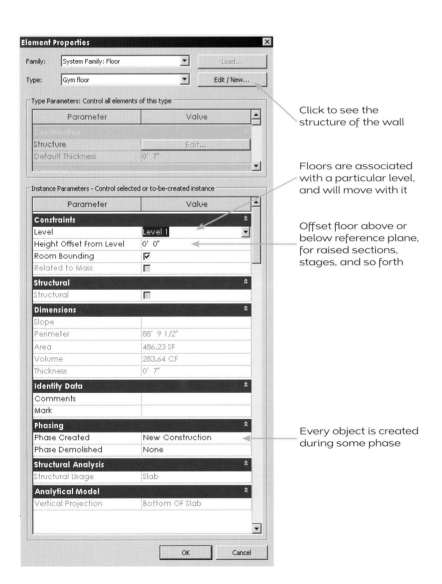

Click to see the structure of the wall

Floors are associated with a particular level, and will move with it

Offset floor above or below reference plane, for raised sections, stages, and so forth

Every object is created during some phase

You can place copies of floors and other objects on multiple levels very easily, which is handy in projects with repeated floor plates, window patterns, and column grids. Select the objects and type CTRL+C. Then choose Edit>Paste>Paste Aligned>Choose level by name... from the drop-down list. You'll find that exact copies of all the stuff you selected show up on the levels you select.

Modeling the Roof

A roof can be drawn in a very similar way. Choose the **Roof>Roof by Footprint** tool on the **Home** ribbon. Once again you enter the Sketch Mode, and again you can select the four walls to draw the purple boundary lines of the roof. Click on the **Roof Properties** button to make sure it's being drawn at the correct level—the roof level—and that the Phase is set to **Existing** (Figure 7.8).

Finally, click **Finish** to draw the roof. Of course, we can't see it in plan view. Double-click on the **Longitudinal Section** view in the Building Sections folder to see the cross section of the building (Figure 7.9).

The walls should have a parapet. Select one, right-click, and then choose **Select All Instances**. Click on the **Properties** button and change the **Top Offset** for the wall to 2'-0" (Figure 7.10).

Figure 7.8 *The **Roof Properties** dialog box*

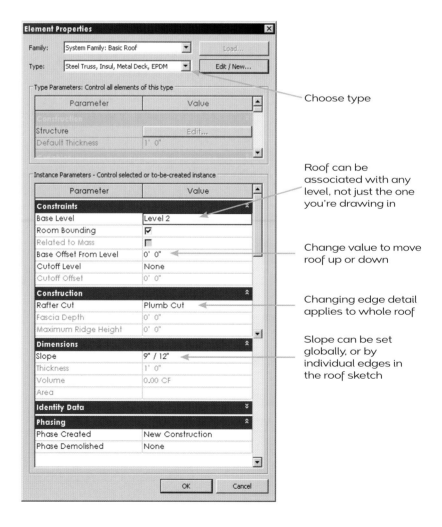

Choose type

Roof can be associated with any level, not just the one you're drawing in

Change value to move roof up or down

Changing edge detail applies to whole roof

Slope can be set globally, or by individual edges in the roof sketch

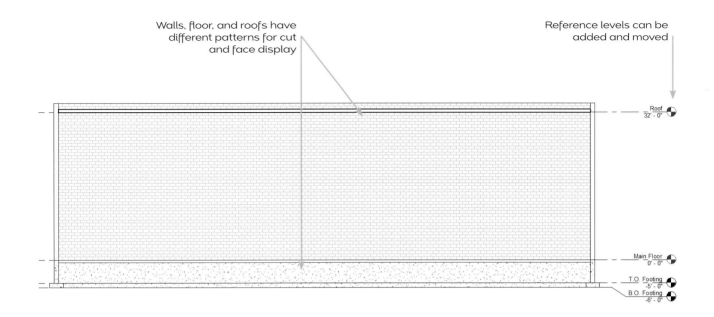

Walls, floor, and roofs have
different patterns for cut
and face display

Reference levels can be
added and moved

Roof
32' - 0"

Main Floor
0' - 0"

T.O. Footing
-5' - 0"

B.O. Footing
-6' - 0"

Figure 7.9 *The
longitudinal section*

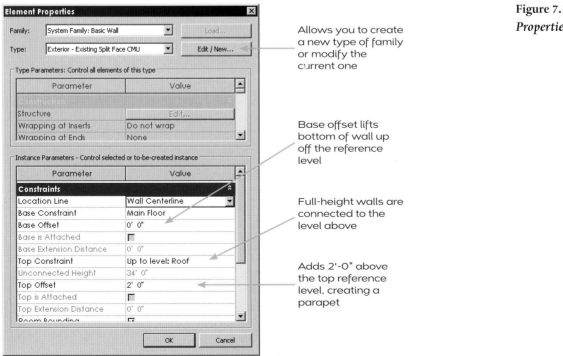

Figure 7.10 *Wall
Properties with offset*

Allows you to create
a new type of family
or modify the
current one

Base offset lifts
bottom of wall up
off the reference
level

Full-height walls are
connected to the
level above

Adds 2'-0" above
the top reference
level, creating a
parapet

You can copy or array almost any entity in any view. If you're working on a multistory project with the exact same floor plate repeated many times, use the **Array** tool in section view.

Interior Partitions

There is a little storage closet built off the north side of the space, but the partitions do not go up to the roof—so you'll have to specify a height.

DRAWING INTERIOR PARTITIONS

1. Return to the **Existing Conditions Plan** view.
2. Click the **Wall** tool.
3. Choose **Basic Wall: 4⅞" Interior Partition (1 hr)** from the Type Selector drop-down list.
4. Start the partition at the middle of the north wall.
5. Draw down 8' and over 40'.
6. Finish the closet back up at the north wall (Figure 7.11).

The north wall and the interior partition are different heights, so they don't join completely. This is represented graphically by a light line at their intersection. If your intent was to have them both the same height, you can change their parameters in the **Element Properties** dialog box.

What about the foundation wall and footings? Interestingly enough, these can be drawn even though you don't really see them—and that is in fact the only way they can be drawn. Click on the wall tool again and choose **Footing wall** from the **Type Selector** drop-down list. Check the wall properties, and you'll see that the top of the wall is at the main level and the base is at the B.O. Foundation level. If you draw the walls now (use a rectangle and just trace over the other walls), you won't see anything in plan. You'll see them in section, though. Try the same with the Footing wall type and watch them appear in section.

LOOK OUT!

*Occasionally, perfectly nice walls just won't join, even when they're exactly the same height. Try using the **Match Properties** tool, which looks like an eyedropper, to copy all the settings from one element to another. If this doesn't work, use grips to drag the uncooperative endpoint away from the adjacent wall. Then drag it back again until a dashed green alignment cue shows up in the middle of the adjacent wall. Click to place, and the join should heal.*

Figure 7.11 *A cute little storage closet*

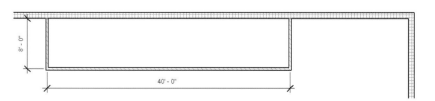

Adding Doors

Of course, this lovely building won't do us much good if visitors can't get in—so let's insert some doors. Like many other elements in Revit, doors come organized into "families," some of which are preloaded into your template and others that need to be loaded from a library. Each family can have several "types," which may have slightly different dimensions or materials. Each family may also have parameters that can be edited once they're inserted into a drawing (again, height and materials are typical, but also level association and offset), which are what you see in the Element Properties dialog box (Figure 7.12).

Does this under-the-hood concept really matter as long as you can just draw stuff that looks more or less correct? Yes, actually, since Revit uses the information about each element or its family to generate handy things like schedules and detail drawings. You could use a schedule to count all the metal doors in a project regardless of size, all the ones that are 3'-0" × 6'-8", or all the metal doors on a particular level. This filtering works only if you're paying attention as you model the building.

MODELING DOORS

1. Click on the **Door** tool in the **Home** ribbon.
2. Choose **Single Glass 36" x 84"** from the Type Selector drop-down list, which can be seen in Figure 7.13.

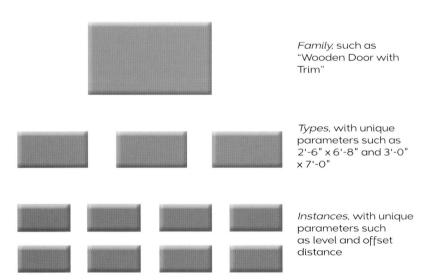

Family, such as "Wooden Door with Trim"

Types, with unique parameters such as 2'-6" x 6'-8" and 3'-0" x 7'-0"

Instances, with unique parameters such as level and offset distance

Figure 7.12 *The Revit family tree*

Figure 7.13 *The **Door**
tool options*

Click for Instance Properties

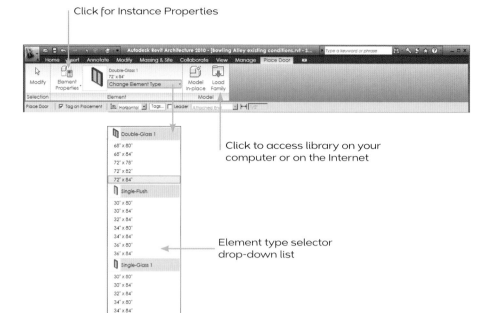

Click to access library on your
computer or on the Internet

Element type selector
drop-down list

3. Click on the north wall 7'-6" in from the NE corner to place the door (scroll to zoom in or out if needed).
4. Click on the **Modify** tool.
5. Click on the door to select it.
6. Click on the blue flippers to change the hand and swing of the door.
7. Type in the correct dimension if you missed it (Figure 7.14).
8. Click on the **Door** tool again.
9. On the **Contextual** ribbon, choose Load Family.
10. Browse the Imperial Library for the **Doors** folder and double-click on it.
11. Browse for **Double Glass 36" x 84"** and double-click on it to load it into your project.
12. Now click 9'-0" in from the NW corner to place the doors.
13. Click on the **Reference Plane** tool. This will draw a handy non-printing line that we can use to orient and mirror object.
14. Use your cursor tool tips to find the midpoint of the west wall and click on it.
15. Move your mouse to the midpoint of the west wall and click to place the other end of the **Reference Plane.**
16. Click the **Modify** command and select the double doors.
17. Hold down the **CTRL** key and click on the single door to add it to the selection set.
18. Click the **Mirror** button on the upper right of the screen.

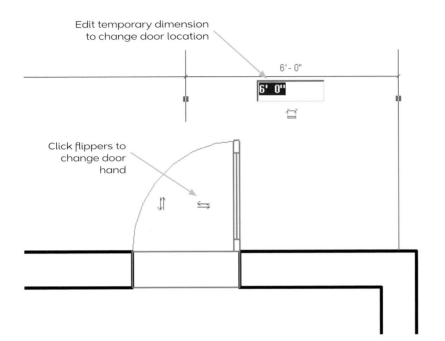

Edit temporary dimension
to change door location

6'- 0"

6' 0"

Click flippers to
change door
hand

Figure 7.14 *The door in position with temporary dimensions*

19. Click on the Reference Plane to mirror the selected objects (Figure 7.15).

Don't like any of the doors in your model? After clicking **Load** in the door tool, click on Web Library. This will take you to a fairly up-to-date online library from Autodesk—be sure to choose the folder for your particular software version. Find the object you want in the Web page, then click on it to download the family. Save the family onto your computer, then load it in by choosing **File>Load from Library>Load Family...**

So that's still not enough choice for you? Then it's time to troll the Web looking for scraps. The best spot I've found is RevitCity.com, which is free to join and has a decent library of various objects. You can download as much as you like, and also upload your masterworks as you create them.

Figure 7.15 *The basic editing commands*

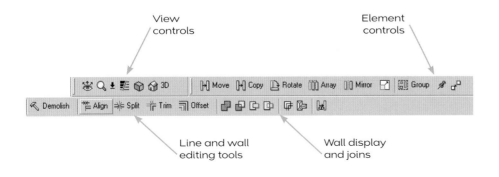

View
controls

Element
controls

Line and wall
editing tools

Wall display
and joins

Inserting Windows

Window components work the same as doors, and also come in families. The existing gym has a row of square, fixed clerestory windows that don't show up in the main floor plan. They can be inserted in plan view anyway, and then edited in section.

ADDING THE WINDOWS

1. Double-click on the view **Longitudinal Section** in the Project Browser.
2. Click on the **Window** tool.
3. Choose **72" x 72" Fixed** from the Type Selector drop-down list.
4. Move your mouse over the north wall and then click to insert roughly in the upper middle of the wall.
5. Click on the window you just inserted.
6. Right-click on it and choose **Element Properties** from the context-sensitive menu (Figure 7.16).
7. Change the sill height up to 15'-0" and click **OK.**
8. Click the **Align** tool.

Figure 7.16 *Window Element Properties*

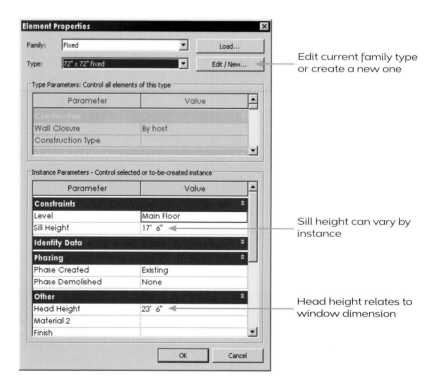

Edit current family type or create a new one

Sill height can vary by instance

Head height relates to window dimension

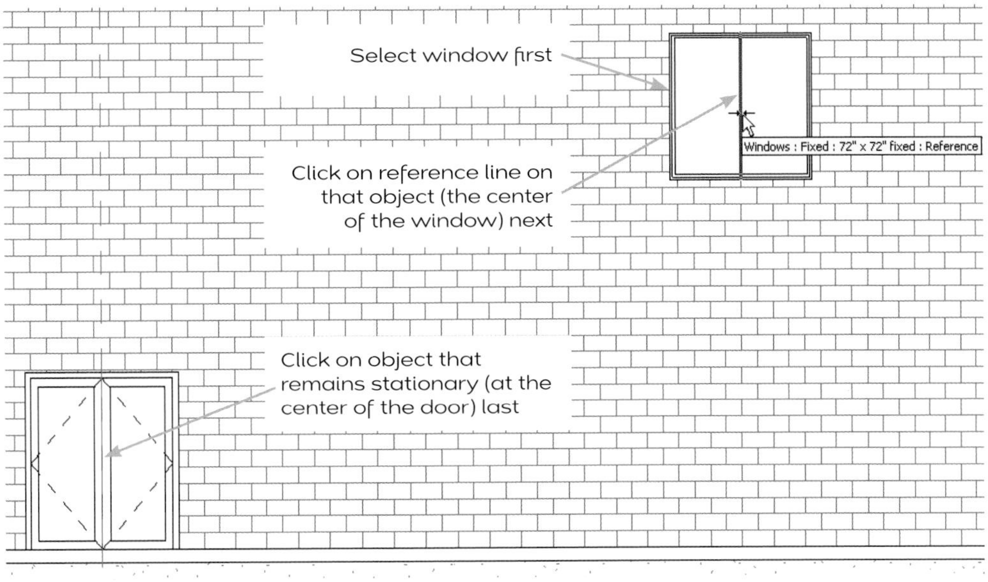

Figure 7.17 *The **Align** tool with the window*

Select window first

Click on reference line on that object (the center of the window) next

Windows : Fixed : 72" x 72" fixed : Reference

Click on object that remains stationary (at the center of the door) last

9. Click on the center of the double doors—this will be where you want the window to move to.

10. Click on the center of the window. A dark bar indicates which part of the window is being used for alignment (Figure 7.17).

11. Select the window again.

12. Click on the **Array** tool.

13. Click to define the base point.

14. Move your mouse to the right and type in **10**, then **ENTER** to create the first copy 10'-0" over.

15. Type in **11** when prompted for the number of copies (this and the separation distance can be edited later).

16. Click the **Modify** tool.

17. Select the array of windows by clicking and dragging from the upper left to the lower right. This is called a selection window.

18. From the Window drop-down menu, choose **Existing Floor Plan** to switch back to that view.

19. Even though the windows aren't visible, they are still selected. Click on the **Mirror** tool.

20. Click on the reference plane drawn earlier to mirror the windows.

21. Don't believe they were copied? Click on the **View** ribbon.

22. Click on the **Elevation** tool.

23. Choose **Interior Elevation** from the Type Selector drop-down list.

24. Move your mouse roughly in the middle of the plan, but a little closer to the south wall—the elevation symbol will point that way.

25. Click to draw the elevation.

26. Open the Interior Elevation folder in the Project Browser.
27. Double-click on the new elevation to see it—it'll be the only one there.
28. Right-click on the name of the new interior elevation and choose **Rename**.
29. Name it something clever like *Existing South Interior Elevation*—you'll see that name next to the elevation symbol in the floor plan, too.

You don't always draw elevations of the existing conditions—only if there is a complicated finish system that needs to be documented, or there's some partial demolition to coordinate. If you need the other interior elevations, just click on the center of the symbol, where there's a horizontal dash (Figure 7.18).

Check the boxes next to the elevations that you create. Unchecking a box will erase the drawing, though, along with any notes or other annotation. It will not remove any parts of the model, however (Figure 7.19).

One downside to this automation is that Revit has some problems with the boundaries around interior elevations. The **Crop Region** is limited to a rectangular shape, even though interior elevations generally don't show anything in section view, such as soffits or casework. If the elevation has areas you need to crop away, use a **Masking Region** to cover them up, which is found on the **Annotate** ribbon.

Once you fix that problem, one section of the interior elevation may no longer be complete. If needed, draw the missing section using **Drafting Lines**, which are also found on the **Annotate** ribbon. For the Crop Re-

Figure 7.18 *Interior elevation symbol*

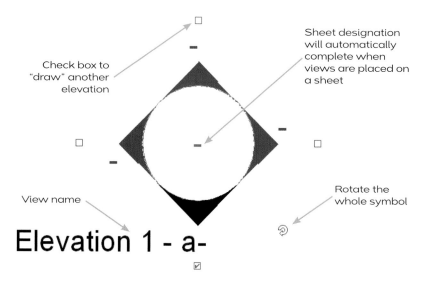

Check box to "draw" another elevation

Sheet designation will automatically complete when views are placed on a sheet

View name

Rotate the whole symbol

Elevation 1 - a-

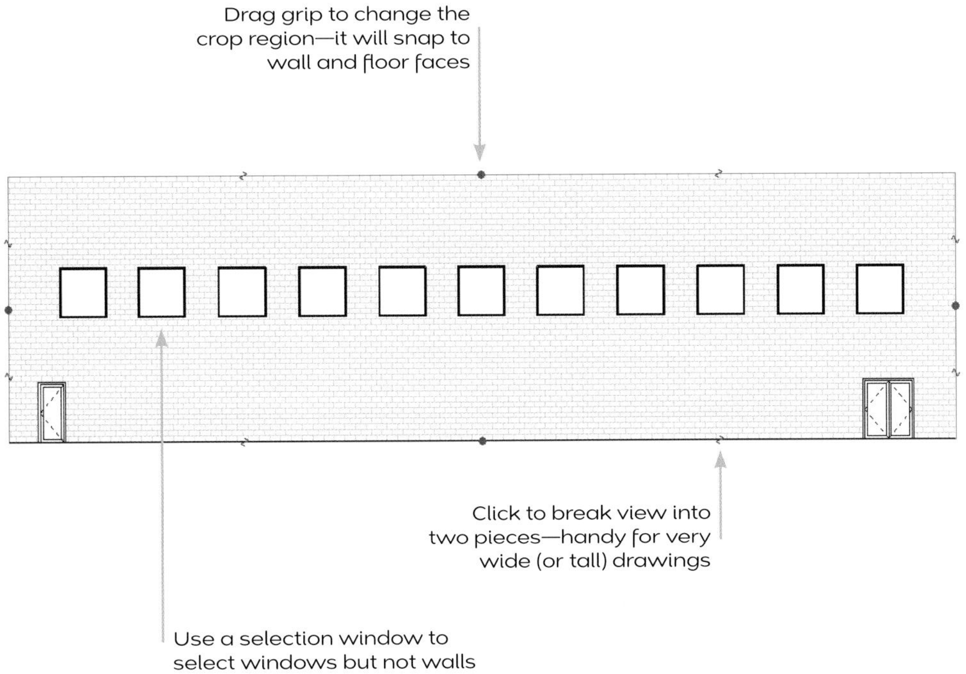

Figure 7.19 *Active crop region*

Drag grip to change the crop region—it will snap to wall and floor faces

Click to break view into two pieces—handy for very wide (or tall) drawings

Use a selection window to select windows but not walls

gion boundaries to print, you'll need to uncheck the hide **Crop Boundaries** button in the Page Setup dialog box.

Tracing from a Raster Image

We happened to know the existing dimensions of the Bowling Alley project, but often you'll have a just a sketch or an existing scan of a plan to trace. This can be done easily in Revit, just as in AutoCAD or in SketchUp. Let's take a lovely historic building, the Wayside Inn in Massachusetts. Drawings and photos of this building are on the Historic American Buildings Survey Web site, which the federal government created to document important buildings throughout the country. I've placed the plan in the **Online Resources** for this chapter.

TRACING A PLAN FROM AN IMAGE FILE

1. Go to the **Online Resources** for this chapter and find *Wayside Inn.bmp*.
2. Save the document onto your computer in your folder for this class.

3. Start a new project using your interior renovation template (On-line Resources file *Interior renovation template 2008.rte*).

4. Switch to the Existing Conditions Plan and click on the **Image** button on the **Insert** ribbon.

5. Browse for the image you just saved and click **OK.** Click to place the image (Figure 7.20).

6. Click the **Modify** command, and be sure to click on the edge of the image to select.

7. Click on the **Resize** tool. Click on a **Base Point**—choose the start of a building element that you know the size of, like the clear dimension string at the top.

8. Click on the opposite end of the dimension string to complete the reference line (Figure 7.21).

9. Revit is now waiting to know how long this reference line is. Move your mouse to resize by eye, or type in the known dimension.

10. Draw using Revit walls, doors, and windows (Figure 7.22).

This is an easy and fairly precise way to generate a base plan. Good fieldwork is critical, however, to check all horizontal and vertical dimensions. Doors have easy measurements to guess, since they are often 3'-0" wide. Dimension strings are also good choices, as are structural grids, as they are often round numbers.

Figure 7.20 *The inserted image with corner grips (Image Courtesy of the Historic American Buildings Survey)*

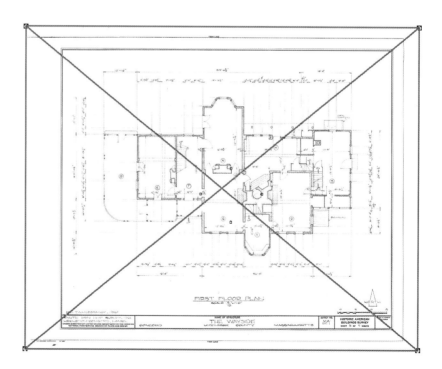

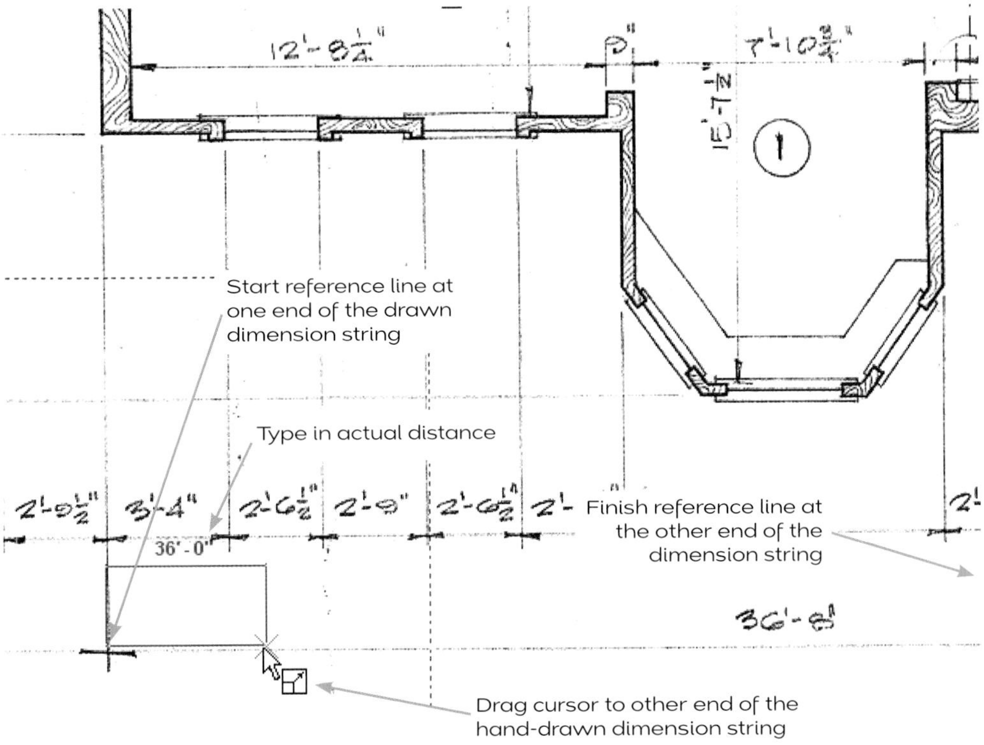

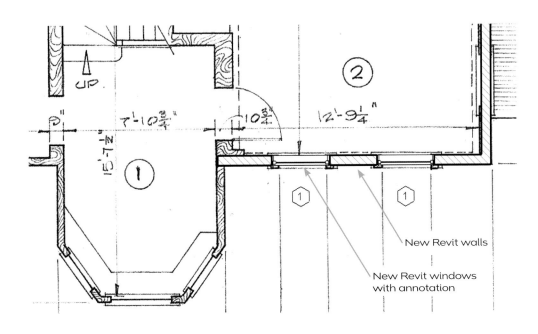

Figure 7.21 *The **Resize** tool in action*

Start reference line at one end of the drawn dimension string

Type in actual distance

Finish reference line at the other end of the dimension string

Drag cursor to other end of the hand-drawn dimension string

36'-0"

Figure 7.22 *Some traced exterior walls*

New Revit walls

New Revit windows with annotation

Online Resources

- Architectural program for the project, *Bowling Alley Program.xls*
- The base model for this chapter, *Bowling Alley existing conditions.rvt*
- *Wayside Inn.bmp*, from the section on tracing a plan
- Template optimized for use in an interiors project, *Interior renovation template 2010.rte*

Term Project Assignments

- Generate existing conditions plans for the Bowling Alley.

Exercises and Further Study

- Trace a raster image of an interesting plan and generate the three-dimensional model with windows and doors.
- Load windows for Andersen windows from www.RevitCity.com.
- Download the directory of furniture from the Autodesk online component library and place it in a custom library folder on your computer.

8

Bubble Diagrams

LEARNING GOALS

- Draw simple lines and shapes
- Create and modify filled regions and groups
- Understand how Revit defines rooms
- Create and apply an automatic color scheme

Bubble diagrams are the first step in the graphic study of a design problem and help to solve the program element adjacency requirements that can be such a puzzle. We'll still draw simple circles, squares, and lines for our diagram as we did using PowerPoint in the previous project, but now we'll define the bubbles from the start as being "rooms" in a project. This allows Revit to keep track of areas and automatically create a color-coded key. Later on, we won't have to re-create the rooms in the block diagram, or again when we actually draw in walls.

Drawing a Bubble Diagram

1. Call up the existing conditions drawing created in the last chapter.
2. Choose **File>Save As** and name it *Bubble Diagram* or something clever like that, so that you won't destroy the blank existing conditions drawing.
3. On the **Home** ribbon, choose the **Room Separation Lines** tool. It's hiding under the **Room** tool (Figure 8.1).

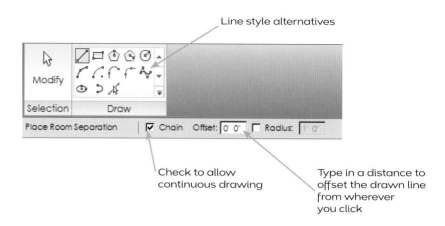

Figure 8.1 *The* **Room** *and* **Area** *toolbar with* **Room Separation Lines** *tool selected*

Line style alternatives

Check to allow continuous drawing

Type in a distance to offset the drawn line from wherever you click

---

MAGIC TRICK

Revit assumes all number entries are in feet—a bit disconcerting when you've just switched from SketchUp. Use apostrophes or decimals as needed.

4. Choose circle from the drop-down list on the **Contextual** ribbon.
5. Click to plant the center of the circle and again to complete.
6. Type in the radius value in feet.
7. Using the **Modify** tool, select the circle and change the temporary dimension as needed to change the size.
8. Type in a new dimension and then **ENTER** to make the change. You can make changes to most dimensions, array element numbers, and other elements this way.
9. To give each bubble an identity as a separate room, click on the **Rooms** tool. Mouse over one of your bubbles—the cursor will highlight the circle with a big X. Click inside the circle to define the room. This places a **Room Tag** into the circle with a name and a number, and each new room you define gets the next number.

Figure 8.2 *Editing a room tag*

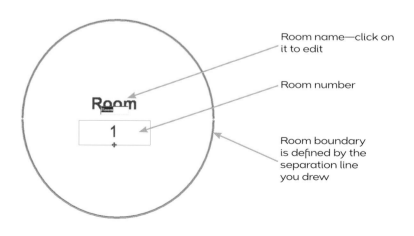

Room name—click on it to edit

Room number

Room boundary is defined by the separation line you drew

10. Click on the **Modify** tool, then click on the word "Room" in the room tag. Click again on the word "Room" to edit (Figure 8.2).
11. Put in the new name and hit **ENTER**.
12. Select the Room Tag with the **Modify** tool again.
13. Define your other bubbles as rooms and rename appropriately.
14. Click on the **Legend** tool.
15. Select the Color Scheme key with the **Modify** command.
16. Choose **Edit Scheme** from the **Contextual** ribbon (Figure 8.3).
17. Change the colors for each room to your heart's desire.
18. **Sort** the list by Name if you don't plan to have room numbers.
19. Add in Area to the **Fields** displayed if you'd like. Click **OK** to return to the re-colored drawing (Figure 8.4).

If you don't want to see the area, just select a room tag and choose a different tag from the Type Selector drop-down list. You can also control the size and font of the schedule text.

Choose schedule field
to color by

Figure 8.3 *The Edit Color Scheme dialog box*

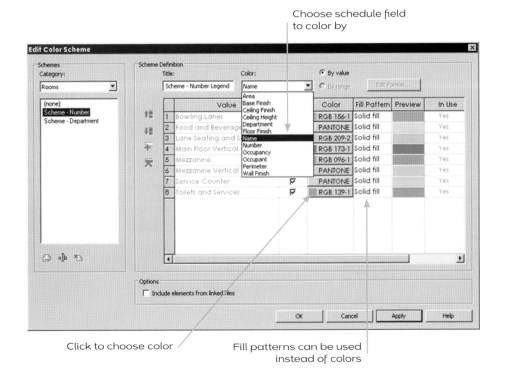

Click to choose color

Fill patterns can be used
instead of colors

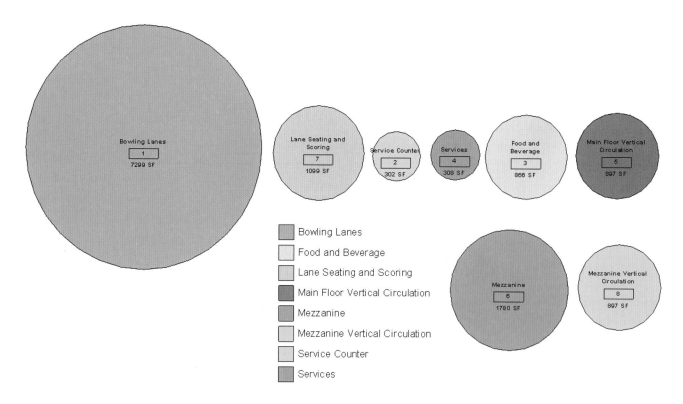

Figure 8.4 *The finished bubbles and key*

Adding Linear Graphics and Hatching

We use all sorts of linear graphics to represent things in bubble diagrams: physical connection, sight lines, acoustical isolation, and more. Revit seems to discourage drawing lines (objects with no built identity or parametric qualities). Nevertheless, there are several standard line types, and you can create your own, and use components like the pair of arrows in the Interior Renovation template.

You can also use filled regions for hatch patterns, which need to be modeled in a special Sketch Mode. Entering this mode causes the rest of the model to become grayed out and unavailable for editing, although objects can be snapped to or used to create boundaries. Those boundaries must form continuous loops for the region to work.

1. Click on the **Annotate** ribbon.
2. Click on **Detail Lines** and choose from **Diagram Heavy Solid Line** from the Type Selector drop-down list (there are even Hidden Lines—dashed, a là AutoCAD).
3. Click once to start a line on the Lanes bubble and again on the Service Desk to define the endpoint.
4. To indicate a strong connection, we'll need a double line. Start a new line next to the first, and move toward the other bubble. The line should snap to parallel (and the first line will become gray). Click to finish (Figure 8.5).
5. Draw another line, but this time choose **Diagram Heavy Dashed Line** from the Type Selector drop-down list.
6. To edit the red arrow, select it with the **Modify** tool. Click and drag on the solid arrows to change its shape (Figure 8.6).

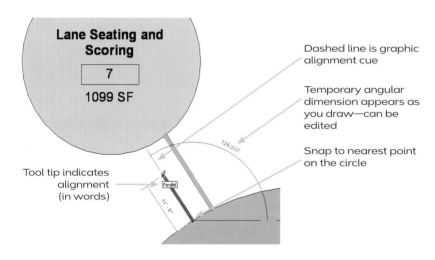

Figure 8.5 *Parallel lines in progress*

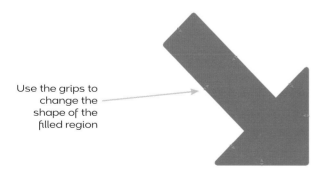

Figure 8.6 *Modifying a filled region*

Figure 8.7 *Sketch mode*
for creating a filled region

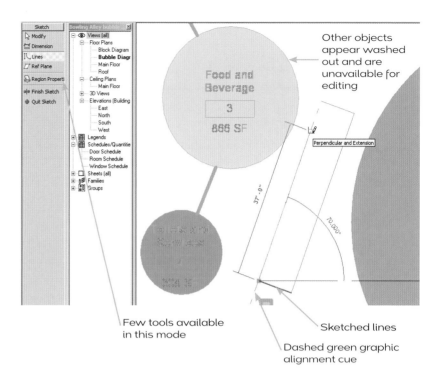

Other objects
appear washed
out and are
unavailable for
editing

Food and
Beverage

3

866 SF

Perpendicular and Extension

Few tools available
in this mode

Sketched lines

Dashed green graphic
alignment cue

Figure 8.8 *The **Filled***
***Region** menu*

Choose from ready-made
fill patterns

Create your own Type definition

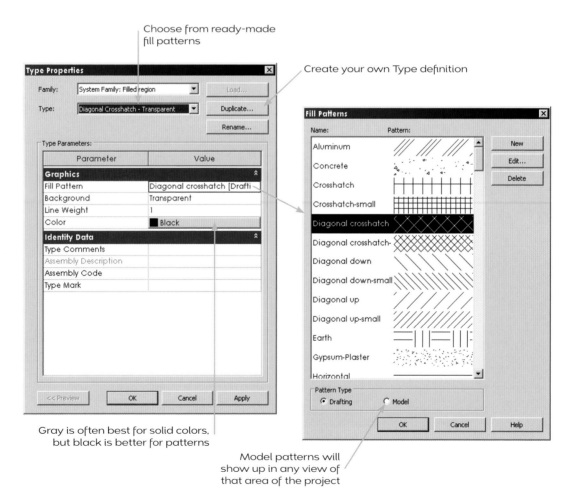

Gray is often best for solid colors,
but black is better for patterns

Model patterns will
show up in any view of
that area of the project

7. Click on the **Filled Region** tool, and the screen goes into a special Sketch Mode to draw the outline of the pattern (Figure 8.7).

8. Choose **Invisible lines** from the Type Selector drop-down list.

9. Draw a rectangle between the seating area and the bowling lanes to indicate a direct connection.

10. Click on the **Region Properties** button to change the kind of region you're inserting to a diagonal cross-hatch (Figure 8.8).

11. Click **Finish Sketch** to complete the region. It will be drawn with an invisible boundary.

12. Modify the region as you did with the red arrow in Step 7.

13. Click on the **Text** button.

14. Choose **¼" Century Gothic** from the Type Selector drop-down list.

15. Click on the Properties button on the **Contextual** ribbon.

16. Click **Edit/New**, then Click **Duplicate** in the new dialog box. Name the new style *My Special Titles Text Style* or something clever like that (Figure 8.9).

17. Choose your own font and click **OK** until you're back in the drawing.

18. Click to place the text, then type "Entrance." Click **OK** when done.

19. Use the grips to move or rotate the text (Figure 8.10).

20. Hold down the **CTRL** key while you click and drag to copy.

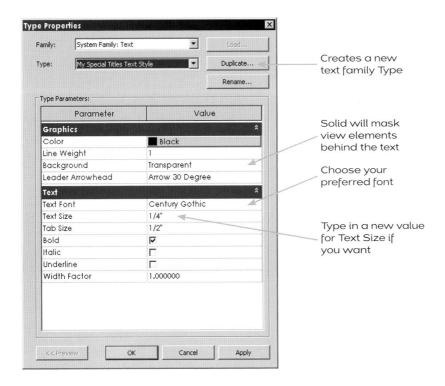

Figure 8.9 *Creating a new text style*

Figure 8.10 *Text modifiers*

Click and drag to move

Click and drag to rotate

Click and drag to change the size of the text window

·Entrance·

21. Continue adding lines and other annotation in this way until the diagram clearly communicates the important design features (Figure 8.11).

The flip of the arrow is called a **parameter**, and parameters are what make BIM powerful. Many objects and components, such as countertop

Figure 8.11 *The finished diagram*

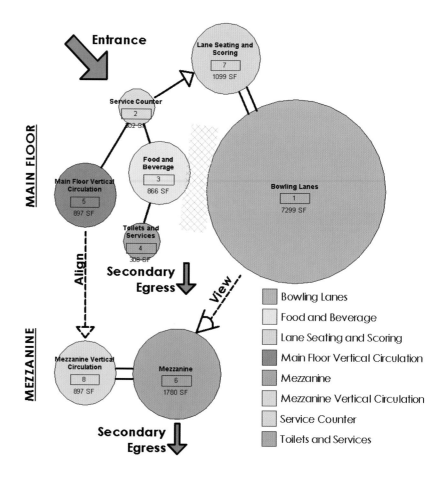

length or wall height in elevation, can be changed using embedded grips (they're usually red) like the filled region. Just select to reveal your options. Other objects, such as the arrow, doors, windows, and even walls, have flippers to change handle location or swing orientation.

The diagram can be saved as a separate Revit drawing or exported to an image file for presentation. Choose **Application Menu>File>Export> Image...**, then browse for where you'd like to save the image file. For the most part, JPEGs set to 100% zoom are fine for onscreen viewing and electronic presentations. If you plan to print, however, choose TIFF, which is lossless, or make the image 200% of the original (Figure 8.12).

You can also change the size of the image, in pixels, which is handy for printed boards where image quality is even more critical. If you're planning to modify or render a plan or other more detailed drawing in Photoshop Elements, you'll get the best results by printing Revit views to a PDF file rather than to an image. This preserves some of the vector information—essentially, the geometry of the drawing—rather than just colors.

You'll be able to choose a much higher resolution upon import in Photoshop Elements, which in turn allows for better print quality. Adobe Acrobat is the most common of converters and virtual printers available.

Many views and sheets can be exported all at once

A simple Web page can be created of multiple sheets and/or views

Figure 8.12 *Export Image dialog box*

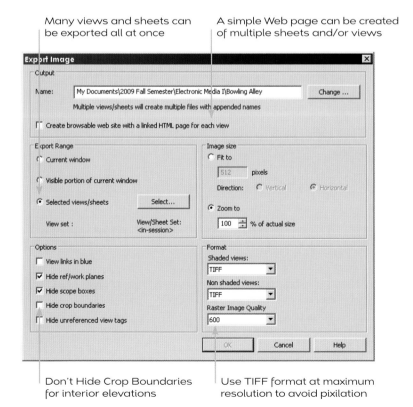

Don't Hide Crop Boundaries for interior elevations

Use TIFF format at maximum resolution to avoid pixilation

Online Resources

- Revit file for the model used in this section, *Bowling Alley bubble diagram.rvt*
- Revit keyboard shortcuts guide, *Revit Keyboard Shortcuts.docx*

Term Project Assignments

- Draw bubble diagrams for three alternate schemes in Revit.

Exercises and Further Study

- Draw bubble diagram for another project and export image for presentation.
- Create a new linetype to graphically indicate two spaces that need an acoustical connection but not a visual connection.

9

Block Diagrams

LEARNING GOALS

- Convert a bubble diagram into a block diagram in Revit
- Understand reference levels and how plans refer to them
- Understand phasing and view phase filters

Now that you've solved all the programmatic adjacencies and other relationships, it's time to start making your design more architectural. Block diagrams are meant as a way to test out the program within the constraints of the existing space. If you're working on a new building, of course, the issues are a little different: You'll want to see what sort of impact the program will have on the overall building form.

Whichever type of project you're working on, producing the diagram is a matter of drawing room separation lines and deleting the arcs and circles. This will make the room shapes more regular and realistic, and keep a color scheme and key that match your bubble diagram. For renovation projects, you'll also need to demolish elements that are in the way—these can then be found on the demolition plan.

Move bubble diagram elements into the Existing Conditions boundaries. You'll also need to create a new level for the mezzanine and draw a diagram for that floor as well.

> **LOOK OUT!**
>
> *Here's one instance where hand drawing has an advantage— sketching with colored markers on a blank plan is quick and immediate. If you want to stay entirely within the electronic realm, but still have the flexibility to sketch and paint, Photoshop works best. Export the bubble diagram from Revit, and use selection tools to move individual rooms around.*

Adapting the Bubbles

BIG PICTURE

You should always save a copy of your project when moving on to another stage, and that would be now. The bubble diagram will be eliminated in this next step, so if you ever want to go back to it, there will be a copy. Other reasonable times to save work are before starting block diagrams, schematic designs, and rendering.

To create the block diagram, you'll want to retain all of the existing room definitions already created, but draw new boundaries that are more regular and architectural. Revit recognizes the exterior walls as valid bounding elements, and you can add Room Separation lines to define the rest of the spaces. The color fill will spill out to complete the new boundaries once you erase the circles that formed the old bubbles.

DRAWING THE MAIN FLOOR BLOCK DIAGRAM

1. Open your bubble diagram from the last chapter and choose **Save As…** Give the copy the name *Block Diagram.rvt* or something clever like that.
2. Double-click on the plan view named *Bubble Diagram*.
3. Click the **Display Crop Region** button.
4. Drag the crop region boundary down and to the right, to show the floor plan.
5. We won't be keeping the storage room, so click on the **Demolish** tool on the **Modify** ribbon.
6. Click on the three walls of the closet to remove them. They're still in the project, but you'll need to look at the demolition plan to see them.

Figure 9.1 *Moving a room bubble*

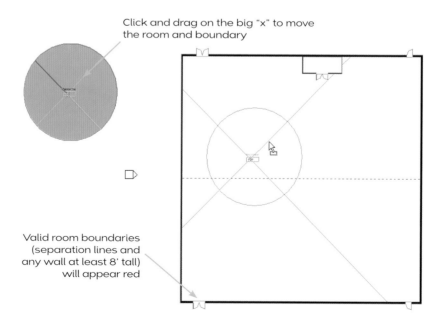

Click and drag on the big "x" to move the room and boundary

Valid room boundaries (separation lines and any wall at least 8' tall) will appear red

7. Click on the **Modify** tool, then select one of the bubbles. Remember that Revit uses the same conventions as SketchUp and AutoCAD: a selection window, dragging from left to right, selects only objects within the selection box. A crossing window, dragging from right to left, selects any object that touches the selection box.
8. Use the move command to move the room and its boundary onto your plan (Figure 9.1).
9. Repeat with the other bubbles, and don't worry yet about the extra spaces that haven't been filled in.
10. Use Room Separation lines to create more regular room shapes. To

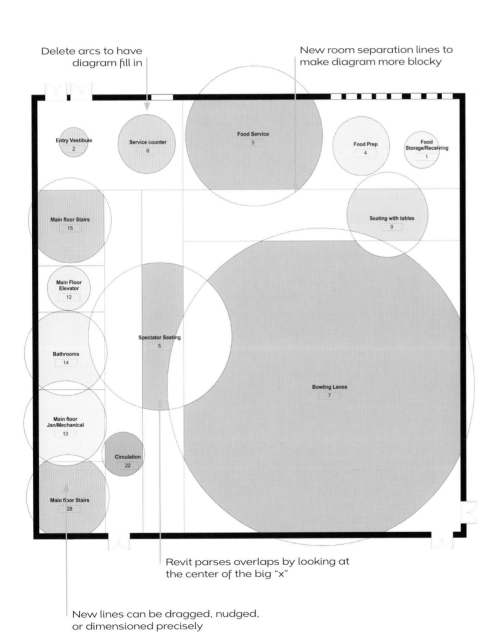

Delete arcs to have diagram fill in

New room separation lines to make diagram more blocky

Figure 9.2 *Creating more regular shapes*

Revit parses overlaps by looking at the center of the big "x"

New lines can be dragged, nudged, or dimensioned precisely

Figure 9.3 *The **Split** tool in action*

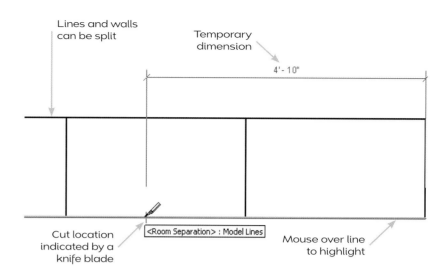

Lines and walls can be split

Temporary dimension

4'- 10"

Cut location indicated by a knife blade

<Room Separation> : Model Lines

Mouse over line to highlight

ensure that the new lines form closed rooms, use snaps to be sure the lines start and finish along another lines, arcs, or walls (Figure 9.2).

11. To make the lines meet at a point, click the **Join** tool, which is on the **Modify** ribbon at the top of the Revit interface.

12. Click the first line, then the section.

13. To make objects line up, click the **Align** tool.

14. Click the object that will move first; the object that stays won't move.

15. To break a line, click the **Split** tool on the **Modify** ribbon (Figure 9.3).

16. Click at some point along the line or arc you want to break.

17. Select extra lines and hit the **DELETE** key—the color fill should spread out to fill the new shape.

18. Add new rooms as needed to increase the sophistication and detail level of your diagram.

19. Modify the color scheme as needed to improve the look of the diagram (Figure 9.4).

Be sure to refer back to the program chart to keep in line with area requirements. Now is also the time to plan for both horizontal and vertical circulation.

Adding a Level

So what about the mezzanine? Well, you can draw a diagram even without a floor—but we'll need to define a new level in the project. Cut and

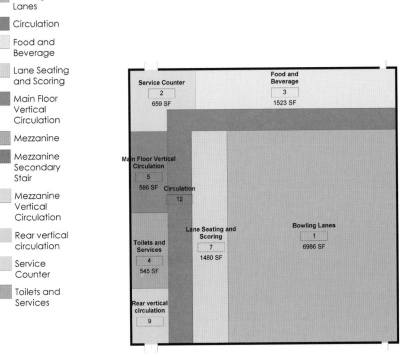

Bowling Lanes

Circulation

Food and Beverage

Lane Seating and Scoring

Main Floor Vertical Circulation

Mezzanine

Mezzanine Secondary Stair

Mezzanine Vertical Circulation

Rear vertical circulation

Service Counter

Toilets and Services

Figure 9.4 *The finished block diagram for the main floor*

paste the upper-level bubbles from the Main Floor plan, and the room definitions will be preserved. To help align spaces with the first floor, from the Mezzanine you can see an underlay of any other level.

DRAWING THE MEZZANINE BLOCK DIAGRAM

1. Open the **Longitudinal Section** view from the Project Browser.
2. Select the Level bullet and line for the main floor.
3. Click the **Copy** button on the **Modify** ribbon.
4. Click once somewhere on the lower level line as a base point.
5. Move your mouse up 13'-0" and click to place the new level.
6. Click to start the new level line.
7. Align your mouse with the other end of the level line and click to create the level.
8. If you mess up, select the level with the **Modify** tool. Click on the grips to stretch or shorten, using the green alignment cues.
9. Check or uncheck the boxes to reveal or hide the bullet and text.
10. Click on the level dimension to edit the height (or click and drag to move graphically).

Figure 9.5 *Editing a level*

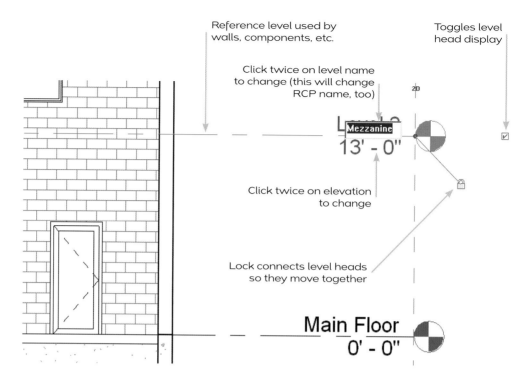

Reference level used by walls, components, etc.

Toggles level head display

Click twice on level name to change (this will change RCP name, too)

Click twice on elevation to change

Lock connects level heads so they move together

Mezzanine

13' - 0"

Main Floor
0' - 0"

11. Click on the name to call it *Mezzanine* (Figure 9.5).

12. Click **OK** to rename the corresponding views.

13. Click on the **Mezzanine** floor plan in the Project Browser and choose **Duplicate with Detailing** from the context-sensitive menu.

14. Right-click on the copy in the Project Browser and choose **Rename**. Call it *Mezzanine Bubble Diagram* or something clever like that.

15. Right-click on the copy again and choose **Apply View Template**.

16. Choose **Block Diagram** from the dialog box.

17. Double-click on the new diagram to open the view.

18. Right-click on the drawing area and choose **View Properties**.

19. Click in the field next to the **Underlay** field.

20. Choose **Main Floor** from the drop-down list.

21. Set the current phase to **New Conditions** and click **OK** to return to the drawing.

22. Open the Main Floor bubble diagram and select the bubbles for the Mezzanine.

23. Type **CTRL+C** to copy to the clipboard.

24. Type **CTRL+V** to paste the bubbles into the view.

25. Select and move the bubbles into place as before.

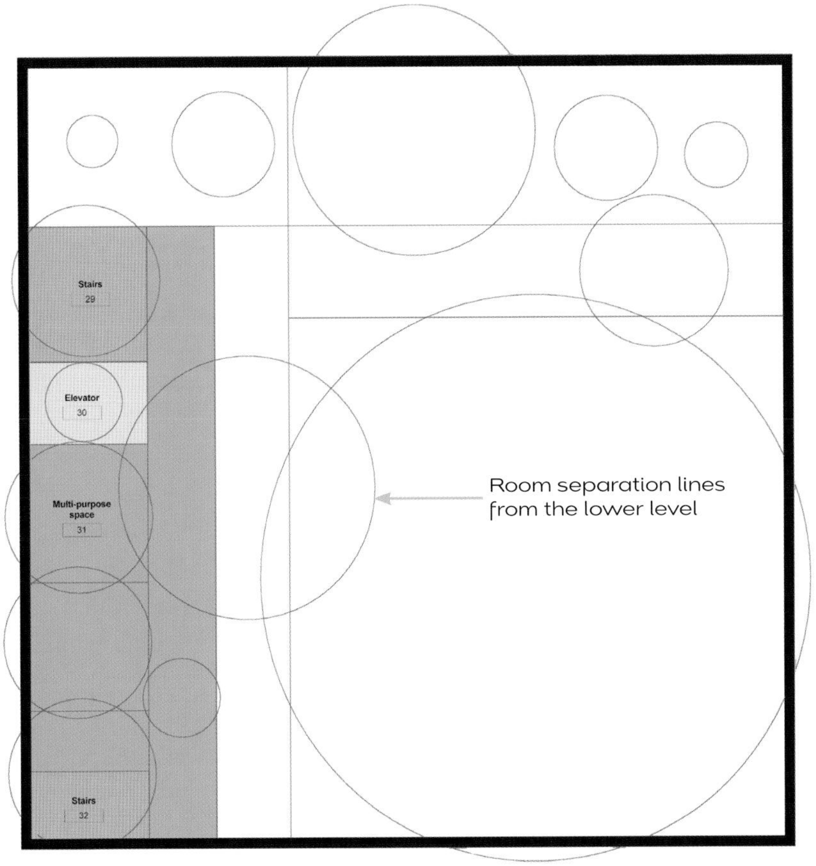

Figure 9.6 *The finished block diagram for the mezzanine*

26. Use the **Align** tool if needed to keep elements such as stairs and elevators coordinated.
27. Evaluate layout and adjust as needed.
28. Add windows on either floor as needed (Figure 9.6).

So the bubble diagram is no more, at least not in this project—if you need to go backward, go back to your back-up. As before, you can export these diagrams to image files or PDFs for easy inclusion in a presentation.

Demolition Plan and Elevations

So you're really mad at some of those walls, and you just won't feel right until you smash them. OK, fine—just don't erase them, though. Revit provides a tool for demolition, and the software helps us out by coordinating the location of new building elements such as windows with the openings they'll need. We'll draw elevations to show those new openings.

MAGIC TRICK

*As in SketchUp and other programs, you can use keyboard shortcuts in Revit to speed up accessing drawing tools. Type **VP** (no **ENTER** necessary) to call up the View Properties dialog box. Check the mouse-over tool tips for other shortcuts—there are quite a few.*

Figure 9.7 *The demolition plan*

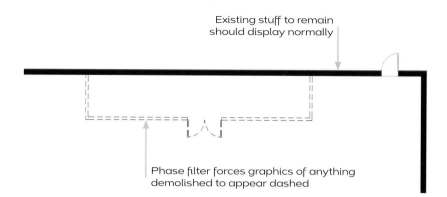

Existing stuff to remain should display normally

Phase filter forces graphics of anything demolished to appear dashed

DRAWING DEMOLITION PLANS AND ELEVATIONS

1. Open the **Demolition Plan** in the Project Browser—you should see the walls of the closet demolished earlier as heavy dashed lines (Figure 9.7).
2. On the **View** ribbon, click on the **Elevation** button.
3. Choose **Interior Elevation** from the Type Selector drop-down list.
4. Move your mouse until the symbol points to the wall where you place a new window. Click to insert the symbol.
5. Open the Interior Elevations folder in the Project Browser.
6. Right-click on the new view and choose **Rename**. Call it *Demolition West Elevation* or something clever like that.
7. Double-click on the new elevation.
8. Click on the crop region to adjust if necessary.
9. Click on the **Display Style** button. Choose **Shaded with Edges**.
10. Click on the **Annotate** ribbon, then on drafting lines.
11. Choose **Demolished** from the Type Selector drop-down list.
12. Draw a rectangle around the demolished section of wall where the new window will be (Figure 9.8).

New views generally take on the view properties from the original view that they were created in. Thus, there are still no new conditions on the demolition elevation because it was created from the demolition plan. To add other elevations, select the center of the symbol with the **Modify** tool and click other check boxes in the other directions. You can also rotate the symbol (Figure 9.9).

Revit guesses about what the boundaries of your interior elevations are supposed to be based on the geometry around the symbol you place. It doesn't always guess right, however, so elevation views sometimes show floor, wall, or ceiling thicknesses. These boundaries are defined by

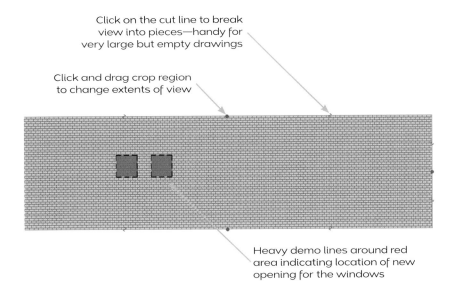

Click on the cut line to break
view into pieces—handy for
very large but empty drawings

Click and drag crop region
to change extents of view

Heavy demo lines around red
area indicating location of new
opening for the windows

Figure 9.8 *Dragging the crop region to show full line thickness*

an adjustable Crop Region, which is a box defining the limits of the view. The box can be expanded or reduced to add or eliminate parts of the view until an appropriate interior elevation view is created.

Revit also has trouble making a nice heavy line for the boundary of the elevation. Right now the Crop Region's lineweight can't be changed, but you can trace over it with heavy weight **Drafting Lines**. These are

Figure 9.9 *An inserted interior elevation symbol*

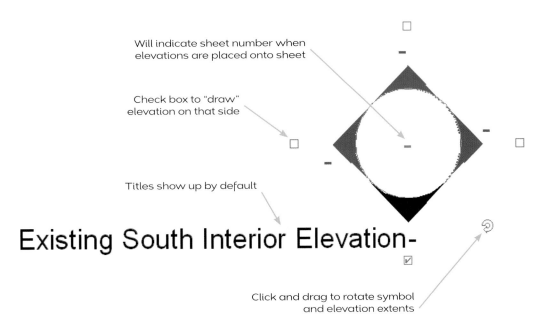

Will indicate sheet number when
elevations are placed onto sheet

Check box to "draw"
elevation on that side

Titles show up by default

Existing South Interior Elevation-

Click and drag to rotate symbol
and elevation extents

LOOK OUT!

Elements are generally demolished in a different phase from the one in which they were created. It's possible to create and demolish in the same phase. This happens if you use the **Demolish** *tool in a drawing set to the Existing Conditions Phase. Those elements will disappear altogether. To bring them back, change the Phase Filter to view to Show All. Find the problem components and, in their* **Element Properties**, *change the* **Phase Created** *or* **Phase Demolished** *fields.*

view specific, which means that if you draw some on the Existing Conditions Floor Plan you won't see them in the New Conditions Plan. **Model Lines** (on the **Annotate** ribbon), on the other hand, will be seen in any view where the surface they're drawn on can be seen. They can be placed on any floor or vertical reference plane.

Phase Filter Graphic Controls

So you're picky about how your poché looks? Or demolition lines have to be a certain lineweight? Objects generally display based on the materials assigned to them and the Detail Level of the particular view. Open your Block Diagram and select one of the exterior walls. Choose Element Properties from the context-sensitive menu, then click on **Edit/New**. Walls in this family are currently set to have no poché, but let's add some to improve the look of our plans and sections. Look for the

Figure 9.10 *Wall* **Element Properties** *cascade to the* **Fill Pattern** *dialog box*

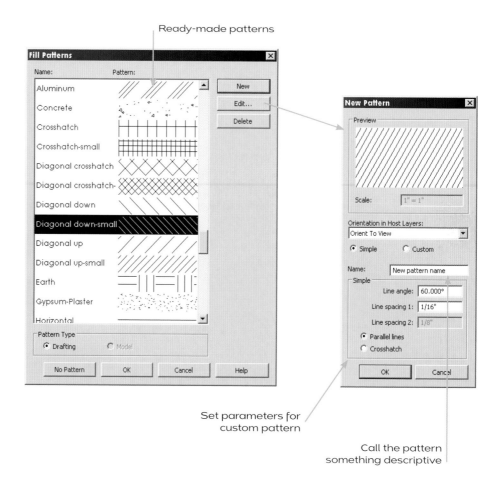

field next to **Coarse Scale Fill Pattern** and click on it to bring up the **Fill Patterns** dialog box (Figure 9.10).

You can choose one of the poché patterns that will display in cut view—plans and sections—on all instances of this wall type. You can also choose a colored, solid fill pattern, or, to create your own, click on the **New** button. Choose a fill pattern and click **OK** until you're back in the drawing. The walls should appear with poché. Any wall family can have poché assigned to it, but you must select each different family individually and assign it as above.

Some offices prefer to have all existing walls have a solid fill pattern, though, to differentiate them from new partitions and walls. How each view looks depends on how the phase filter is set up to display objects. To do this we need to override the wall's display properties. From the **Manage** ribbon, choose **Phases** (Figure 9.11).

On the **Phase Filter** tab, you'll see the preset project filters, and you can add more if needed. Your new conditions plan will use the **Existing to Remain + New** filter, where objects created in the **Previous** phase are overridden. To control what Overridden objects look like, click on the **Phase Filter** tab. Each filter has a different way of controlling how objects with different phases are seen. Classification **By Category** means that objects will show whatever their material assignments are. VCT will

Options for element display include by the original category, hidden, or overridden for specific line properties

Figure 9.11 *The **Phasing** dialog box with the **Phase Filters** tab*

Phases in the current project

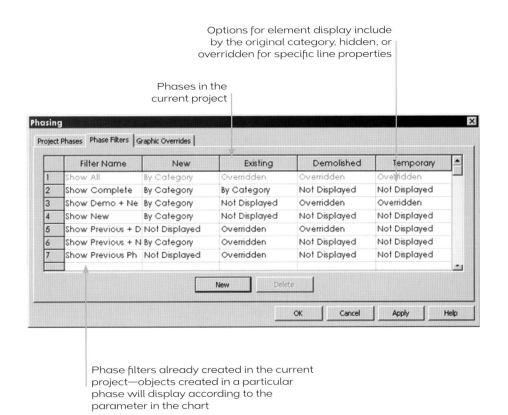

Phase filters already created in the current project—objects created in a particular phase will display according to the parameter in the chart

have a 1' square pattern, for example, or concrete will have the appropriate hatching. **Not Displayed** means that those objects are turned off, like demolished items in the new conditions plan. All objects of a particular phase can be **Overridden** to display whatever linetype, lineweight, or color that you choose—which is why lines on a demolition plan appear heavy and dashed.

If you want existing objects in your main floor plan to display with a black fill pattern, first find the Phase Filter for the new conditions plan—**Existing to Remain + New**. Click in the Existing cell and choose Overridden. Now click on the Graphic Overrides tab and click on the Existing cell. Revit overrides objects in a given phase, assigning a material to all of them. Click on the Cut Fill Pattern cell to choose whatever pattern you'd like. Click **OK** until you're back in the drawing. Note that walls created in the new phase will display by their normal properties, as shown above.

Online Resources

- Revit file used in this chapter, *Bowling Alley block diagram.rvt*

Term Project Assignments

- Adapt your bubble diagram from the previous chapter to a block diagram.
- Create block diagrams for a total of three alternative schemes.

Exercises and Further Study

- Change plans to have solid poché for existing walls and diagonal poché for new walls.
- Make a plan that is filtered such that it only shows demolished elements and nothing that's meant to remain.

10

Starting the Design

- Generate new walls from the block diagrams
- Develop basic editing skills
- Understand inserting and manipulating components
- Understand creating and modifying ceilings

The goal of schematic design is to test out whatever sort of partí or big idea you might have, to see if the architectonic reality can match the conceptual notion you've come up with. Foremost, then, is letting the computer model help you evaluate the design as it develops, and producing drawings that communicate your intentions to others. Slow and steady development, with plenty of opportunities for reflection and analysis, generally produce the most successful designs.

Drawing New Partitions

The quickest way to build up the model is to create walls from the room separation lines you've already drawn. You can also add walls the same way we drew the exterior of the building. As always, check the wall parameters before drawing so you won't have to change them later. We'll have to destroy the block diagram, though, so be sure to save a copy somewhere, just in case.

BIG PICTURE

As usual when moving on to a new phase of design, start by saving a copy of your model. Use or create Revit-native components and other elements whenever possible, so that they'll show up in schedules and legends more reliably later on. Custom objects from SketchUp may be quicker, but only for one-off elements.

UNDER THE HOOD

Revit tries hard to help you learn its various tools. Just hover over a button to see a descriptive tool tip. Wait another few seconds, and a more complete description will pop up.

1. Open your project and choose **Save As**. Give the new file the name *Schematic Design* or something clever like that.
2. Open the **Main Floor Plan New Conditions** view.
3. Right-click on the center of the Demolition Interior Elevation and choose **Hide Elements in View** (Figure 10.1).
4. Room tags from the bubble diagram won't automatically show up, so you'll have to add them. Click on the **Room Tag** tool.
5. Click in each of the rooms to add room labels as needed.
6. Click the **Wall** tool on the **Home** ribbon.
7. Choose 4⅞" Interior Partition from the Type Selector drop-down list and set the top of the wall to go up to the mezzanine.
8. Click the **Modify** button on the **Contextual** ribbon.
9. Click on one of the room separation lines—this creates a wall in that location—and ignore the error warning beep (Revit treats the new wall as a duplicate room separation). A new wall will appear on top of the Room Separation line.
10. Add walls along the other locations.
11. Choose different wall types where needed, such as for a plumbing chase or a furred-out wall.
12. If two walls don't join, click and drag the end grip until they "heal," forming a clean joint.
13. Click when you see the dashed green alignment indicator of the adjacent wall.

Figure 10.1 *Context-sensitive menu*

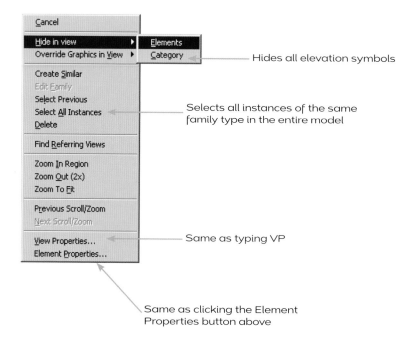

Figure 10.2 *The floor plan with walls and doors*

Walls created from the block diagram

Leave room separation lines for areas where you don't intend to have a dividing wall

14. Add new rooms with walls and the room tool for smaller divisions, such as for the elevator, toilets, and so forth.
15. Add doors or openings to each of the rooms and spaces.
16. Add borrowed lights where needed in your design (Figure 10.2).

There are several of the editing tools that come in handy here—keep the Quick Reference Chart handy to remember what they all do. In particular, Split, Move, Copy, and Mirror are useful, because walls can't overlap.

> **MAGIC TRICK**
>
> *Where did those hidden elements or categories go? Click the lightbulb at the bottom of your screen to display them. Right click on a hidden object to un-hide it or the whole category.*

Modeling Ceilings

Once the walls are in, you can add ceilings quickly—they use the room boundaries to figure out where the ceilings should go. Like many automated Revit features, they can create elements that you can't see if your views are not set up correctly. Ceilings set too high may not be visible because of a floor slab in the way. Gypsum ceilings have a solid white surface pattern assigned, so they won't appear any different from open sky in your Reflected Ceiling Plan (RCP). Check in a section view if you suspect you've lost a ceiling or other element somewhere.

1. On the **Home** ribbon, click on the **Ceiling** tool and choose **Compound Ceiling: 2x2 ACT System** from the Type Selector drop-down list.
2. To set the ceiling height, click the **Element Properties** button (Figure 10.3).
3. Move your mouse over your plan until a room boundary is highlighted.
4. Click inside a given room to draw the ceiling.
5. Click the **Modify** command.
6. Click on a grid line.
7. Click the **Rotate** tool. Angle the grid as desired.
8. If the room is not properly bounded or the ceiling doesn't go all the way to the edge of the room, click the **Sketch Ceiling** button.
9. This is the same sketch mode we saw with floors and roofs. You can now draw any continuous boundary your heart desires with lines, so long as it forms a closed loop (Figure 10.4).
10. Click the slope button to draw a slope arrow.
11. Get the arrow's properties to set the exact slope.
12. Click **Finish Ceiling** to have the software draw the ceiling.
13. To change a ceiling that's already there, select one of the ACT lines,

Figure 10.3 *The Element Properties dialog box*

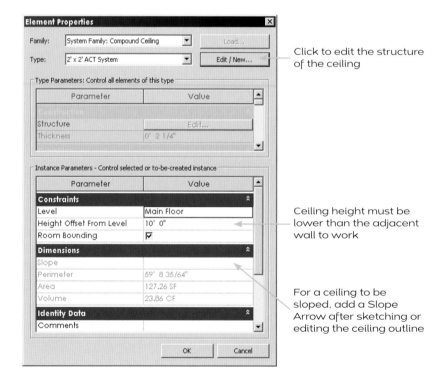

Click to edit the structure of the ceiling

Ceiling height must be lower than the adjacent wall to work

For a ceiling to be sloped, add a Slope Arrow after sketching or editing the ceiling outline

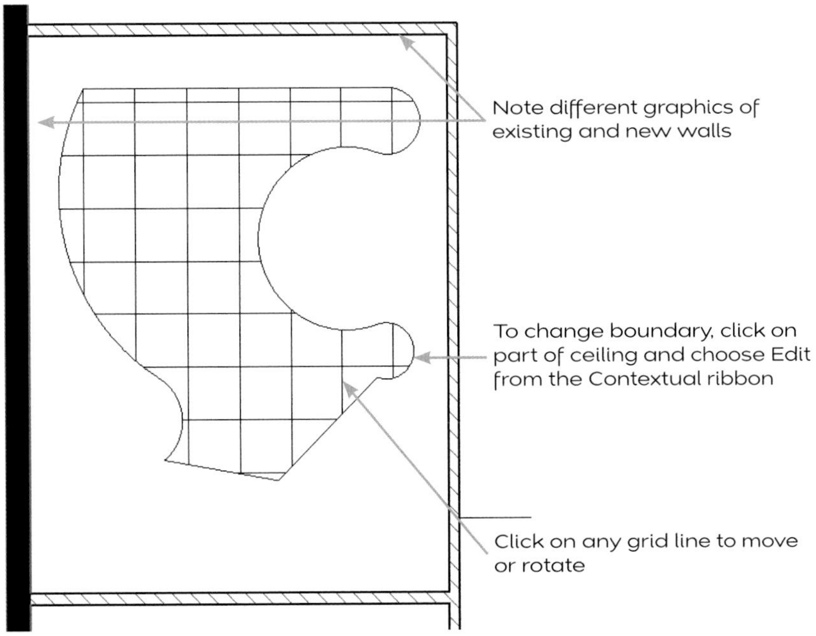

Figure 10.4 *A ceiling with an irregular boundary*

Note different graphics of existing and new walls

To change boundary, click on part of ceiling and choose Edit from the Contextual ribbon

Click on any grid line to move or rotate

right click, and choose **Element Properties** from the context-sensitive menu.

If I'm not sure what sort of ceilings I want yet, but only that I do in fact want ceilings, I'll choose a 2 × 2 ACT. This allows me to select it more easily later on. With Generic and Gypsum ceilings, you won't actually see anything in the RCP, although you will find them in the section. It's very easy to accidentally click several times in a given room to add more than one ceiling—I've seen as many as 20 in a given room. It's easiest to select them in section and delete.

Custom ceilings can be a dramatic effect within an interior, helping to define space and lighting conditions, and assist in wayfinding. There are many ways to experiment, including interesting shapes, edge conditions, materials, and slope.

What about drawing soffits? This is a common design feature, even at this early stage of design. You'll need to create a new ceiling type from one of the ceiling families. It will have extra thickness so that it looks like a soffit. Finally, you'll need to cut an opening in the middle so we can see the original ceiling.

MAGIC TRICK

Ceilings can be hard to select—move your mouse over what looks like the edge of the ceiling. The pop-up information box will tell you what object it thinks you want to select. Hit TAB to toggle through any objects in the vicinity. The pop-up box will tell you what the object is. Left-click when you get to the ceiling. This technique works in any view with any type of object.

DRAWING A ROOM WITH A LOWERED PERIMETER SOFFIT

1. Click on the Ceiling tool. Choose **Compound Ceiling: GWB Soffit** from the Type Selector list.

2. Click the **Properties** button. Set the ceiling height to 8'—lower than the other ceilings you've been putting in.
3. Click **OK** until you're back in the drawing.
4. Choose a room with a 2 × 2 ceiling at 10' above the floor.
5. Click in a room to draw the new ceiling in it—the new ceiling will obscure the other one because it's below it.
6. Now click on the **Openings>Openings by Face** tool on the **Modify** ribbon. Just click **OK** when prompted to choose an object type to allow you to select a ceiling. Move your mouse over the edge of the ceiling until it's highlighted, then click on it.
7. You're now in sketch mode again. Type 2'0" for the offset value.
8. Click on the lower left corner of the room. The purple boundary will start 2'-0" inside the room.
9. Click on the upper left corner, then on the other two corners.
10. Click **Finish Opening**—you should see the 2 × 2 ceiling through the new opening (Figure 10.5).

The simple opening shown above is fine for situations where you have only one or two elements that you're cutting through. In a multi-story building, where you'll have many floors and ceilings, use a **Shaft Opening** instead for stairs and elevators. The start and end heights are set when you create the opening, and it will cut through any objects in its way.

Figure 10.5 *The GWB soffit with 2 × 2 ACT above it*

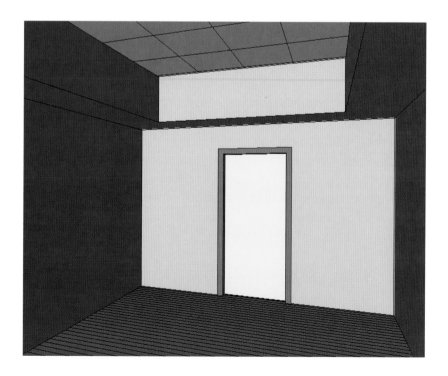

Populating the Model with Stuff

Inserting components is basically the same as doors and windows, except that they're not usually host based. Click on the **Components** tool and choose from the Type Selector drop-down list or load from the library (Figure 10.6).

Browse in the folders to find the components that you need. Once you select one and click **OK**, the component will become available under the Type Selector drop-down list.

Some components are a little tricky. Elevator doors and wall openings, for example, are found in the Doors folder and need a wall host just like other doors. Once loaded into your drawing, however, you'll need to insert them using the **Component** tool.

Some components have different flavors of basically the same thing— these are called family types. For example, when you load in a double-hung window, you end up with a dozen different sizes listed in your

Figure 10.6 *The **Imperial Library** that comes with Revit*

Folders in the Imperial Library installed with Revit

Click to see AutoDesk's online library, which has just a few more components

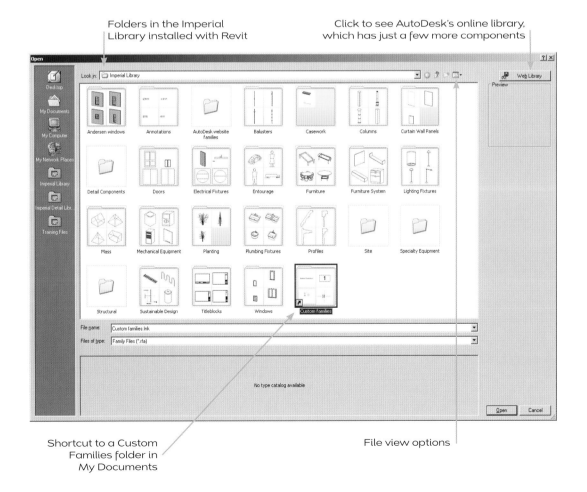

Shortcut to a Custom Families folder in My Documents

File view options

Type Selector drop-down list. To add a new family type, choose **Edit> New>Duplicate**—be sure to give the new instance a good name. Now change the dimension in the **Properties** dialog box. Click **OK** to return to the drawing.

Not every component has different instance types—some have parametric elements that you can change directly in the **Properties** dialog box. Others, like kitchen counters, have many different **grips** that allow an infinite number of configurations for length, width, and location of the sink opening.

File Management

I'm pretty compulsive about backing up my work, and this includes my library of downloaded components and custom materials. I have all of my data stored on a partition of my hard drive, for easier backups, and that's where my Revit Library folder is located. The Imperial Library, however, is on my other drive. To link my personal Revit Library folder for convenience, I'll use Windows Explorer to find the Imperial Library folder.

Now, while holding down the **ALT** key, click and drag on your personal library folder (located in My Documents) into the Imperial Library folder—this creates a link to the original folder. Now, when you go to load in a component, you'll see your folder in the list.

Loading components in from the Autodesk online library is also easy, and you can download whole directories. These come in as zip files, which are compressed folders that package a bunch of files together for easy transfer. Go to the Web Library, then browse for your version of Revit— it may be under the Archived Versions link if you're not running the latest and greatest version. Then, under **Accessories**, click on **Toilet Specialties** to reveal bathroom partitions of various sorts.

The Toilet partitions you just downloaded are a type of component that must always have a wall host. To load a bunch of different component families at the same time, choose **Application Menu>Load from Library>Load Family...** and then browse for your folder. Then select as many of the families as you think you'll need (use **CTRL** and **SHIFT** while clicking to select multiple items), and click **Open**.

Choose the partition family you want from the Type Selector drop-down list of the **Component** tool. As you mouse over a wall, Revit will show a preview of where the component will go. Click on the wall to insert. Select the partition with the **Modify** tool and change to orientation of the door and toilet with the blue flippers.

Another good place to get components is at RevitCity.com. You can

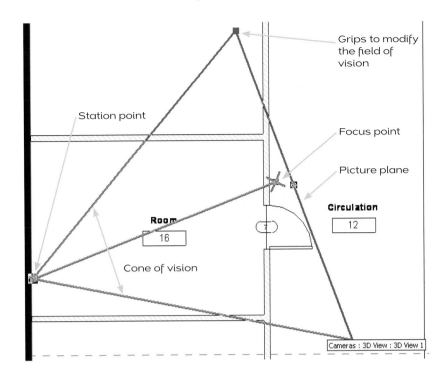

Station point

Grips to modify the field of vision

Focus point

Picture plane

Circulation

12

Room

16

Cone of vision

Cameras : 3D View : 3D View 1

Figure 10.7 *Perspective construction "triangle" in plan*

upload as well as download for free, and you can even add multiple files to a ZIP file for easy transfer. Just unzip into your local Revit Library folder.

Perspective Views

Now it's time to look at the project in perspective. On the **View** ribbon, choose **Camera**. Click once in the drawing to place the camera, and again to place the focus. Note that Revit places a 30° cone of vision on your plan, and that any of the perspectival elements (station point, picture plane) can be moved here in plan (Figure 10.7).

You can find the new view under the 3D views in the Project Browser. Interior perspectives often need much wider fields of view than exterior ones, since you are generally limited in the distance you can get from any part of a space. Click on the edge of the visible area to change the Crop Region. Click and drag the grips to make the field of view wider.

To orbit, click and drag your scroll wheel while holding down **SHIFT**. For more advanced controls, click on the **Navigation Wheel** button at the top of the screen (or hit the **F8** key) to bring up a little interactive toolbar with a variety of different view modification options (Figure 10.8).

Mouse over a command to highlight it, then click and drag to execute the command. The view tools are very sensitive, so it takes some practice

LOOK OUT!

Revit crops away everything beyond the picture plane, even if it crosses a wall. If part of your model is invisible in a perspective view, this is usually the problem. To move it, go back to the plan you created the perspective in, right-click on the perspective in the project browser, and choose Show Camera. This will reveal the perspective triangle again, so you can drag the focus point out of the room.

Figure 10.8 *The Navigation Wheel controls*

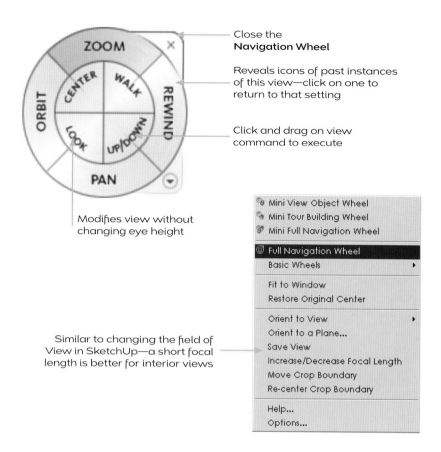

Close the **Navigation Wheel**

Reveals icons of past instances of this view—click on one to return to that setting

Click and drag on view command to execute

Modifies view without changing eye height

Similar to changing the field of View in SketchUp—a short focal length is better for interior views

to make more subtle changes. Compose the perspective to show off your interior, with a balance of floor, wall, and ceiling shown. You should also consider if you want more of a one-point, two-point, bird's-eye, or worm's-eye view. Interior views tend to have wider fields of view, so don't worry if there's some perspectival distortion. If you totally mess up the view, use the **Rewind** feature to return to previous states of this particular view.

The View Control Bar

As Revit first creates them, perspectival drawings often need a little help to read well, and this is where the **View Control Bar** comes in handy (Figure 10.9). Most of these basic controls also show up in the **View Properties** dialog box.

Most perspectives look better as shaded views, so switch to **Shading with Edges** under **Model Graphics**. Colors are based on the finish materials assigned to objects in the model, and can be altered from the **Materials** dialog box. Want to turn off the furniture to make some wall edits? Select a component and click on the **Temporary Hide/Isolate**

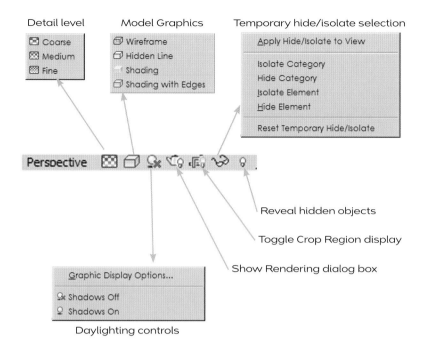

Detail level
- ☒ Coarse
- ☒ Medium
- ☒ Fine

Model Graphics
- Wireframe
- Hidden Line
- Shading
- Shading with Edges

Temporary hide/isolate selection
- Apply Hide/Isolate to View
- Isolate Category
- Hide Category
- Isolate Element
- Hide Element
- Reset Temporary Hide/Isolate

Figure 10.9 *View Control* bar

Perspective

Reveal hidden objects

Toggle Crop Region display

Show Rendering dialog box

Graphic Display Options...
- Shadows Off
- Shadows On

Daylighting controls

Figure 10.10 *Sun and Shadows* settings dialog box

Use sliders to adjust sun and shadow intensity

Pre-set sun conditions for commonly used conditions

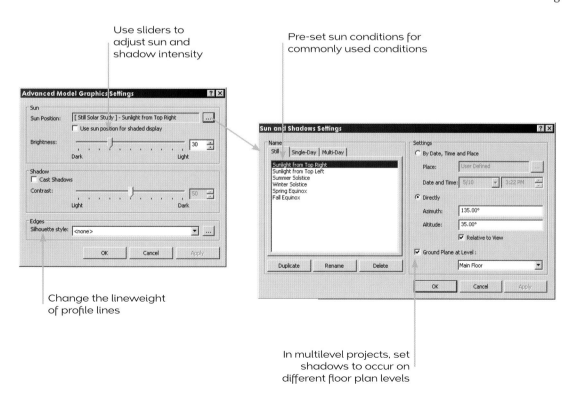

Change the lineweight of profile lines

In multilevel projects, set shadows to occur on different floor plan levels

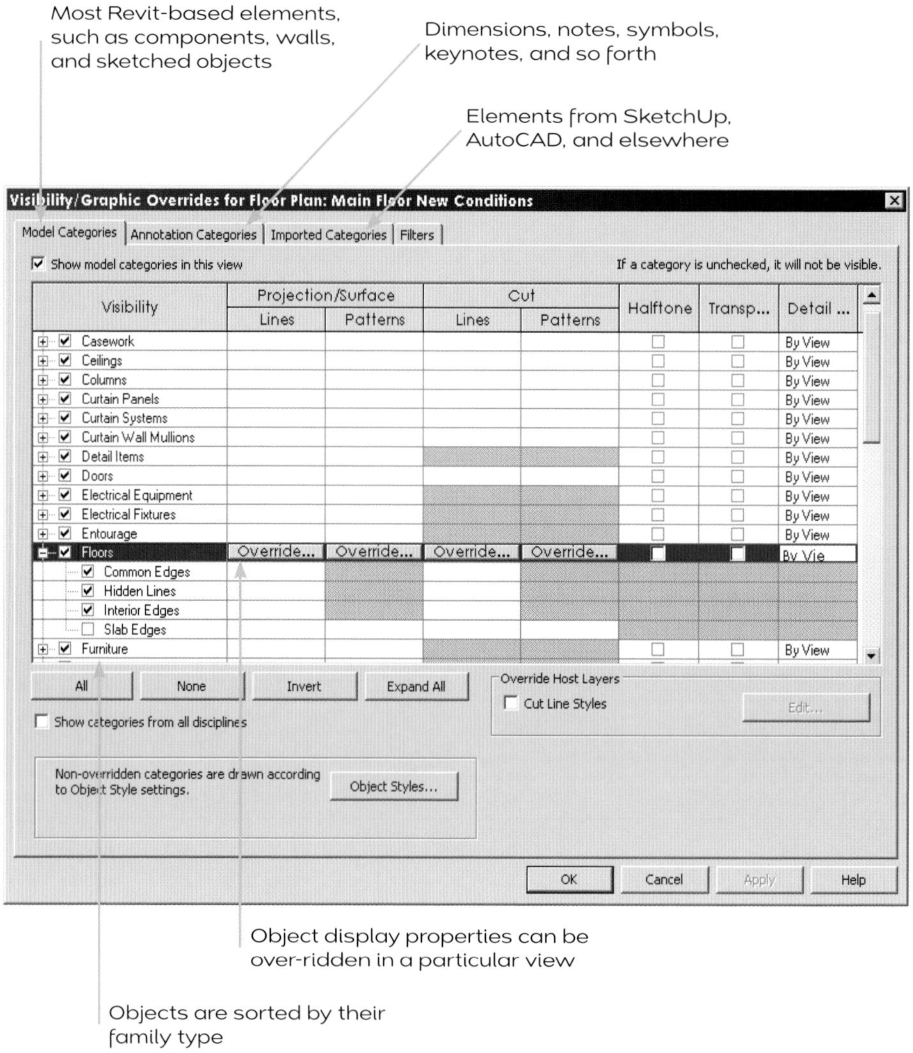

Figure 10.11 *The Visibility/Graphic Overrides dialog box*

Most Revit-based elements, such as components, walls, and sketched objects

Dimensions, notes, symbols, keynotes, and so forth

Elements from SketchUp, AutoCAD, and elsewhere

Object display properties can be over-ridden in a particular view

Objects are sorted by their family type

Shadows show up on whatever level is defined as the ground plane in the model. To make shadows show up properly on the mezzanine, you'll need to define it as the ground plane (be sure to export the lower-level plan first). On the Mezzanine Plan, choose Advanced Model Graphics. *Click on* Sun and Shadows *settings and make shadows display on the ground plane at the second level.*

button and choose **Hide Category**. These objects will print, however, so if you don't want them to show up again, choose **Apply Hide/Isolate to View** and Revit will make the view changes permanent.

Plans and axonometrics will appear to have greater depth if the sun appears to be on—just choose **Shadows On**. You can control sun and shadow intensity in the **Advanced Model Graphics** menu. To change the daylighting settings, open the **Sun and Shadow Settings** dialog box—there are several standard options for date, time, and geographic location. Custom conditions can be created by modifying any of the parameters for date, time, and location (Figure 10.10).

Want to turn on (or off) that **VCT pattern** in a particular view, or all the furniture? Different classes of items are automatically assigned to a family type, and so their visibility can be turned off or changed en masse.

Choose **Visibility/Graphics...** from the **View** ribbon (this menu is also in the View Properties dialog box). Or just type **VG** from your drawing (Figure 10.11).

This is similar to the Layer Properties Manager in AutoCAD, and allows you to turn on and off different classes of elements within an individual view. On the Model Elements tab, click the little **+** sign next to floors to reveal the different pieces of a floor that can be controlled. Click the radio button next to **Surface pattern** to turn on any floor patterns you may have in your project.

Complex Parametric Objects: Stairs

Somehow when I say "complex parametric objects" I think of the spaceships my son makes out of Legos. In the world of BIM, however, this refers to any object that is generated using a combination of sketching, compositional rules, and ready-made parts. Stairs are a good example, and are one of the more dramatic things to model in Revit. They come complete with railings, landings, and calculation rules to combine them. The overall shape is defined by a sketch of the stair outline and risers.

Stairs are sketched, just like floors and roofs—either as a whole run or step-by-step with custom boundaries. And, like other complex objects, they can be edited later. Let's start with a fairly standard out- and back-type stair, then modify to have a more interesting profile.

MODEL A STAIR

1. On the **Home** ribbon, click on the **Stair** tool—you'll enter sketch mode.
2. Click the **Stair Properties** button to make sure you're using the appropriate rules (Figure 10.12).
3. Click **OK.**
4. Click once on the screen to start drawing a run of stairs.
5. Move your mouse north until the green **Risers Created** message shows that you've completed half the needed steps.
6. Click to finish the run.
7. Move your mouse to the west of the last riser line created—note the dashed green alignment indicator (Figure 10.13).
8. Click again to start the next run. Head south this time, and click when you don't need any more treads.

Figure 10.12 *Stair properties*

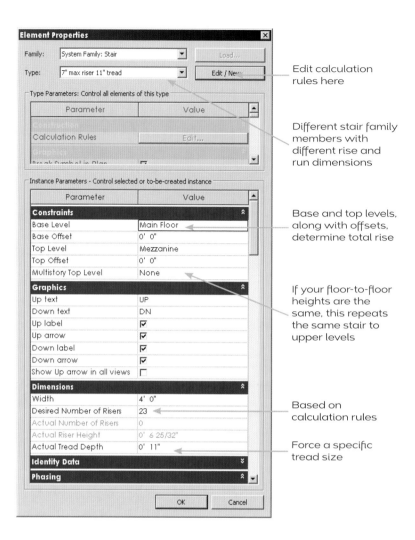

Edit calculation rules here

Different stair family members with different rise and run dimensions

Base and top levels, along with offsets, determine total rise

If your floor-to-floor heights are the same, this repeats the same stair to upper levels

Based on calculation rules

Force a specific tread size

9. Click **Finish Stair**, and you'll see your stairs shown appropriately, with up arrows, cut lines, and all.
10. Select the stair with the **Modify** command.
11. Choose **Edit** from the **Contextual** ribbon—you'll enter Sketch Mode.
12. Use the **Modify** command to select one of the green boundary lines.
13. Use the grip to move it out, spreading the run of stairs.
14. Click **Finish Sketch** and Revit redraws the stair with the splayed run.
15. Edit the stair again, but this time click the **Boundary** tool from the **Contextual** ribbon.
16. Draw an arc along the flared side.
17. Delete the original border and click **Finish Sketch**—again, Revit redraws the stair with the new boundary (Figure 10.14).

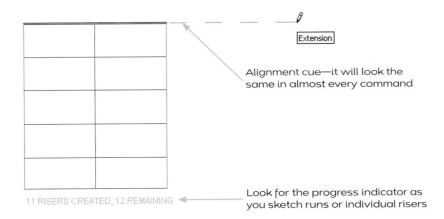

Figure 10.13 *The alignment cues for the first run of stairs*

Alignment cue—it will look the same in almost every command

Extension

11 RISERS CREATED, 12 REMAINING ← Look for the progress indicator as you sketch runs or individual risers

You can keep changing the boundary this way, making curved landings and grand staircases.

Revit will try to follow the rules you've set up, but it can't account for local code compliance, so be careful. In Massachusetts, for example, a single run of stairs can go a maximum of 12' vertical before needing a landing—so we need at least one landing in this project. If the same stair design repeats for several levels in a multilevel project, choose the **Multistory Top Level** option in the Stair Properties dialog box.

MAGIC TRICK

If you just need to move an object like a stair or a component a little bit, select it and use the arrow keys to nudge it one way or another.

Figure 10.14 *Stairs of various layouts*

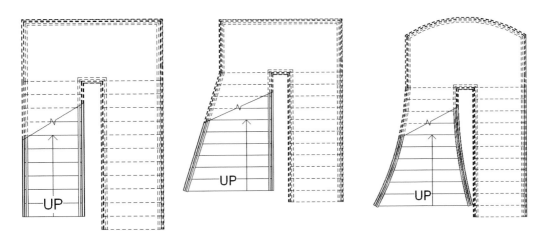

Circular Stairs

Circular and winding stairs are basically the same process. After starting the Stair command, click the **Circular** button in the **Contextual** ribbon. Drafting lines marking the center point and the arc center are handy when sketching the runs, especially if you need a landing (Figure 10.15).

Don't forget that you'll need to cut an opening in the first-floor ceiling and the mezzanine floor. Go to the Mezzanine Plan view, but turn on an underlay of the first-floor plan from the View Properties menu. After starting the **Opening** tool, you can use the **Select** option to use the already created boundaries of your stair to define the new opening (Figure 10.16).

Be sure to leave a landing in the correct location, and consider head height as well as design. You'll also need to cut a hole in any ceilings below. You can turn off the underlay again when you're done. Even with

Figure 10.15 *The curved stair sketch*

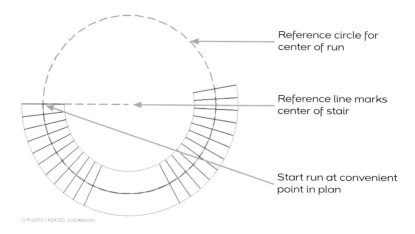

Reference circle for center of run

Reference line marks center of stair

Start run at convenient point in plan

23 RISERS CREATED, 0 REMAINING

Figure 10.16 *Boundary of the second-floor opening for a circular stair*

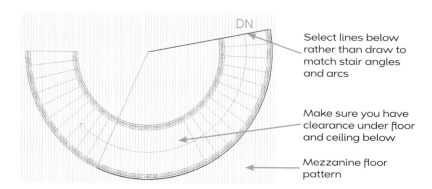

DN

Select lines below rather than draw to match stair angles and arcs

Make sure you have clearance under floor and ceiling below

Mezzanine floor pattern

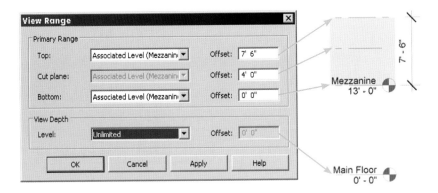

Figure 10.17 *The View Range dialog box*

the opening cut, you may not be able to see the stair. But where is the stair? From the **View Properties** menu, scroll down and click on the **Edit** next to the View Range field (Figure 10.17).

This menu controls the height where the cut plane occurs. Change the View Depth to Unlimited and click **OK** until you're back in the drawing. This displays the ceiling below the opening you've just made, so you can cut an opening like before.

Exporting Images for Presentations

Exporting a batch of views for a quick presentation is pretty easy. Choose **File>Export>Image...** like we did with the bubble diagram. This time, however, click on the **Selected views/sheets** button. This brings up a list of all exportable views in your drawing—just check off the ones you'd like in your presentation. Click OK, then be sure to click the Output button and choose a folder for all of these images. Be sure to make subfolders to collect these images, as Revit will name them generically and they can pile up very quickly.

So now that you have all of these images, you'll probably want to assemble them into a PowerPoint slide show. For a linear slide show, on the **Insert** menu, choose **New Slide Show** (Figure 10.18).

Browse to select all the images you'd like to include and choose a layout. Individual images can be moved up and down, rotated, and given titles. Click **Create** to produce a new slide show with each of your images on a different slide. If you're making presentation boards, remember that you can select more than one image at a time by holding down **SHIFT** (for a continuous group) or **CTRL** (for noncontiguous files) and click to build your selection. They'll come in all on top of each other, but you'll have to arrange the board anyway.

> **MAGIC TRICK**
>
> *Revit will save incremental backups of your project—each time you click* Save, *in fact, a new one is created. In the directory for your project, they're all marked with an .0000# extension. Don't delete these, as you may need them in case of a catastrophic crash. Don't open them either, because if you hit* Save, *it will overwrite the original (and more recent) file.*

Figure 10.18 *Menu for creating a new slide show*

Browse for text pictures

Select (can be more than one) to change slide order

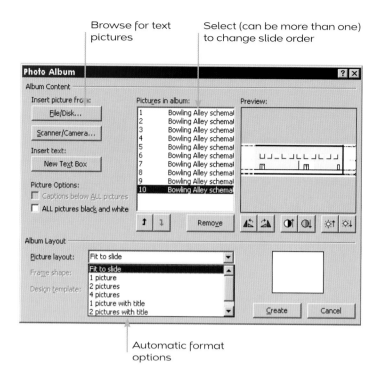

Automatic format options

Animated Walkthroughs

Just as in SketchUp, you can create an animation of your project fairly easily—it's just another view (or really a bunch of views strung together) of your completed model. You can even choose the visibility settings when exporting to a file, so advanced rendering can be applied for photo-realistic walkthroughs.

CREATING A WALKTHROUGH ANIMATION

1. Open the Main Floor Plan.
2. On the **View** ribbon, click **3D View Walkthrough**.
3. Click on the plan at the location you'd like to start the walkthrough.
4. A 30° cone of vision is now attached to your cursor. Click again to define the next frame of the walkthrough.
5. Keep clicking to trace a path through the project (Figure 10.19).
6. Double-click to end the path.
7. Open the view under the Walkthroughs folder of the project browser—it will show the view from the last frame.
8. Click on the edge of the view to change the Crop Region—a wide field of view is generally most effective.

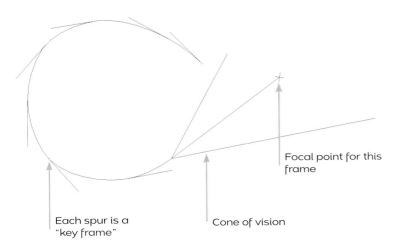

Figure 10.19 *The walkthrough path in plan*

Focal point for this frame

Each spur is a "key frame"

Cone of vision

9. To preview the movie, click **Edit** on the **Contextual** ribbon (Figure 10.20).
10. Use the double-arrow buttons to navigate to the beginning of the movie.
11. Click the **Play** button. Change the settings to individual key frames as desired.
12. To export, choose **Application Menu>Export>Walkthrough** (Figure 10.21).
13. Choose the view settings you'd like. If you've defined a rendering scene, you can apply it here, or a standard **Display mode**.
14. Choose the frame rate and frame transition time. Click **OK**.
15. The export process can take a very long time, depending on your settings. Go have dinner, get a good night's rest, and take a look at your movie in the morning.

When exported using standard **Display Modes**, the animation will display a ticker as the frames pass by. Choose Photorealistic Rendering to get rid of that ticker and produce a dramatic walkthrough with materials and lighting fully rendered.

You may select the path drawn in plan and make changes to individual nodes by clicking and dragging. Select the edge of the walkthrough

Figure 10.20 *Playing a walkthrough*

Playback controls

Returns all camera key frames to their original placement

Figure 10.21 *The walkthrough **Export** dialog box*

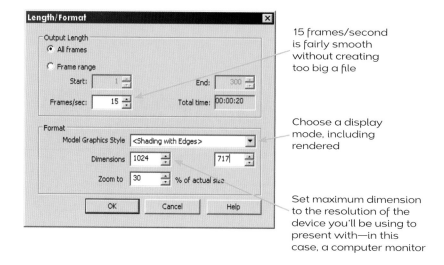

15 frames/second is fairly smooth without creating too big a file

Choose a display mode, including rendered

Set maximum dimension to the resolution of the device you'll be using to present with—in this case, a computer monitor

preview to change the size of the **Crop Region** using grips. You can also click on the **Size** button on the **Contextual** ribbon and specify exact dimensions—just be sure to check the **Scale (locked proportions)** button. To make the animation longer, click on the **Properties** button. At the bottom of that menu, you can change the number of frames, which is 300 by default. This is especially important when you've created a large number of nodes, because otherwise the motion will occur too quickly.

Daylighting Studies

Revit can produce daylighting studies for a single day, just as we saw in SketchUp. Choose the **Settings>Sun and Shadow Settings...** dialog box and go to the Single Day tab. Choose one of the standard solar studies, or duplicate one to create your own. Click **Apply**, then **OK** to return to the drawing (Figure 10.22).

Switch to plan view, then choose **File>Export>Animated Solar Study...** Unlike an animated walkthrough, there's no way to increase the number of frames, but you can decrease the frame rate down to five and still have a decent study. Click **OK** to export the file.

Online Resources

- Revit file used for illustrations in this chapter, *Bowling Alley schematic design.rvt*

Choose a standard
solar study

Click to change location,
either by name or by
longitude and latitude

Figure 10.22 *The Sun and Shadows Settings dialog box for a solar study*

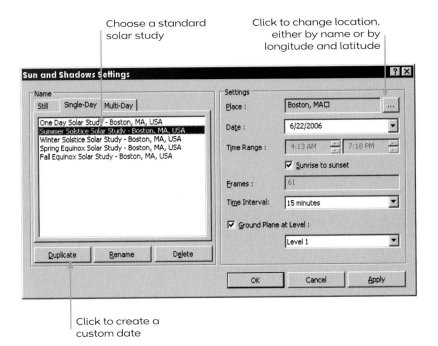

Click to create a
custom date

Term Project Assignments

■ Create a schematic design presentation in PowerPoint that includes:
  ▼ Visual Concepts Board
  ▼ Partí Board
  ▼ Program Analysis Board
  ▼ Building Codes Board
  ▼ Accessibility Regulations Board
  ▼ Project Constraints Board
  ▼ Floor plan, section, and reflected ceiling plan
  ▼ Walkthrough animation

Exercises and Further Study

■ Lay out an auditorium with arcing seats.
■ Make a custom stair border.
■ Create solar studies for the winter and summer solstices for an interior perspectival view.

Unit 4

Working Drawings and Documentation

11

Design Development Drawings and Diagrams

- Understand wall types and how to represent them
- Model complex elements within Revit
- Understand how to import SketchUp-based custom objects
- Create code analysis drawings
- Create and complete various schedules
- Understand egress compartmentalization

Once you (or your clients, or your instructors) are happy with the direction of your schematic design, it's time to start looking at your project with greater precision and subtlety. This is when you need to make more careful study regarding the constructability of your project—assigning real materials and dimensions to systems you may have just improvised earlier on. You'll also need to do diagrams to calculate code-based occupancy loads and verify egress capacity.

Dimensioning the Drawing

Open up your drawing from the previous chapter. I like to put in dimensions at this point—somehow it makes the project seem more real. The **Dimension** tool, like Reference Plane and Text, appears on several tabs of the **Home** ribbon. Click on the **Dimension** tool, and be sure to set the Options appropriately for the type of walls you'll be referencing (Figure 11.1).

Figure 11.1 *Dimension Contextual ribbon*

Modify the current style, or create a new one, under **Family Properties**.

Choose a dimension style.

Click on a wall centerline or face at one side of the project, then click on the next wall down. You may change options in the middle of the string. Click on the next wall, and the next, to build the string. Click in a clear area above the plan to place the dimensions. Select the dimensions to edit or to add or remove subdivisions.

As a general rule, existing and exterior walls are dimensioned to their face, while new interior partitions are typically dimensioned to the centerline. Doors and windows take dimensions to their centerlines, except in masonry construction. Try to keep the dimensions off the plan, and avoid overlapping lines for different strings (Figure 11.2).

Figure 11.2 *A fully dimensioned area of the plan*

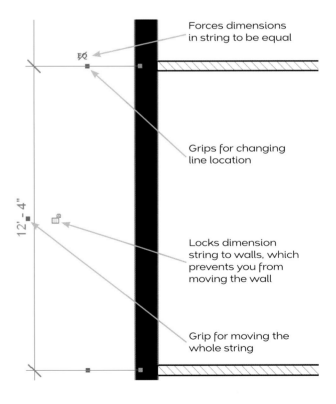

Forces dimensions in string to be equal

Grips for changing line location

Locks dimension string to walls, which prevents you from moving the wall

Grip for moving the whole string

Defining Wall Construction

Adding detail to a Revit drawing is more about setting scale and view properties than it is about drawing more lines and hatch patterns. Wall construction needs to be finalized so that partition types can be identified and detailed. Base moldings and reveals are applied to walls globally using sweeps—linear, horizontal bands of a predefined profile.

ADDING BASE AND TRIM TO A WALL

1. In your Main Floor Plan, select a wall and choose **Element Properties** from the context-sensitive menu.
2. Click **Edit/New.**
3. To make a wall with a sweep, click **Duplicate** (to avoid messing up the original).

Selected layer highlighted in preview

Selected layer can be added, subtracted, and moved up and down

Materials chosen here will apply to all instances of this type

Figure 11.3 *The wall structure*

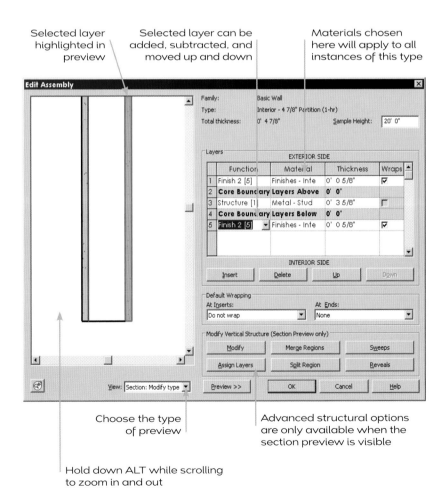

Choose the type of preview

Advanced structural options are only available when the section preview is visible

Hold down ALT while scrolling to zoom in and out

4. Give the new wall a name like 4⅞" Interior Partition with wall base (or something clever like that) and click **OK**.

5. Next to the Structure field, click on the **Edit** button.

6. Click on the **Preview** button. Choose **Section** from the drop-down list below the preview (Figure 11.3).

7. To change the dimension of a structural element, select it in the chart and type a new dimension—all instances of this wall type will change.

8. Click on the **Sweeps** button to activate the Sweeps menu.

9. Click on the **Load** button. This brings up what looks suspiciously like the **Component Load** dialog box, where you can browse in the Profiles folder for different bases, crowns, and chair rails.

10. Choose a wall base and click **OK**. Back in the **Sweeps** dialog box, click the **Add** button.

11. Click the select button in the Profile field to choose the shape of the base you'd like to use.

12. Choose a wall base from the drop-down list.

13. Select the new sweep in the chart and click the **Duplicate** button. On the new sweep, change the location from Interior to Exterior.

14. Zoom in on the base of the wall to see what the sweeps look like. Move the sweep up or down by changing the offset heights.

15. Add other sweeps or reveals to one or both sides of the wall until you've put your carpenter's kids through college.

16. Click **OK** until you're back in the drawing.

17. Go to an interior view to see the sweeps applied to the walls.

LOOK OUT!

This will add sweeps to ALL instances of this wall type! If there are spaces where you don't want the sweep but do want this wall construction, be sure to duplicate the original wall type. If there's a sweep on only one side of the wall, select the wall in plan and use the blue flippers to mirror the wall (and thus the side with the sweep). Click on a wall, and grips will appear for changing the length of any sweeps.

Figure 11.4 *Axonometric view of a wall with a sweep*

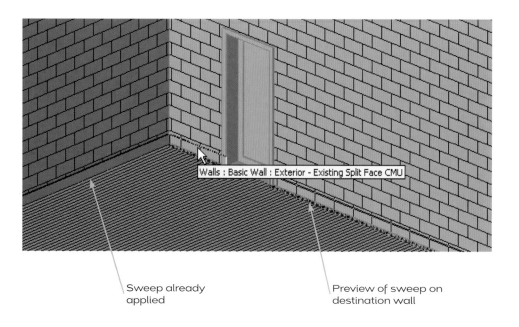

Walls : Basic Wall : Exterior - Existing Split Face CMU

Sweep already applied

Preview of sweep on destination wall

Sweeps can be added or removed at any point in the drawing process. Select one in an orthographic view (I prefer axonometric) and you'll see grips to shorten or lengthen individual sections of trim. These sweeps can be painted, just like walls, but this can be a bit of a pain for more complex traditional profiles. It would be better to assign materials in the sweeps dialog box (Figure 11.4).

The sweep can be moved up and down by dragging or through its **Element Properties**. You can also change the profile and material from this menu. This can get tedious, but is easier than changing the whole wall type when trim only occurs in one or two spaces.

A set of construction drawings almost always has a sheet of *Partition Types*, and often these are tried-and-true drawings from a dusty archive somewhere. If you don't have a vast library of CAD drawings, you'll just have to create the details from scratch, using enlarged sections of the wall types you're already using. To see the detail information, draw a section through a given wall: Choose **Wall Section** from the Type Selector drop-down list, then click on either side of a wall to place the section symbol.

Up the **Detail Level** to *Fine* and the scale to at least 1½" = 1'-0", then all of the structure should show up nicely. It's now a matter of providing notes and dimensions where appropriate. On the **View** ribbon, click on the **Section** tool (Figure 11.5).

Select the **Crop Region** of the section to control the extents of the section. Use the section dividers to crop away the middle part of the wall—and don't worry, this won't leave huge gaps in the middle of walls throughout your project. Each half can then be moved up or down (Figure 11.6).

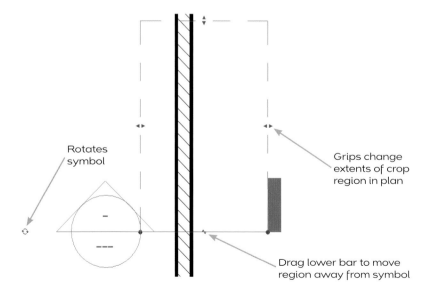

Rotates symbol

Grips change extents of crop region in plan

Drag lower bar to move region away from symbol

Figure 11.5 *Inserted section symbol*

Figure 11.6 *The cropped partition type*

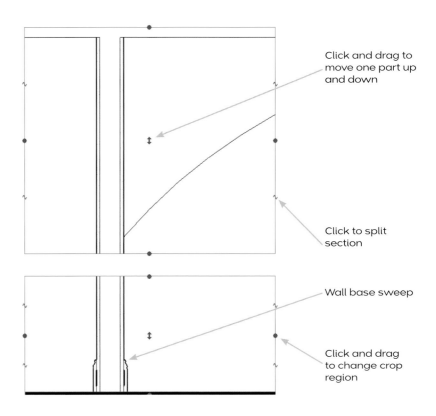

Click and drag to move one part up and down

Click to split section

Wall base sweep

Click and drag to change crop region

Add annotation and dimensions to fill out the basic assemblies, and use detail components as above for objects that don't display as desired.

Curtain Walls

Curtain walls are put together quite differently than regular walls, both literally and in terms of electronic modeling in Revit. Use the **Wall** tool to draw a length of the Curtain Wall type, then take a look at it in elevation. It should look like a solid sheet of glass. Select it in elevation, and select **Storefront** from the Type Selector drop-down list. You should see a wall with vertical and horizontal mullions (Figure 11.7).

The Storefront wall type has a regular pattern of grids and mullions already applied, and are locked in place. All basic curtain walls start life as a single piece of glass, which can be broken up either in a regular grid from the **Family Properties** menu or by placing them one by one (Figure 11.8).

You can choose a mullion profile you'd like, too, and they can be added or deleted individually. Regular doors won't work, however—you'll have to replace one of the panels with a special door component.

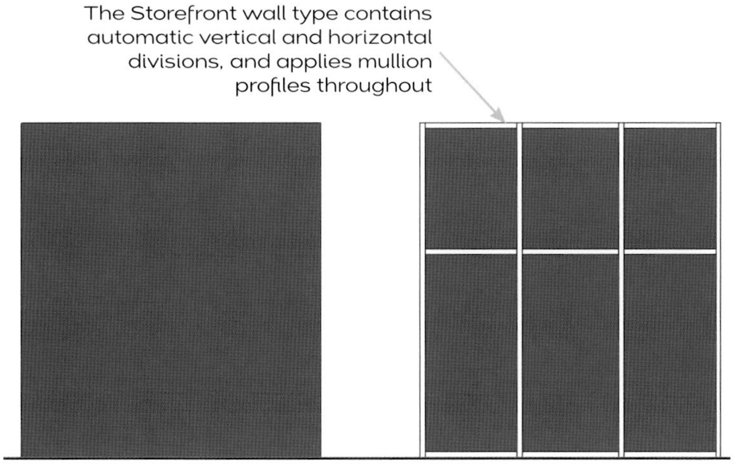

The Storefront wall type contains automatic vertical and horizontal divisions, and applies mullion profiles throughout

Figure 11.7 *Curtain wall and Storefront wall types*

MODELING A CUSTOM CURVED CURTAIN WALL WITH A DOOR

1. In your Main Floor Plan, click on the Wall tool.
2. Choose **Curtain Wall** from the Type Selector drop-down list.
3. Draw a 12' length, 10' high with a pleasant arc to it—it will look straight in plan for now, though (Figure 11.9).
4. Go to (or create) an interior elevation view of the wall.
5. Click on the boundary of the wall.
6. Click on the **Properties** button on the **Contextual** ribbon.

Figure 11.8 *Curtain wall* **Properties**

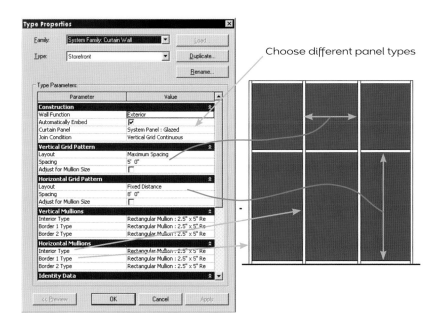

Choose different panel types

Figure 11.9 *The suspiciously straight curved curtain wall*

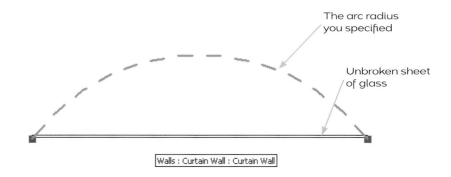

The arc radius you specified

Unbroken sheet of glass

Walls : Curtain Wall : Curtain Wall

7. Click on **Edit/New.**
8. Click on **Duplicate.**
9. Name the new type *Segmented Curve* or something clever like that.
10. Add vertical grids at 2' on center.
11. Add a horizontal grid 8' above the floor. Click **OK** (Figure 11.10).
12. Create an elevation view of the wall.
13. To add mullions to selected segments, click on the **Mullion** tool.
14. Choose **2.5"x5" Rectangular** from the Type Selector drop-down list.
15. Uncheck the **All Open Grids** radio button (or you'll apply mullions everywhere).
16. Move your mouse over the segment you want to add a mullion to and click to add (Figure 11.11).

Figure 11.10 *The faceted curtain wall*

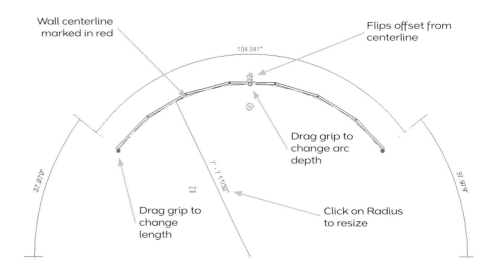

Wall centerline marked in red

Flips offset from centerline

Drag grip to change arc depth

Drag grip to change length

Click on Radius to resize

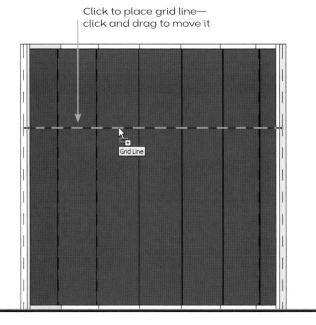

Click to place grid line—
click and drag to move it

Grid Line

Figure 11.11 *Adding mullions*

17. To add a set of double doors, select the vertical and base mullions where you'd like to put a door.
18. If there is a lock icon visible next to the panel, it won't be editable. Click the icon to unlock it, and hit the **Delete** key.
19. From the **Insert** ribbon, choose **Load Family...** Double-click on the **Doors** folder.
20. Choose the Curtain Wall Sgl Glass.rfa door, and click **OK** to load it into your drawing.
21. Draw a selection window around the panel to be changed, and don't worry about selecting other things like mullions.
22. Click the **Filter** button on the **Contextual** ribbon.
23. Deselect everything but Curtain Panels and click **OK**.
24. Unlock the Panel if need be.
25. Click the **Properties** button. Choose Curtain Wall Sgl Glass from the Panel Type drop-down list. Click **OK**, and you should have doors.
26. The handing can be changed with flippers in plan view like other doors.

Curtain walls are a little harder to edit, and should always be coordinated with adjacent ceiling heights. When you're not sure about a construction detail, a good place to look for further information is one of the standard reference manuals, like *Interior Design Graphic Standards*.

LOOK OUT!

In any ready-made grid system, such as Storefront, the panels, mullions, and grids will be locked. Select one and you'll see a little closed padlock. Click it to unlock the element for modification or deletion. Note that this is a good way to lock elements you don't want edited easily, such as structural grids or chase walls.

Automated Schedules

Schedules in Revit are just another view of the data that's already in your project. The Interior Renovation Template we're using already has a Room Finish Schedule in it, and while you were busy drawing block diagrams and making rooms, the software was filling out your schedule. Open the schedules group in the Project Browser, double-click on the room finish schedule, and you should see a list of all the spaces in your project. To edit, just type in any of the fields. You'll find that Revit remembers what you've typed, so in the next room down, there will be a drop-down list of the different notes or materials.

These fields can be sorted in various ways, the text can be formatted, and you can add or delete fields. Right-click on the schedule name in the Project Browser and choose **Properties** from the menu. Click on the characteristic you'd like to change. For instance, you typically sort

Figure 11.12 *The new schedule dialog box for a wall take-off*

Available fields are defined by the family

Sort by any of the fields available, itemize every instance, and calculate totals

Adds another custom field

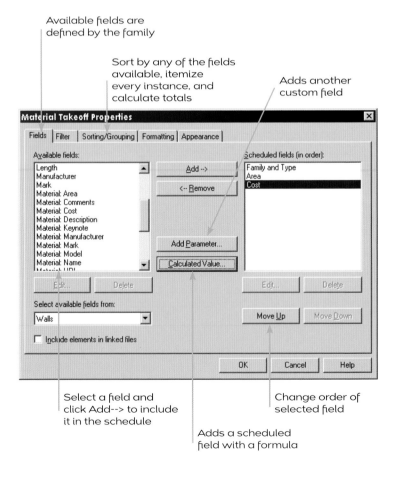

Select a field and click Add--> to include it in the schedule

Adds a scheduled field with a formula

Change order of selected field

the schedule by room number. You can also change the text size, font, and even the line type used.

New schedules of your own configuration can be added from the **View** ribbon. A variation on a schedule is one where you have Revit add up the total amount of some element of your project, such as light fixtures, furniture, or floor areas. These are often used for cost estimating or producing purchase orders. To make a new one, choose **Schedules> Materials Take Off...** from the **View** ribbon. Let's create a schedule that lists each type of wall in the project and the total area of each (Figure 11.12).

Add the fields for what you'd like to count, and sort it if needed. Be sure to uncheck **Itemize Every Instance** to just get totals. Click **OK** to create the schedule. Once a schedule is dragged onto a sheet of drawings, select it and you'll see wedge-shaped grips to change the width of columns (Figure 11.13).

If the schedule is not showing what you expected, right-click on your view and choose **View Properties**—you'll return to the dialog box in Figure 11.12. Text size and formatting is controlled in the **Properties** dialog box. Be sure to match the font of other elements in your project. In a room finish schedule, you'll want Revit to display each instance of the family type, so on the **Sorting/Grouping** tab, check the box next to **Itemize Every Instance**.

Drag grip to change column width

Click in a cell to change value

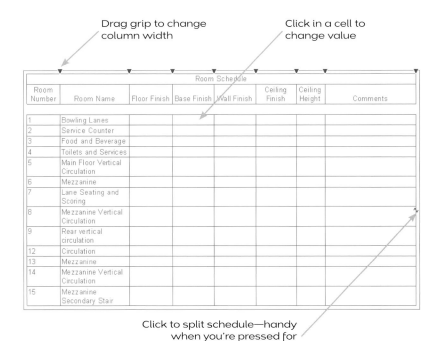

Click to split schedule—handy when you're pressed for space on a sheet

Figure 11.13 *Schedule with adjustable columns*

Complex Custom Components—
Keep Colors for Clarity

Often you'll want something more cool and funky than is available from any of the sources mentioned previously. For anything complex and custom, the easiest thing to do is draw it in SketchUp.

Purists out there may complain that Revit has the ability to "solid model" just about anything, but I find those tools slow and cumbersome. SketchUp drawings can be imported directly into a Revit drawing but need a little preparation for use in Revit.

A CUSTOM SERVICE AND CHECK-OUT COUNTER

1. Draw the counter in SketchUp as you would normally.
2. Do NOT paint anything—all entities should have the **Default** paint.
3. Add layers for anything that's supposed to be a different material: the countertop, the cabinet, and the base.

Figure 11.14 *The import dialog box*

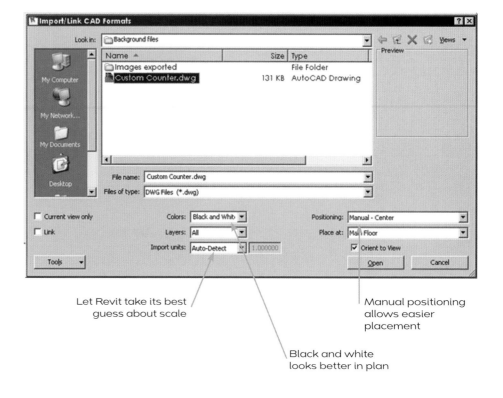

Let Revit take its best guess about scale

Black and white looks better in plan

Manual positioning allows easier placement

4. Click the **Color By Layer** option, so you can visually distinguish which objects are assigned where.

5. Turn off all those new layers except Layer 0, the current one (and the one that everything is probably drawn on).

6. Put the different parts of the drawing on the appropriate layer—they should disappear.

7. When nothing is left, you're done (sometimes curvy objects will have residual edge lines that won't go away—don't worry about it).

8. Turn the other layers on one by one to see your drawing reappear.

9. Save the SketchUp file in your project folder somewhere.

10. Back in Revit, on the **Insert** ribbon, choose **Import CAD** (Figure 11.14).

11. Choose SketchUp drawing from the File of Type drop-down list, and browse for your file. Select it and click **OK** (Figure 11.14).

12. It's best to manually place the drawing and let Revit choose the scale.

13. Sometimes the object will come in HUGE. If it's drawn correctly in SketchUp, scale it down to $\frac{1}{12}$ the size.

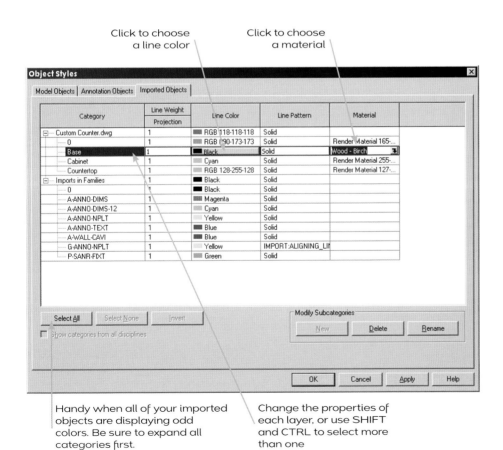

Click to choose a line color

Click to choose a material

Handy when all of your imported objects are displaying odd colors. Be sure to expand all categories first.

Change the properties of each layer, or use SHIFT and CTRL to select more than one

Figure 11.15 *Changing properties in the **Object Styles** dialog box*

Figure 11.16 *The properly colored display counter*

Segmentation on curved objects will not render, but it's sure annoying in shaded views

Remember that patterns don't necessarily represent rendering materials

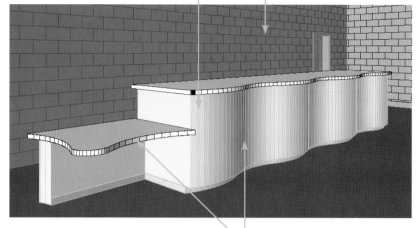

Different materials should display different colors in shaded model, if your layering is working right

14. To make the lines show up black, choose **Object Styles** from the Settings drop-down menu.
15. On the **Imported Objects** tab, find the Countertop drawing and click the **+** next to it to see the layer (Figure 11.15).
16. Make the Line color for all the layers black.
17. Click to choose a material for the countertop.
18. Click **OK** until you're back in the drawing (Figure 11.16).

Colors displayed in this mode will now be based (approximately) on the assigned materials. To lessen the impact of the facet lines imported on curved objects, change their color. These lines won't show up in the rendered version of the view, so don't worry about them too much.

Imported objects sometimes behave unpredictably. They'll show up in Existing Conditions floor plans and Reflected Ceiling Plans. Turn the whole category off using the **Visibility/Graphic** dialog box. If the lines are annoying in plan view, you can always make them white in the **Object Styles** dialog box, if you can figure out which layer they're on.

Sometimes these SketchUp objects can make your Revit model crash. If so, try exporting to DWG format first and then importing. You might also import the object into a new Family, which has the advantage of making the object available to schedules.

Solid Modeling

Sometimes it's necessary to create new objects within Revit. One example is a barrel-vaulted ceiling, which you'd like to be able to receive ceiling-hosted light fixtures. The simplest way to do this is with the Revit solid modeling feature, which is like electronic Play-Doh.

Revit needs to know where, in three dimensions, you plan to draw the profile or new object. You must start by creating a **Reference Plane**, which defines where the object will start. If there's a structural grid, each grid line is automatically a Reference Plane, but we'll need to make our own here.

DRAWING A BARREL VAULT UNDER THE MEZZANINE

1. Draw a reference plane along the north (top) wall of the plan.
2. Select it and get its **Properties** from the context-sensitive menu.
3. Give it a name like *Barrel Vault Start* and click **OK.**
4. Go to the Longitudinal Section view.
5. On the **Modeling** tab, click the **Create** tool.
6. Choose **Ceilings** and click **OK.**
7. Name it *Barrel Vaulted Ceiling*, or something clever like that, and click **OK.**
8. On the Modeling tab, click **Solid Form>Solid Extrusion.**
9. Choose the reference plane you just created from the drop-down list.
10. Now you're in that familiar Sketch Mode. Use lines to sketch the outline of the ceiling.
11. Sketch the ceiling thickness, as well—lines must form a closed loop (Figure 11.17).

BIG PICTURE

Masses can be created using extrusions, revolved profiles, or other simple techniques, and can be assigned materials. Choose a family that matches what you intend to do with the object—a new door, ceiling, or whatever. SketchUp models imported into Masses can be used to create walls and roofs, using the **Model By Face** *feature, but they're not as foolproof as those created in Revit.*

Figure 11.17 *The ceiling profile sketch*

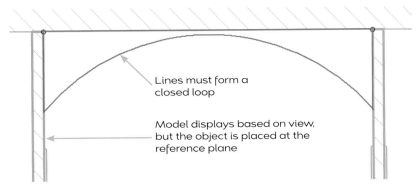

Lines must form a closed loop

Model displays based on view, but the object is placed at the reference plane

Note: a positive depth will extrude out toward us, a negative value will burrow into the screen

Figure 11.18 *Perspective of the barrel vault*

12. Click **Finish Sketch** to create the mass.
13. Select the mass with the modify tool—you can use grips to make modifications.
14. Go to the RCP for the first floor, and you should see the mass.
15. Use the grip (or the rotate command) to change the mass to fit in the space provided.
16. Use the grips to stretch the mass, and other tools to move or rotate it.
17. Click **Finish Family** on the **Contextual** ribbon to complete the ceiling (Figure 11.18).

This mass can be rotated, moved, copied, and arrayed, or even opened back up in Sketch Mode. Use the **Cut Geometry** tool to subtract different masses from one another. Also, you can copy and paste it into a different project, adapting the length and width as needed.

Cropping Walls Under Stairs

A similar technique to modeling the custom ceiling can be used when aligning a wall to the underside of a stair. A straight stair is a simple matter. Get an elevation view of the wall and stair, and select the wall. From the **Contextual** ribbon, click **Edit Profile** and you'll enter Sketch Mode (Figure 11.19).

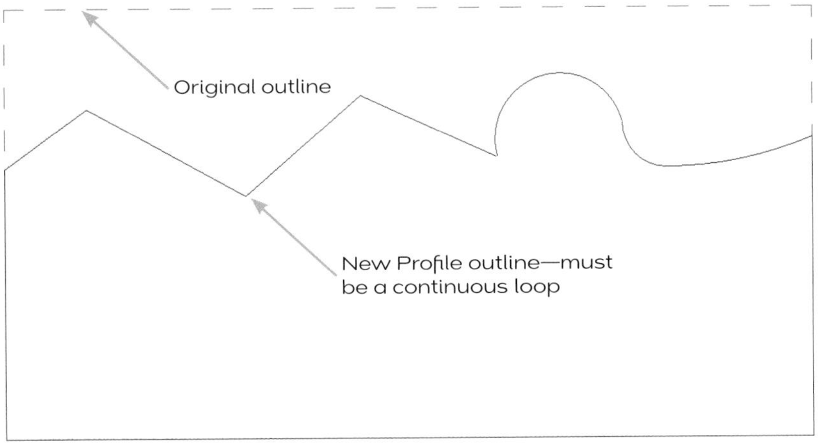

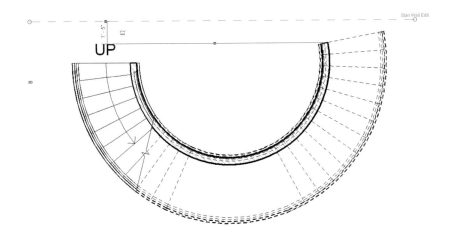

Figure 11.19 *Editing the profile of a wall*

Original outline

New Profile outline—must be a continuous loop

The purple lines are the boundary of the wall—so long as they remain in a closed loop; you can change the boundary to be any shape. Click **Finish Sketch** to apply the changes. You can still select the wall and use the grips to change its height, but now the top will have chamfer to it.

Curved walls are a little trickier. You'll need to create a new mass for this, with a solid form for the curved wall, and then a void form for the irregular top profile. Then, use the void from the solid. This is not the most precise technique, but most visual problems will be covered up by the stringer. As with the ceiling, you'll need to create a reference plane to draw the profile on.

CROPPING A CURVED WALL UNDER A STAIR

1. Draw a **reference plane** close to the wall to be changed (Figure 11.20).

Figure 11.20 *Plan of the stair*

UP

Figure 11.21 *The void-wall profile*

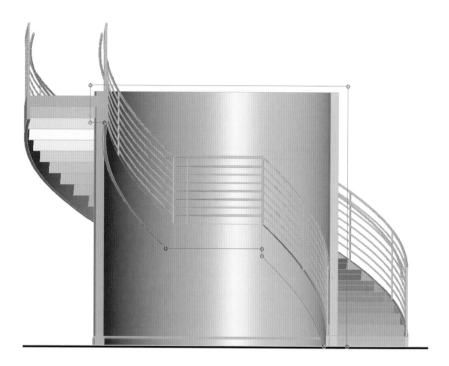

2. Select the reference plane and get its **Properties.**
3. Give it a name like *Stair Wall Edit* and click **OK.**
4. Go to the elevation or section view of the stair.
5. Under the **Massing and Site** ribbon, choose **In-Place Mass.**
6. Name it *Wall Void* or something clever like that.

Figure 11.22 *The void in your plan*

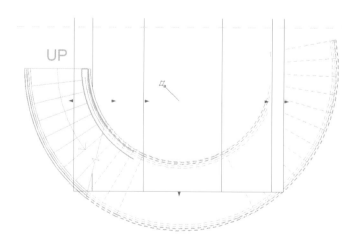

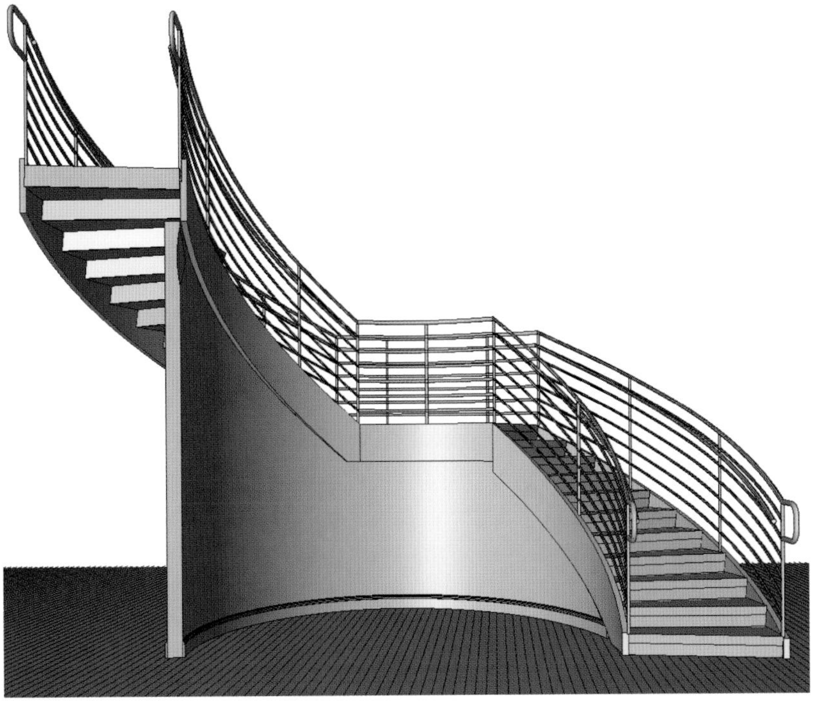

Figure 11.23 *The cropped curved wall under the stair*

7. Use Pick Lines and Offset to match the outline of the stair, and be sure to draw a closed loop.

8. Select the lines, and choose **Create Form>Form**.

9. Go to elevation view, and give the form enough height to cover the underside of the stairs.

10. Now draw the outline for the part of the wall that must be cut away (Figure 11.21). Revit will prompt you to specify which reference plane you'd like to use.

11. Select the lines and choose **Create Form>Void Form**.

12. Return to plan (or RCP) view and make sure the void is overlapping the solid form (Figure 11.22).

13. Choose **Finish Mass** to complete the wall.

14. Nudge the mass until you can't see any rough edges, if there were any (Figure 11.23).

This method isn't totally, completely, obsessively perfect—the cropped wall will have little slivers left as it curves toward us.

If your stringers are deep enough to cover up the messy parts, you can get a decent-looking cropped wall in no time. If not, you might consider bringing the stair into SketchUp, modeling the wall within a component, and then bringing that wall back into Revit.

MAGIC TRICK

There's an even quicker and sloppier method, which only works with curved walls: Select the wall in elevation, and click **Create Opening** *on the* **Contextual** *ribbon. Click and drag across the wall to define the opening dimension. Draw as many rectangular openings as you'd like. The openings can be selected using the modify tool, and have grips to change their size.*

Axonometric Views

Axonometric views are revealing at this point in the design process, as they allow you to have an undistorted overview of at least one level of your project. Click on the **Axonometric** view under the 3D section of your Project Browser. You should see a gray box around a scale 3D view of the exterior of your model. This is the **Section Box**—click on it to expose the crop boundary grips. With these you can clip away part of the model, opening up the inside for an impressive view. To get rid of it, open the View Properties dialog box, scroll down until you find a field marked **Section Box**, and uncheck it. Click **OK**.

Select the section box to reveal arrows that allow changing the bounds of the section box. Drag until the upper part of the project is cropped away. Rotate the model so that the rooms are more prominent. These section boxes won't print, by the way. Hold down **SHIFT** while clicking the scroll wheel and dragging to orbit the view (Figure 11.24).

So what about the Mezzanine? Well, you've gone to the hard work of setting up the first floor plan. In the Project Browser, right-click on the name of the view in the Project Browser and choose **Duplicate**. Drag the **Section Box** grip to crop away everything but the Mezzanine.

Figure 11.24 *The cropped axonometric*

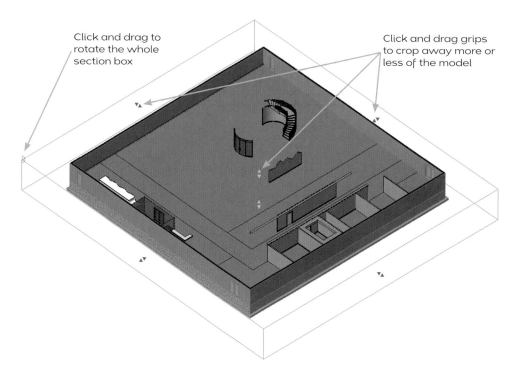

Click and drag to rotate the whole section box

Click and drag grips to crop away more or less of the model

Interior Elevations

All the work of adding sweeps, defining wall construction, setting ceiling heights, and the like comes to fruition when you go to create interior elevations. As we've seen, Revit has its limitations. Also, for complex volumes, changing the Crop Region boundaries isn't always enough, though, so sometimes the Lineweight tool on the **Modify** ribbon is what's needed. Select the lineweight you'd like from the Type Selector drop-down list. Then just click on the line and it should change to the chosen line type. Choose Invisible Lines to make the line go away, or Heavy Lines to make it darker. These changes are view specific, by the way, so other views will have to be changed separately.

After you've inserted a few hundred interior elevations into your drawing, it can get a little muddy with all the titles. To hide them on the **Manage** ribbon, choose **Settings>Elevation Tags** menu. Be sure to choose the ½" circle from the Type drop-down menu, as this is the one used for interior elevations. Then just deselect the radio button next to the Show View Name field.

Bigger projects can often have dozens of interior elevations, so you'll want to get in the habit of naming them immediately after drawing them. Most typical is to use the name of the room plus the appropriate cardinal direction—for example, *Storage Room East*, *Storage Room South*, *Storage Room West*, and so forth.

Legends

Legends are views that can be inserted onto multiple sheets. To create a Legend for the Reflected Ceiling Plan, click on **Legends** from the **View** ribbon. Be sure the legend is the same scale as your RCP. From the **Annotate** ribbon, choose the symbols needed to this legend, such as section callouts, etc. Insert a piece of text describing each one.

Code Analysis Diagrams

The tough part of designing a real project is that you have to comply with constraints like building codes and public health and safety. Code Analysis drawings are an essential part of your design process, and being absolutely clear and comprehensible can smooth things along with the building inspector. Revit can make calculations based on data it already knows about your project, such as the area of different rooms. You'll have to enter the correct multipliers, based on your local code, so that Revit can calculate the occupant load.

There are usually type drawings you'll do during this stage: an occupancy plan and an egress plan. Both are copies of your floor plan, and are typically at 1/32" = 1'-0". The best way to diagrammatically show this information is to create a custom line type, which is usually red to stand out. The occupancy plan should show hatched areas for the different specific occupancies (Figure 11.25).

To create a chart with the specified occupant load per net or gross square foot, you'll need to create a new schedule that can calculate the number of occupants in a given room for you. Choose **View>New> Schedule/Quantities...** from the drop-down menu. On the Fields tab, choose Add Parameter and make an integer value called SF/Occupant. Then click the **Calculated Value** button to add a formula (Figure 11.26).

Click **OK** and order and rename the fields as you desire. As you fill in the occupancy calculation values, the chart should calculate the number of occupants in each room for you. Alas, there's no way to have it calculate the grand total for you.

The egress plan should show the exit location, the path of egress, the separation of exits, and the maximum length of travel from the deepest part of the plan (Figure 11.27).

Figure 11.25 *The occupancy plan*

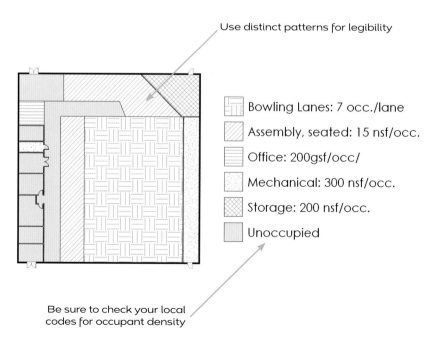

Use distinct patterns for legibility

Bowling Lanes: 7 occ./lane
Assembly, seated: 15 nsf/occ.
Office: 200gsf/occ/
Mechanical: 300 nsf/occ.
Storage: 200 nsf/occ.
Unoccupied

Be sure to check your local codes for occupant density

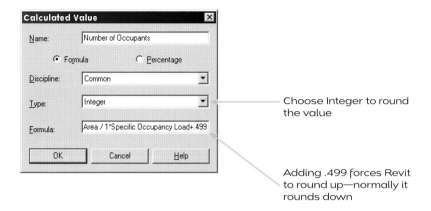

Figure 11.26 *Adding a calculated value*

Choose Integer to round the value

Adding .499 forces Revit to round up—normally it rounds down

The final piece is to calculate the required width for corridors and doors. Microsoft Excel is our friend here. Be sure to check your local codes for the correct multipliers, which usually change based on **Use Group** (as defined in the building code) and whether or not you have sprinklers. You'll also need the total occupant load to calculate the number of toilets, urinals, lavatories, and drinking fountains you'll need. Unfortunately, Revit can't cope with Excel files, so you'll have to convert it to a JPEG and import it right onto the final sheet.

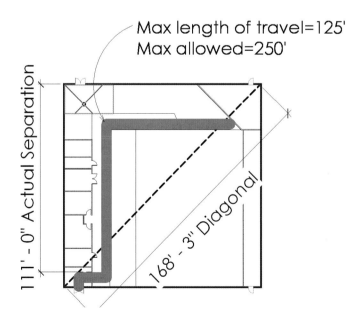

Figure 11.27 *The egress plan*

Compartmentalization Diagrams

An egress system needs to be simple and wayfinding clear enough that, in an emergency, everyone can have a protected route to the exit of the building. The system must allow a protected tunnel of sorts—a fire-rated corridor leading to a fire-rated stair tower (or area of refuge), and then out to grade. This is much easier to visualize in three dimensions, and since it's a diagram, let's use SketchUp to approximate the building geometry.

I color my model by layer, then use those same layers to sketch the different egress components: the existing building, vertical circulation, and horizontal circulation (Figure 11.28).

Be sure that you indicate how occupants exit to grade, and not just to the first floor. Like all design work, make sure you follow local codes for fire ratings of egress components, lobbies, and fire separation of Use Groups within your project.

Figure 11.28 *Compartmentalization diagram*

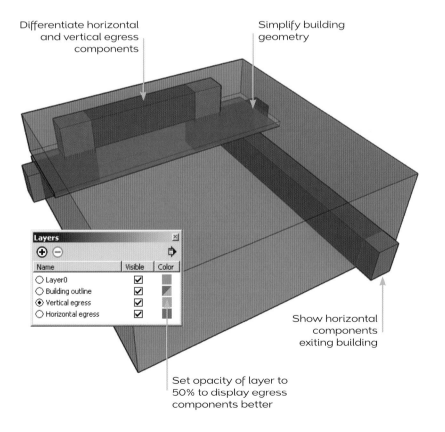

Differentiate horizontal and vertical egress components

Simplify building geometry

Show horizontal components exiting building

Set opacity of layer to 50% to display egress components better

Printing a Set of Drawings

At this stage of the design process, it's a good idea to print out your progress for review. Your instructor, boss, or client will certainly need to see the level of detail you've developed, and you also may want to visit the building inspector if the project involves tricky code issues. Printing a whole set of model views is pretty straightforward. Click the **Print** button, then check to make sure you've chosen a printer that can handle the size sheets you're using—usually a large-format machine (Figure 11.29). Print the current view, or select the sheets you'd like to print as a batch. You can even let Revit remember that set, in case you need to print your design-development drawings again.

Click on the **Setup** button to control how the sheet is laid out (Figure 11.30). Some options, such as nesting and final print quality, may be controlled at the plotter itself. When you're all set up, click **OK** until Revit sends the drawings to print.

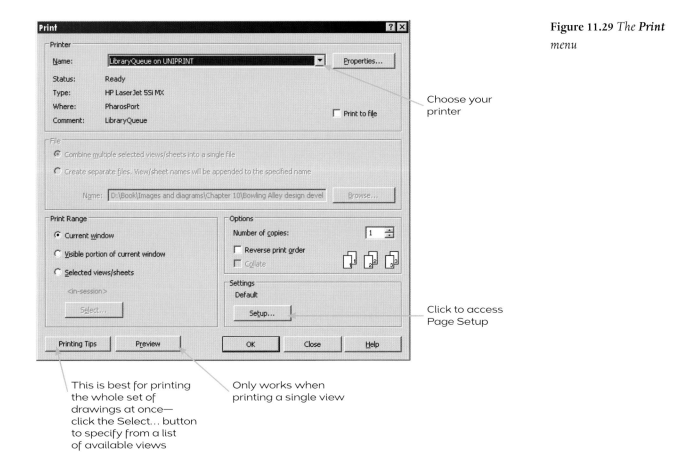

Figure 11.29 *The **Print** menu*

Choose your printer

Click to access Page Setup

This is best for printing the whole set of drawings at once— click the Select… button to specify from a list of available views

Only works when printing a single view

Figure 11.30 *Print Setup*
dialog box

For non-scaled drawings, choose a small sheet size and check the Fit to Page radio button

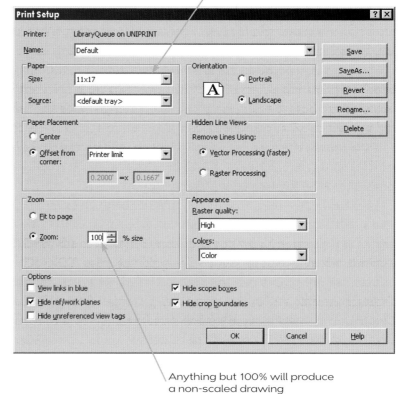

Anything but 100% will produce a non-scaled drawing

For handling mark-ups, views placed on a sheet can be opened up for editing to make quick changes without clogging up your list of open windows. Right-click on a view and choose **Open View**. The rest of the sheet becomes gray and all editing commands are available. When done, right-click on the screen again and choose **Close View**.

Online Resources

- Revit file used for illustrations in this chapter, *Bowling Alley design development diagrams.rvt*
- Building compartmentalization diagram in SketchUp, *Egress compartmentalization diagram.skp*
- Custom counter in SketchUp and AutoCAD formats

Term Project Assignments

- Give all partitions a wall base and other millwork, as appropriate to the design.
- Study construction of floors, walls, and ceilings in detail.
- Calculate occupancy load in project, and produce a diagram showing specific occupancy areas.
- Draw an egress plan diagram.
- Model building compartmentalization in SketchUp.
- Complete room finish and lighting schedules.
- Produce a design-development drawing set: code analysis, plans, sections, elevations, and perspectives.

Exercises and Further Study

- Generate a furniture schedule for an office-planning project.
- Add fixture counts to your Lighting schedule.
- Create a room with wood wainscoting and cornices.
- Model a groin vault.
- Import a warped ceiling created with SketchUp's Sandbox tools.

Construction
Documents

LEARNING GOALS

- Modify standard Revit elements for unique configurations
- Create and modify construction detail views
- Lay out and print a set of drawings

The goal of the construction documents phase of design is to analyze and communicate the exact materials and configuration of the project to a contractor. This is when doorjamb details and paint schedules get created, and when about 50 percent of the designer's fee is spent. But it's also where all the hard decisions about which family types to configure pay off, as a large amount of detailed construction information is generated more or less automatically by Revit.

Modeling during schematic design is often imprecise, and complex or difficult-to-create elements are often left for a later date. Some custom elements are easiest to create in SketchUp and imported, but others can be created with dimensional accuracy from right within the Revit interface. Sloped ceilings (and floors), dormers, and railings are common things to modify to make the design more refined.

BIG PICTURE

Keeping as much information as possible within the main model means much simpler and more efficient coordination. Everything from site plans and code diagrams down to full-scale details should be kept within the same model. The only tradeoff is that the model size will increase rapidly as the number of drawing elements and loaded families grows, slowing down your computer.

Sloped Ceilings

Any ceiling in your model can be made to slope. While editing the ceiling, you have to draw a special element called a slope arrow. The slope angle is

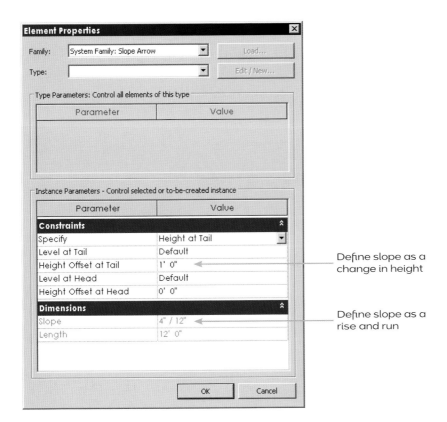

Figure 12.1 *The slope arrow in the floor sketch*

controlled in the element properties of the arrow. Let's start a sloped ceiling from scratch, where one side is 10" lower than the other side.

MODELING A SLOPING CEILING

1. Click on the **Ceiling** tool.
2. Click on the **Sketch** button on the **Contextual** ribbon.
3. Click on the **Lines** tool.
4. Draw the outline of the ceiling.

Figure 12.2 *Slope arrow* **Properties** *dialog box*

*Floors can be sloped, too—select one and choose **Edit** from the **Contextual** ribbon. Click on the **Slope** tool, draw and edit the arrow the same way you do with the floor. Be aware of local codes regarding sloped floors. Generally, a 1:20 slope is the maximum angle allowed without handrails, guard rails, and periodic landings.*

LOOK OUT!

There's no way to place ceiling-mounted lights in or on a roof, no matter how hard you click. To get around this, you could create a new freestanding luminaire, and copy and paste in the geometry from the ceiling-based fixture you like. You could also model a ceiling, and then align it just under the roof, or you can always Photoshop in those recessed cans.

5. Click the **Slope** tool.
6. Click once on the middle of one of the short segments (use the purple triangular tool tip).
7. Click again on the middle of the other short segment to draw the slope arrow (Figure 12.1).
8. Select the arrow with the **Modify** tool.
9. Right-click on the arrow and choose **Element Properties** (Figure 12.2).
10. Change the top offset to 10" and click **OK**.
11. Click **Finish Sketch** to draw the ramp.

The sloped ceiling can be moved around in section to align with the top and bottom with different parts of the project. The slope of the ceiling, as well as the whole sketch, can be changed again by selecting it and clicking the **Edit** button.

Dormers

When is a roof like a sloped ceiling? When it's a dormer, of course, because you use the same slope arrows to create gabled dormers. To put a transverse dormer in a simple gabled roof takes a little planning; you'll have to draw extra lines for the gable-end side of the dormer. In this case, each half of the dormer roof requires its own slope-defining boundary. Then it's a matter of drawing the slope arrows (Figure 12.3).

If you want a shed dormer, or something more complex, it's easier to just draw separate roofs. Then use the Join Roof tool to make them connect. You'll have to cut openings in the lower roof if you want cathedral ceilings on the inside.

Figure 12.3 *Sketch for a roof with dormers*

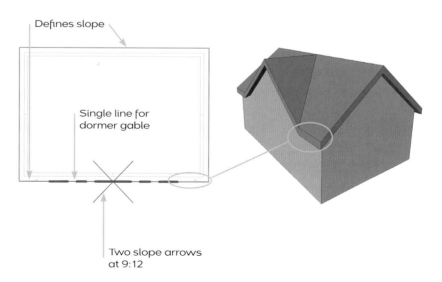

Defines slope

Single line for dormer gable

Two slope arrows at 9:12

Ramps

Modeling a ramp is just like modeling a stair. You have to set the vertical distance the ramp must bridge, and choose a handrail and guardrail. As always, check and comply with all local codes.

MODELING A RAMP

1. On the **Home** ribbon, click on the **Ramp** tool—you'll enter the all-too-familiar sketch mode.
2. Click on the ramp **Properties** (Figure 12.4).

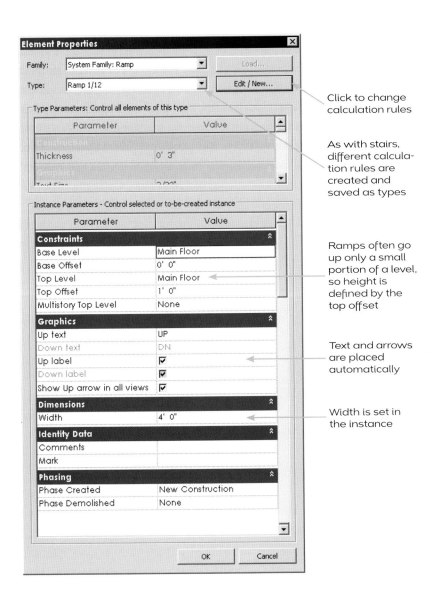

Figure 12.4 *Ramp Properties*

Click to change calculation rules

As with stairs, different calculation rules are created and saved as types

Ramps often go up only a small portion of a level, so height is defined by the top offset

Text and arrows are placed automatically

Width is set in the instance

Figure 12.5 *Ramp outline*

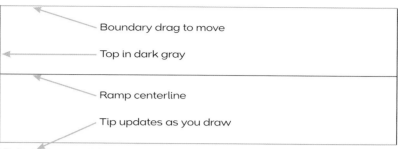

Boundary drag to move

Top in dark gray

Ramp centerline

Tip updates as you draw

12' of inclined ramp created, 0" remaining

3. Change the offset to whatever your raised section of floor is at. Click **OK.**
4. Click once in the drawing area to start the ramp—the cursor will cue you for the distance remaining.
5. When the cue indicates that there are 0" remaining, click to finish the ramp (Figure 12.5).
6. Click the **Modify** tool.
7. Use a selection window to grab the sketched ramp.
8. Drag it into alignment with the landing.
9. Click **Finish Ramp** to complete the sketch (Figure 12.6).
10. The default handrails may not be code compliant. Select them with the **Modify** tool.
11. Choose **Ramp Handrails** from the Type Selector drop-down list.

Just as with stairs, the ramp and railings can be selected, moved, nudged, or aligned.

Figure 12.6 *The finished ramp*

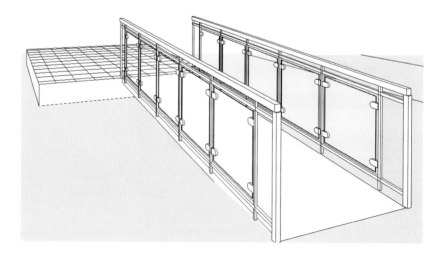

Railing Construction

As discussed when we went through modeling a stair, guardrails are generally needed any time there's a change in height greater than 29". Revit provides a bunch of options, with many different editable parts—so many options that Autodesk provides a drawing loaded with sample configurations (Figure 12.7).

Some of the railing types form a "ladder" of sorts, which is generally forbidden by the commercial building code. The glass ones are very nice but pose some modeling problems, as they often won't wrap properly around stairs and landings that don't exactly match their spacing increment. At least it's easy to change a railing from one type to another, but modifying an existing one can be complex, to say the least.

Figure 12.7 *Railing examples drawing from Autodesk*

1. Switch to your Mezzanine plan.
2. On the **Home** ribbon, click on the **Railing** tool—you'll enter the familiar Sketch Mode.
3. Click on the **Set Host** tool.
4. Click on the edge of the Mezzanine floor.
5. Choose **Glass Panels** from the Type Selector drop-down list.
6. Click on **Railing Properties.**

Figure 12.8 *The rail structure*

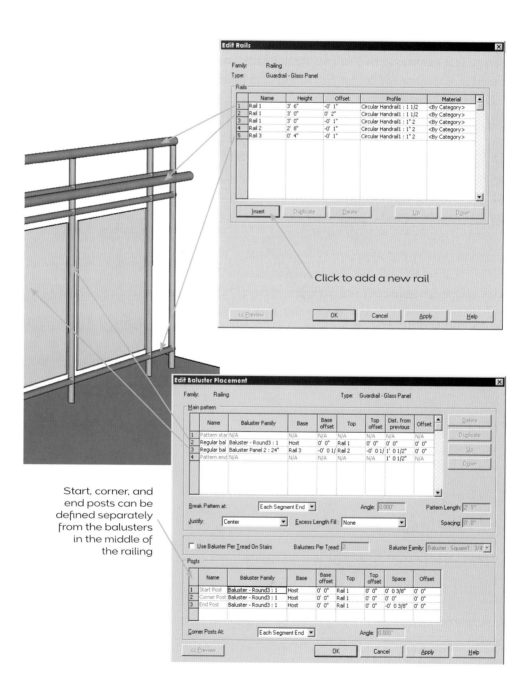

Start, corner, and end posts can be defined separately from the balusters in the middle of the railing

7. Click on the **Edit/New** button.

8. Click on **Duplicate** and name the new one.

9. This is where you can change the design to your heart's desire, adding panels, rails, or changing the height.

10. Click on the **Rail Structure** button (Figure 12.8).

11. Click **Add** to make another railing.

12. Click the down arrow next to the Baluster and Rail profiles field to choose a different material.

13. Click **OK** until you're back in the drawing.

14. Click once to start the railing sketch.

15. Continue drawing with the pencil tool, or use the select and edit tools (lines don't need to make a continuous loop).

16. Click **Finish Railing** to complete the sketch.

There are a few different ready-made railings. Take a look at the railing examples drawing from Autodesk posted in the **Online Resources** for this chapter (*Railing Samples.rvt*).

Inserting AutoCAD Details

One of the quickest ways to draw a detail is to have someone else do it. There are plenty of offices with disks filled with old AutoCAD details, and these can be inserted into a Revit drawing. Open a new Drafting View from the **View** ribbon, and set it to the same scale as the original CAD drawing. Then choose **CAD File** from the **Insert** ribbon. Browse for the file, and just like with SketchUp drawings, be sure to manually place the object.

After import, use the **Measure** tool (on the **Modify** ribbon) to check the size of the drawing—if it's off, it's often by a factor of 12. Also, if the line colors are wacky, change them all at once in the **Object Styles** dialog box on the **Imported Objects** tab. There are plenty of manufacturer's standard details available this way. Just as when tracing a raster image, you can draw Revit objects such as drafting lines and filled regions on top. You can control colors and line types with layers, just like with inserted SketchUp drawings. Use the **Imported Objects** tab of the **Element Properties** dialog box.

AutoCAD drawings often have all sorts of elements in there, and it can be confusing to figure out what's what. You can get limited information about imported objects within the drawing by selecting the import and clicking on the **Query** button on the **Contextual** ribbon. Then click on a line or arc, and Revit will tell you everything it knows about it, which is generally just its layer name.

MAGIC TRICK

Generally, you can't directly edit the lines of an imported AutoCAD drawing because they come in as a group. Depending on how the original drawing was created, they might be available to edit if you explode them. This is particularly useful if there are blocks for furniture or other elements in the CAD plan that you'd like to manipulate. Select the CAD drawing using the **Modify** *tool, and choose* **Partial Explode** *from the* **Contextual** *ribbon. This usually breaks the drawing into lines and text. A full explode can sometimes make everything disappear, so* **Undo** *is your friend.*

The elements of the drawing are developed using a combination of the existing linework, detail components, detail lines, and filled regions. Often, lineweights have to be adjusted or lines hidden altogether. Elements that you want to display in the model, like the front and side of the fascia, must be modeled using mini walls and ceilings or extra-thick ceiling construction.

Complex Details: The Fascia

Detail sections of complex design situations are quite common at this stage and can be tricky. Let's develop a detail for the mezzanine fascia, a tricky design problem where ceiling, floor, railing, and the fascia finish all come together.

For this detail, you will have to have completed several pieces of the project, including the first-floor ceilings, the mezzanine floor, and railing, and considered what sort of look you want the fascia to have. In our case, let's stick with a simple painted drywall meeting a concrete slab on metal decking and acoustical ceiling tile below.

DRAWING A DETAIL OF THE MEZZANINE FASCIA

1. Open the First Floor RCP.
2. Sketch a **GWB** ceiling for the bottom of the fascia.
3. Now open the Mezzanine Floor Plan.
4. Choose the wall tool, and choose 1½" furred wall from the Type Selector drop-down list.
5. Make the bottom of the wall at 3'-0" from the mezzanine, and the top right at the mezzanine. This will create the front of the fascia.
6. Draw the wall along the length of the mezzanine.
7. Click on **Section** tool on the **View** ribbon.
8. Choose **Detail Section** from the Type Selector drop-down list.
9. Click on one side of the mezzanine edge and then the other to draw the section indicator.
10. In the Project Browser, open the new section—it's in the Detail Sections folder.
11. Make sure the scale is set to at least 1½" = 1'-0".
12. Set the detail level for the view (at the bottom of the drawing area) to **Fine**.
13. On the **Annotate** ribbon, choose **Component>Detail Component.**
14. Choose **Bar Joist End** from the Type Selector drop-down list.
15. Click on the underside of the floor structure.
16. Insert a W24 × 96 in the same way.
17. Insert detail components for ⅝" GWB, the pieces of an ACT ceiling, and three ⅝" metal studs.
18. Move, elongate, and arrange until you're happy with the design.
19. Draw a solid white-filled region for the mortar pocket that holds the railing base channel.
20. Add notes and dimensions (Figure 12.9).

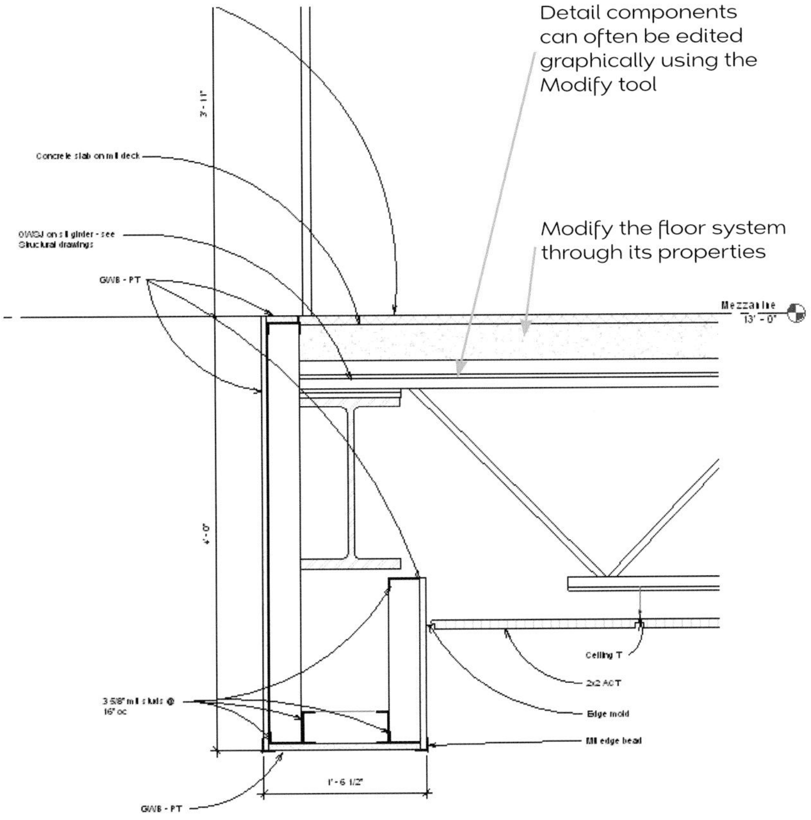

Detail components can often be edited graphically using the Modify tool

Modify the floor system through its properties

Concrete slab on mtl deck

OWSJ on st girder - see Structural drawings

GWB - PT

Mezzanine
13' - 0"

3' - 11"

4' - 0"

3 5/8" mtl studs @ 16" oc

Ceiling T

2x2 ACT

Edge mold

Mtl edge bead

1' - 6 1/2"

GWB - PT

Figure 12.9 *The finished detail*

If you like a nice heavy line to indicate the section outline, use the Linework tool on the **Modify** ribbon. Choose the line type you'd like (wide lines), then click on the lines you'd like to change. You can also hide lines this way by choosing the Invisible line type.

The modeling process is more or less the same for most types of enlarged details, whether in plan or section. Casework, for example, often requires enlarged plans in addition to sections. Choose **Callout** on the **View** ribbon and draw a rectangle around the area of casework to be enlarged. Add in detail, annotation, and even new sections in this drawing.

Sometimes you just can't get one of the model elements to match the detail—this is particularly true of railings, which can be hard to make work exactly as the manufacturer specifies. In this case, make sure you draw the details correctly (or import CAD drawings), and just hide the Railing family in this view.

LOOK OUT!

You don't always want section indicators to show up on both your main plan and your detail section. Select the repeated annotation in the main plan and choose View>Hide Annotation in View.

Rendered Details

Details of a project are where the theory of a project meets the reality of constructability, and that's the ultimate test of a good design. To see if what's in your head at 3 A.M. is really as good as you're hoping, try doing a simple rendered detail of some prototypical design element of your project. This can be something wild and unusual, but you can also just take a standard detail and project it back in axonometric or perspective to see what it looks like when you've applied materials (Figure 12.10).

The example above is straight out of *Interior Design Graphic Standards* (Wiley & Sons), a valuable reference filled with commonplace construction assembly details. Adding a little color, along with some Photoshop filters, gives you a better sense of whether or not your detail idea is really working. Modify the materials and/or construction as needed to refine the detail.

Figure 12.10 *A standard detail rendered to test a design scheme*

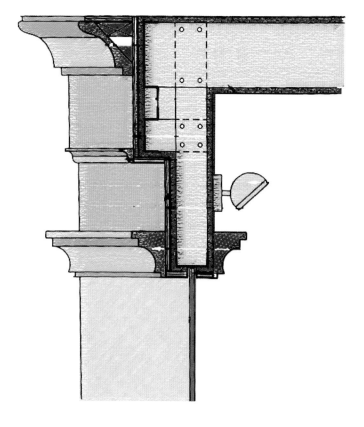

Creating Similar Details

There are often several slight variations of an architectural element, such as different locations on the fascia that you need to detail—perhaps at a slightly larger duct enclosure or beam. These are indicated in the same view where the typical detail was created but with the note "similar" next to the call-out. In our case, the railing detail was called out in the Mezzanine plan, so in that view, click on the **Section** button on the **View** ribbon. To refer to the already-created detail view, on the **Contextual** ribbon check the box for **Refer to Other View**, then choose the view from the drop-down list. Draw the call-out and it will automatically fill with the number of the original detail and will be noted with the abbreviation SIM.

For more substantial differences in conditions, you'll want to create an entirely different detail. Create the new view with a call-out, and copy Revit-based detail components and drafting lines from one view to another. Revit provides an opportunity to align the elements just right in the new view before committing to the operation.

Don't worry that you might accidentally make a copy of your floor or ceiling—only drafted elements like lines and detail elements will be copied, not the underlying building components. You can also use the **Filter** option to specify exactly which elements you'd like to copy.

LOOK OUT!

Why not just right-click on the view in the Project Browser and choose **Duplicate with Detailing**? *Well, you could, but you will have to deal with manually placing the call-out—a section indicator—at the correct place in plan. It will not be linked to the detail, which means it won't auto-complete when the view is placed on a sheet.*

COPYING DETAIL ELEMENTS

1. Select objects in the detail you'd like to copy with a Selection or Crossing Window, or with **SHIFT** and **CTRL.**
2. Click the **Filter** button on the **Contextual** ribbon (Figure 12.11).

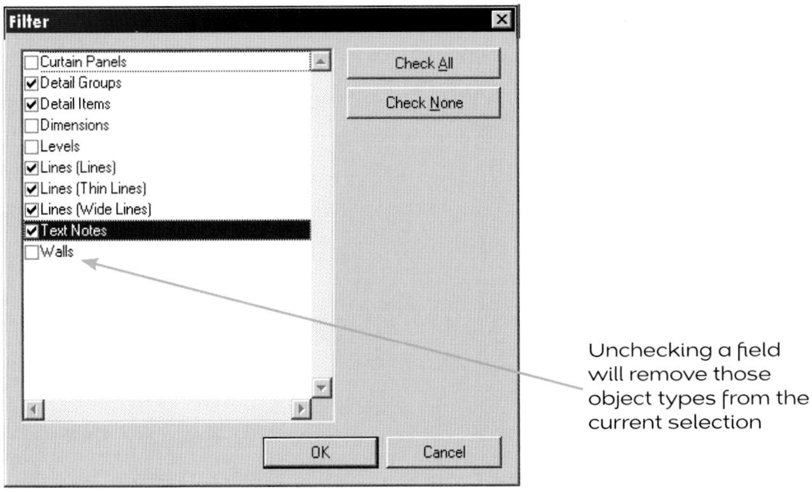

Filter

☐ Curtain Panels
☑ Detail Groups
☑ Detail Items
☐ Dimensions
☐ Levels
☑ Lines (Lines)
☑ Lines (Thin Lines)
☑ Lines (Wide Lines)
☑ Text Notes
☐ Walls

Check All
Check None

OK   Cancel

Unchecking a field will remove those object types from the current selection

Figure 12.11 *The* **Filter** *dialog box*

Figure 12.12 *Moving the pasted elements*

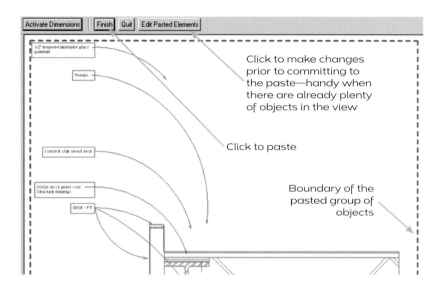

Click to make changes prior to committing to the paste—handy when there are already plenty of objects in the view

Click to paste

Boundary of the pasted group of objects

3. Leave selected only drafting lines, detail components, and text.
4. Type **CTRL+C** to copy to the clipboard.
5. Switch to the detail view of the new project.
6. Make sure the scale matches the source drawing.
7. Type **CTRL+V** to paste (Figure 12.12).
8. Move the objects as a group into position.
9. Click the **Finish** button when done.

You can now edit the pasted objects in the new view. It's a good idea to remove any elements you won't need before completing the paste operation, as they can sometimes be hard to select afterward.

Specialty Plans: Switching

As your floor plans and reflected ceiling plans get populated with components and dimensions, they can get challenging to read and understand. Thus, we often break conceptual pieces out into separate drawings. A switching plan is a good example of this process, and it's more or less the same for finish plans, furniture plans, or even enlarged detail plans of, say, a toilet room. It's a matter of copying the original view and changing the Visibility / Graphic Overrides settings to control the visibility of drawn elements. Draw in added notes and details as needed.

Lighting is a complicated subject, of course, and there are a number of different ways of showing switching, power, voice / data, and all other advanced technology that goes into our projects. Some offices will label individual circuits rather than draw loops, while others will schedule everything.

A SWITCHING PLAN

1. Right-click on the Main Floor RCP in the Project Browser.
2. Choose **Duplicate with Detail** (to copy filled regions, text, and drafting lines you may have used).
3. Type in **VG** to open the Visibility / Graphic Overrides dialog box.
4. On the **Annotate** tab, turn off Dimensions and Ceiling tags if you used them (and anything else you don't want to show). Click **OK**.
5. Click the **Components** tool. Choose Two-pole Switch from the Type Selector drop-down list.
6. Move your mouse over a wall and click to place.
7. On the **Annotate** tab, click on the **Drafting Lines** tool. Choose **Switching Loops** from the Type Selector drop-down list.
8. Draw loops as splines or arcs, per your taste.
9. For home runs, use lines for arrows and text for circuit labeling (Figure 12.13).

One of those great geek moments is when you discover that the light switches you just put into the switching plan actually show up in other views too, like perspectives and elevations. OK, so they're just toggle switches, but you have to admire that level of detail in a project.

LOOK OUT!

Remember that editing a soffit or light fixture in this view will be reflected in other views, including the RCP and perspective views. Check other related views before deleting an object that seems to be out of place, especially when they're imported.

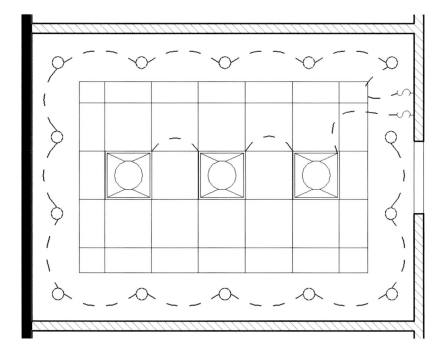

Figure 12.13 *Partial switching plan*

Automated Material Annotation

Keynotes are a commonly used form of annotation, and can have notes attached to them, reference drawings, or user-defined notes. The basic kind are used in detail drawings and note the materials used based on the object definition. On the **Annotate** ribbon, in the **Tag** grouping, choose **Material.** Move your mouse over an element in your detail and the cursor will type to figure out what it is. Click once to place the leader line, again to start the tail, and one more time to finish the tail (Figure 12.14).

Some offices use Construction Specifications Institute (CSI) standard section format numbers and descriptions, which are often seen on public projects. For these, choose **Keynote>Material.** Click on an object as before, but now you'll be prompted to choose from a standard list of CSI sections. This is particularly handy if you have many details to annotate, as Revit will remember the next time what section you applied to a given material (Figure 12.15).

Figure 12.14 *Automatic material tag*

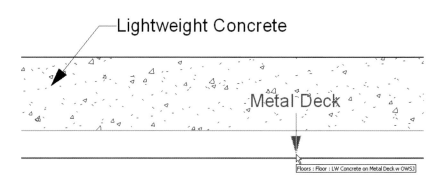

Figure 12.15 *CSI standard keynotes*

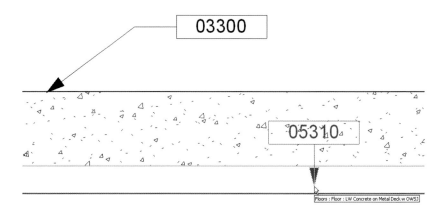

Demolition Keynotes

Demolition plans often employ keynotes, but these need to be more generic, so you'll have to use a symbol rather than an automated system. Click the **Symbol** tool and choose **Keynote**. Click to place it in the drawing.

Right-click the inserted keynote and choose **Element Properties**. There you'll see a description of what the keynote is meant to represent—in this case, removing the interior partition and bracing entirely. This text can be edited, and there are many other numbers available from the Type Selector drop-down list, each with its own note (Figure 12.16).

These notes can be used to generate a legend, and even count the number of instances if you're so inclined. Choose **View>New>Note Block** and choose the Demolition Keynote (Figure 12.17). Set up which elements will be included and how the list will be filtered. Click **OK** to complete the legend.

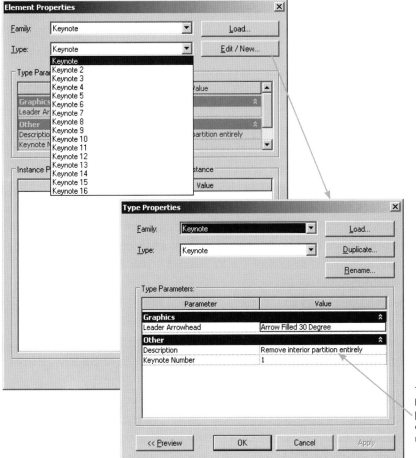

Figure 12.16 *Keynote properties*

Type description here, or choose from the drop-down list and modify

Figure 12.17 *The Note Block dialog box*

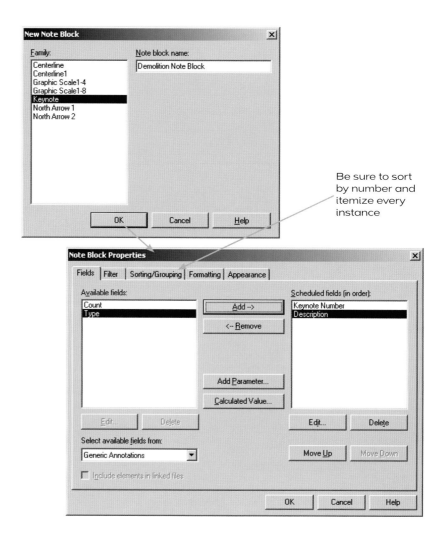

Be sure to sort by number and itemize every instance

You can type right into the different fields, and it's a good idea to have this view open while working on the Demolition plan, to edit as you go. Close all other views besides the Demolition plan and the Key, and then choose **Window>Tile** from the drop-down menu—you'll be able to see both views at the same time. If I'm feeling a little indecisive as to which tag I plan to use, I will put all the tags into a Legend instead, so I can use notes from a previous project.

Tag, You're It

Revit can also tag entire assemblies for you, such as walls or ceilings. On the **Annotate** ribbon, click on the **Tag>By Category...** tool. Choose Walls and click **OK** (Figure 12.18).

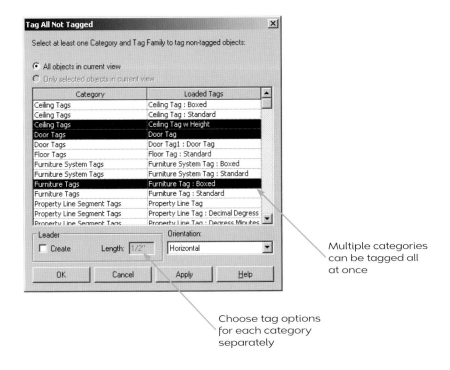

Figure 12.18 *The plan with walls tagged*

As you mouse over a wall in plan, Revit will indicate a wall tag—click to place. Click inside the tag to give it a name or letter. Every time you click on a wall of the same type, the software will automatically fill out the new tag for you (Figure 12.19).

This is handy, since you generally tag EVERY new interior partition, which can be quite a few. Different wall types will need another letter or number filled out, and all unlabeled tags will update as you fill them out.

MAGIC TRICK

When tagging light fixtures on an RCP, the tags themselves will sit right on top of the luminaire. Right-click on one, select all instances, and then move them all down and to the right of the luminaire symbol.

Figure 12.19 *Tag options*

Multiple categories can be tagged all at once

Choose tag options for each category separately

All the new doors, windows, and walls need to be tagged. Some offices become tag-happy, applying them to ceilings, floors, equipment, furnishings, and lighting. These tags can help generate schedules for imported objects that otherwise are unknown to Revit.

Composing the Title Sheet

First things are often done last, and this book is no different. I always seem to put off doing the title page until everything else is done. Fortunately, many elements are either automatic or can be cut and pasted from past projects. And, as always, follow the graphic standards of the office you're working in or the written requirements of the project if you're in school.

To get a view onto the title sheet, first you have to open up the view in the Project Browser. Then drag whichever view you'd like from the browser into the open sheet (Figure 12.20).

Revit will warn you if the view is already in use, although legends can be used over and over again.

Figure 12.20 *Dragging a view onto a sheet*

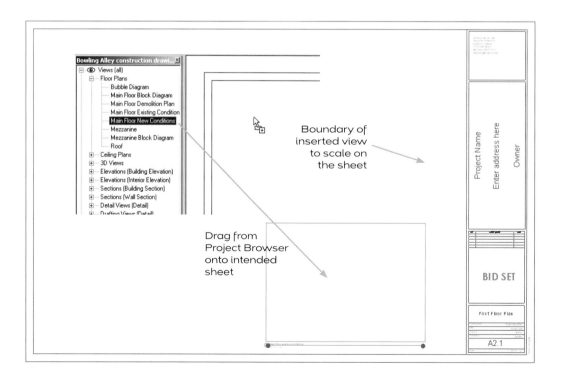

Typically there are six things that go on a title sheet, although this too varies a great deal both by project and by office graphic standards: a perspective drawing, a list of sheets, general construction notes, a list of abbreviations used, a key to symbols used, and a code analysis. Let's look at how to generate each below.

PERSPECTIVE DRAWING

Your best-looking perspective from the project is great to have right in the middle of the title sheet—somehow this seems to set the tone for the set of otherwise dull and technical drawings. If the image is too small, select it and click on the Image Size button on the **Contextual** ribbon (Figure 12.21). Be sure to lock the proportions, or it'll end up looking funny. The title block can be changed, too—select it and choose **Viewport: No Title** from the Type Selector drop-down list. The title can be moved, and the line underneath can be shortened using grips (Figure 12.22).

Generally, the **Crop Region** is hidden when you print, so if you want a border, uncheck the **Hide Crop Boundary** box in the **Page Setup** dialog. If you've got crop regions that you don't want in other views on the sheet (or in your project, if you're printing multiple sheets), you can either open each view and hide it, or you can draw in the border on this one view with heavy drafting lines, just as with interior elevations.

LIST OF SHEETS

A handy list of the sheets in your project can be had by choosing **View>New>Drawing List** from the drop-down menu. Drag it onto the sheet from the Project Browser.

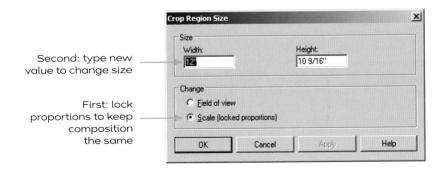

Second: type new value to change size

First: lock proportions to keep composition the same

Figure 12.21 *Image size options*

Figure 12.22 *Editing the viewport and title*

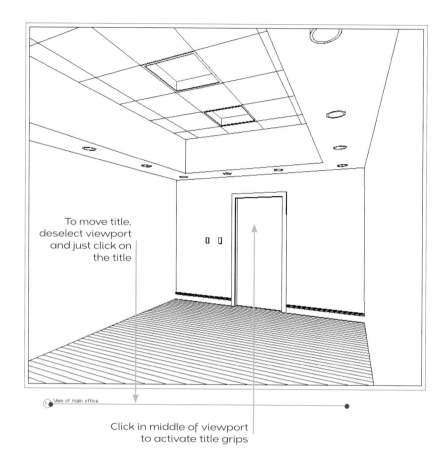

To move title, deselect viewport and just click on the title

Click in middle of viewport to activate title grips

View of main office

MAGIC TRICK

*Text can be copied and pasted in from any program. After copying text in another program, click on the **Text** tool in Revit. Then click in the drawing area to start the text. Then just type **CTRL+V** to paste in the text.*

GENERAL NOTES AND LIST OF ABBREVIATIONS

Inserting a list can be done several ways. You can just create a piece of text right there on the title page, or you can type them up in a new **Drafting View** (on the **View** ribbon). I like the latter, since I often insert a note block for my library of CAD drawings.

CODE ANALYSIS

Excel charts are often needed for a simple code summary, and there really isn't a simple way to do this. For highest resolution, I'll often print the chart to a PDF file, then rasterize the PDF into a JPEG. The latter can be inserted right onto the title sheet. If relevant to the project, a site plan is usually included here. Also, include both the occupancy and egress plans. In a larger project, code analysis will have a sheet all to itself, but here, it fits nicely onto the complete sheet (Figure 12.23).

You're finally ready to print. Be sure to save the set of chosen sheets

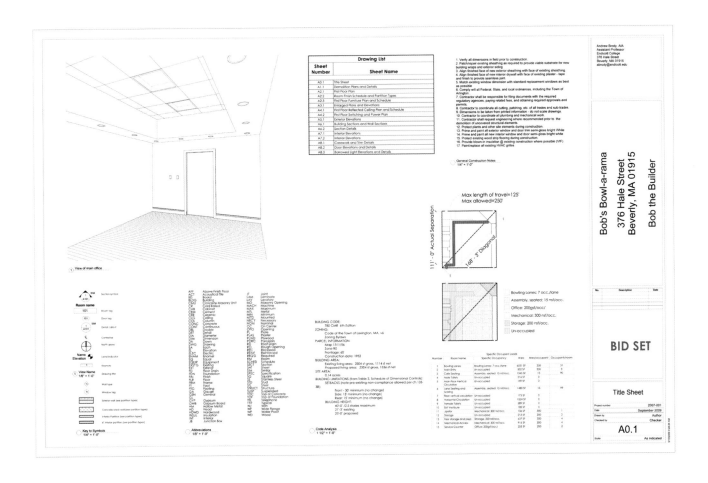

Figure 12.23 *The finished title sheet*

in the Print Setup dialog box, since you often have to make changes before the project can be issued for construction.

Checking Your Work

Go through sheet by sheet, adding views, legends, and schedules. In an office setting, a senior-level manager will review a check set (yes, physical prints are really best for checking your work) and make redlines (yes, you will have mistakes and oversights). The easiest way to make small but critical changes is editing within viewports right on the sheets. Right-click on the problem viewport and choose **Activate View**. This is just like opening the view for editing, but quicker. To exit this mode, right-click again and choose **Deactivate View**. Other common mistakes to look for are detail symbols that haven't filled in or schedules that are missing some room numbers, light fixtures, or the like, where they should be in a sequential list.

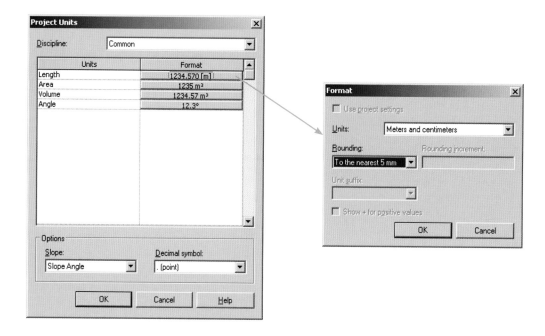

Figure 12.24 *Revit **Units*** *settings*

Working in Metric

Revit projects can be switched to metric also, and like SketchUp, require only that you consider if you'll be working in soft or hard metric. Choose **Project Units...** from the **Manage** ribbon (Figure 12.24).

Just as in SketchUp, you can control the precision of the drawing, and dimension strings in particular, by changing the rounding setting. Note that you should change units prior to laying out sheets or all of your viewport scales will be off.

Online Resources

- Revit file used for illustrations in this chapter, *Bowling Alley construction drawings.rvt*
- *Rendered detail.psd*
- *Railing Samples.rvt*

Term Project Assignments

- Create a complete set of construction drawings for the bowling alley project, including:
  - ▼ Title sheet with code analysis

- ▼ Demolition plans and details
- ▼ Main- and upper-floor plans and RCPs
- ▼ Building sections
- ▼ Dimming and switching plans
- ▼ Room finish, lighting, and furniture schedules
- ▼ Construction details
- ▼ Complete elevations for the entire project
- ■ Render a large-scale detail important to the aesthetics of your project.

Exercises and Further Study

- ■ Create axonometrics with shadows of both the main and mezzanine levels.
- ■ Create a detail drawing with note block, using CSI annotation.
- ■ Create a large-scale set of casework drawings for the bowling alley front desk, including enlarged floor plan, elevations, and all needed detail sections.
- ■ Generate a construction detail for a custom light fixture created from a model imported from SketchUp.

Unit 5

Advanced Rendering

13

Photo-Realistic Images with Revit

LEARNING GOALS

- Apply materials directly to different types of objects
- Create custom materials from the standard library
- Understand rendering controls
- Understand light sources and lighting controls
- Understand image adjustment and capture options

R evit can produce a fairly simple but effective photo-realistic rendering just using standard materials and lighting components that are already in your model. The rendering "engine" applies colors, patterns, and photographic images from its library to the geometry of the model—a process known as "mapping." Luminaires use photometric data to produce light distributions that mimic real performance. Color, texture, and reflective characteristic of materials can be modified to better replicate different finish qualities. All this effort produces a convincing photo-realistic representation of your view.

Greater depth and subtlety can be achieved with customized components, unique photograph-based material mappings, and using photographic images for people and flat entourage. Custom lighting can be created using light-distribution templates, imported geometry, or even just glowing surfaces. There are four basic steps:

1. Apply materials to all visible elements
2. Adjust rendering setting for draft, to test rendering settings

3. Adjust materials, lighting, and so forth
4. Revise settings to produce final high-quality rendering

As before, we will to focus on interior views. Let's create a rendering of the conference room in the bowling alley project. Open up your project, or go to the Online Resources for this chapter to download the base file used for this section.

The Materials Library

Materials for a given element or finish layer are selected from the **Materials** library. Each definition applies both a shaded color and a rendering material, and the two are vaguely related. The shaded color should be set to take its properties from the rendering materials, so the shaded view looks

Figure 13.1 *Choosing door materials*

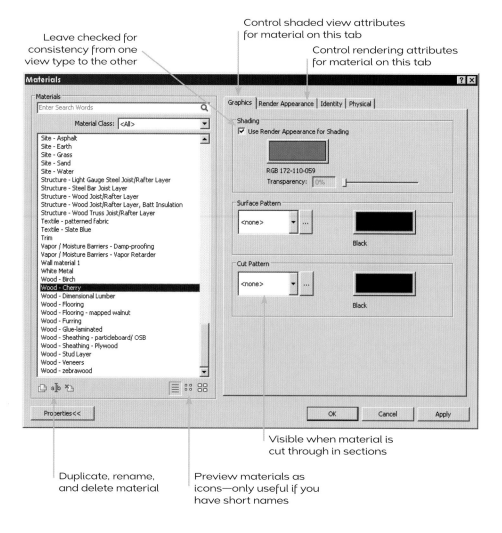

Leave checked for consistency from one view type to the other

Control shaded view attributes for material on this tab

Control rendering attributes for material on this tab

Visible when material is cut through in sections

Duplicate, rename, and delete material

Preview materials as icons—only useful if you have short names

a little bit like the rendered one. When you execute the rendering, however, the only setting that will make a difference is the Render material.

For every different type of finish in the model, even if it's just a paint color, you'll need a different entry in the **Materials** library. To open, click **Materials** on the **Manage** ribbon (Figure 13.1).

There are quite a few ready-made material definitions, each one with graphics defined that control normal, nonrendered display. Revit is not always consistent about having the **Render Appearance** set, though, and more often than not, the material is "Default," which will render gray. To create your own definition, select one of the existing ones and duplicate it. You can then apply graphics and rendering characteristics that fit your project.

The first step is to assign materials to all the different types of elements in your project.

Applying Materials to Components

To see what materials are already applied, select a door and get its **Element Properties**. Click on the **Edit/New** button to see how this particular door type is assembled (Figure 13.2).

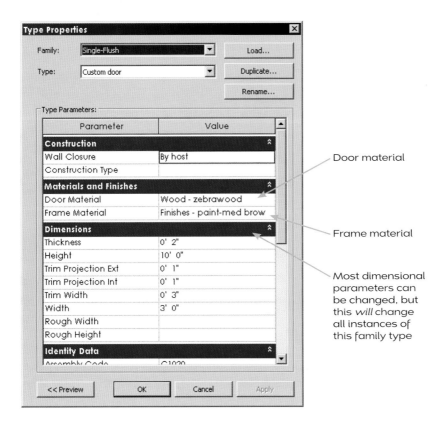

Figure 13.2 *The* ***Materials*** *library*

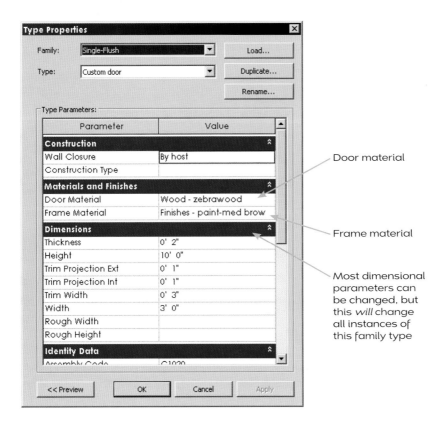

Click on the arrow in the **Door Material** field to choose a material from the **Materials** library. Most Revit-based components will have parameters for their main materials, although sometimes they don't. If not, select the component in an orthographic view and click on **Edit Family** on the Options toolbar. This opens up the component as a separate file in the **Family Editor**, where you can take a look at the pieces of the object to see how materials are assigned. Select an object and get its **Element Properties** to see if any material has been assigned. If not, assign it, or better yet, create a parameter so that the materials can be placed within your main model. When done, choose **Load into Model** from the Design bar. You'll have to override the existing components in your model.

Objects that have been imported from SketchUp or AutoCAD can have materials applied to them in the **Object Styles** menu—but they won't allow painting with the Paint Bucket. Each layer can have a separate material, and once the image is rendered, the edge lines will disappear. You can also apply materials to other model categories, but beware that these are generally global changes.

LOOK OUT!

*You can edit the materials of a wall, floor, or ceiling from the **Element Properties** dialog box, too. First click the **Edit/New** button and then, in the **Type Properties** dialog box, choose **Edit Structure**. Materials can be chosen here for any layer of construction, Remember, this will change the material of ALL walls, floors, or ceilings of this type. Duplicate the type if you don't want a global change.*

Applying Materials to a Wall Family

Materials can be applied to an entire family in one fell swoop. Select one of the walls in your project and get its **Element Properties**. Click **Edit/New** to see the **Type Properties**, then click on the **Structure** button in the dialog box. This will show you the actual construction of the wall—Figure 11.3 shows this dialog box. Each part of the wall construction is shown here, and each can have materials assigned to it. Only layers defined as Finish will render, though.

Click inside the **Material** field to select materials for both the interior and exterior finish layer. If the two sides of the wall are different, be sure you have them oriented correctly in plan. Selecting a wall will reveal a special flipper to switch the inside of the wall with the outside.

Creating New Materials

To make a custom rendering material, you'll have to duplicate one of the existing materials. Each material definition has a **Render Appearance** tab, which defines how the mapping will behave during the render. This includes both the image used for mapping and finish characteristics applied to the image. Some materials, like Wood-Cherry, are based on an image file, while others, like Paint, are based on a solid color (Figure 13.3).

The selection of materials that come with Revit are fine for basic rendering, but generally designers are going to want custom ones that indicate the actual products used in the project. Select a material, such as Paint, and click the **Duplicate** button. It's a good idea to name it something descriptive of its category and finish, such as *Paint-Blue*, so it will be easy to find in the future. For this new material, you can choose from Revit's large library of preset rendering materials. Click on the **Replace...** button to open the **Render Appearance Library** (Figure 13.4).

Each render appearance material has a preview—a sphere, a corner of a building, and so forth—that shows it off best. You can sort by class or search by name. Browse to find a blue paint with a color and finish that you like and click **OK** to return to the **Materials** library. It's now available for application to any element in the project. We won't be able to see the actual material until the view it shows up in is rendered. The shaded view should reflect this new render appearance if you've checked the **Use Render Appearance for Shading** button.

Opens the Render Appearance Library

Figure 13.3 *The **Render Appearance** tab for Wood-Cherry and Paint*

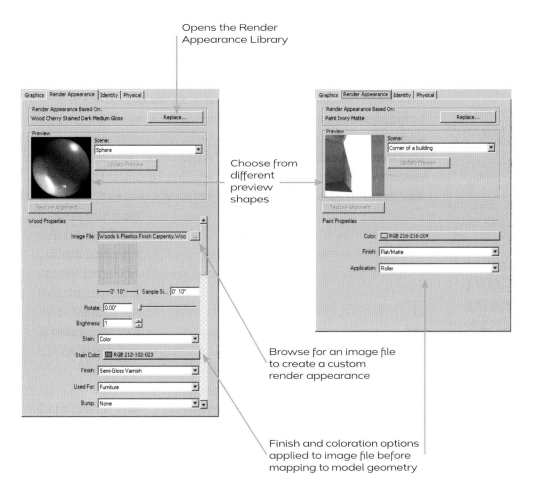

Choose from different preview shapes

Browse for an image file to create a custom render appearance

Finish and coloration options applied to image file before mapping to model geometry

Figure 13.4 *The Render Appearance Library*

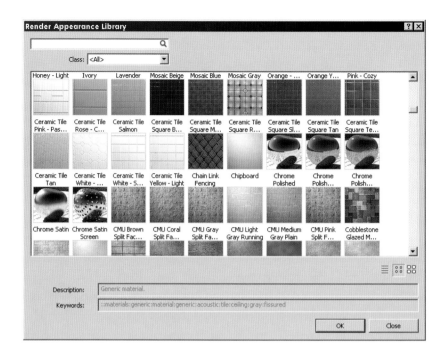

Figure 13.4 *The Render Appearance Library*

MAGIC TRICK

If you want your new material definition in another project, you'll have to import it. Open the source file and, from within a view of the destination project, choose File> Transfer Project Standards... If you have more than one project open, be sure to choose the right one from the drop-down list. Uncheck all categories except Materials, and click OK to import any materials in the source project.

The process is the same for creating a custom image-based material. To get good images for rendering, go to the manufacturer's Web site of the finish material you'd like to use and you should be able to find high-quality electronic samples. On the **Render Appearance** tab, click on the **Image...** button and browse for the new photo.

Finish quality and the base image file can be modified or changed for the particular conditions you'd like to create in your design. Using actual images as a basis for a rendered material is especially effective if you want to study the effect of a particular fabric, carpet, or custom finish, and ties a presentation drawing nicely with a finish board. Once a material is loaded in from the library, it becomes part of the project. Any changes to the appearance of render material will be contained within this project only—the **Render Appearance Library** will not be affected.

Since I'm so obsessive about backing up my work, I keep a custom materials folder on my data drive and store all images used for custom materials there. If I need to render my project on another computer, I copy the materials folder over to the new machine, and then reassign the maps.

Using the Paint Bucket

Now that you have a good selection of material definitions, it'd be nice to be able to paint walls, floors, and ceilings without having to create new family types every single time. **Paint Bucket** (on the **Modify** ribbon) to the rescue! Whole walls and floors can be painted by mousing over the edge until the area you want is highlighted. The trick is finding that edge, as it's often cropped away in elevation. Use axonometric views for best results, and mouse around the drawing until the face you want is highlighted. Once it is, click to dump paint.

So what if you want to paint a lower portion of a wall a different color from the top? You can break that face into different regions using the **Split Face** tool (on the **Modify** ribbon). Put your project in an elevation or plan view where you see the surface you'd like to split. Click the **Split Face** tool and move your mouse over the edge of the face you'd like to split—it will become highlighted (use the arrow part of your cursor). Click on the face edge and you'll enter the Sketch Mode. Draw a region using lines—it must form a closed loop, so either draw a continuous boundary or connect to the edges of the face—they'll appear to be an orange color. Click **Finish Sketch** on the Design bar and you'll see the boundary show up in elevation. You can now dump paint over a delineated region on that face.

People

In Revit, scale figure components will have only a wireframe outline until you Render the view they're in. There are a few very nice RPC people (stands for Render Plus Content, a separate company that provides photo-realistic rendering content), found in the Entourage folder of the Imperial library. They will cast shadows and can be rotated somewhat for slightly different profiles.

You can download a special piece of software to create your own RPC people from pictures of your mom or your dog. To create one requires a nice, cropped image of a scale figure (obviously) and a mask of that image, which is basically a reverse silhouette. Both of these can be created and sized properly using Photoshop Elements. Go to www.archvision.com/RPCCreator.cfm to download a useful, free RPC creation tool.

Fixing Light Fixtures

OK, so nothing ever really goes that smoothly. The most common problem in rendering is that the lighting isn't doing what you want, due either to problems with the luminaire or problems with your design. Well, I can't help you with the design here, but I can show you how you might fix the lighting. The most obvious problem would be that the fixture is not producing enough light. You can increase the lumen output of a luminaire by going to **Edit/New>Element Properties**.

More likely, though, is that the geometry of the fixture itself is blocking the light source. You can select the luminaire in RCP and choose **Edit** from the Options toolbar. This will open the **Family Editor**, where you can switch to any view to locate the problem (Figure 13.5).

In elevation view, you'll see a reference plane indicating the light source elevation. Make sure it's not embedded in a tube or other solid object, as in Figure 13.5. In plan, make sure the crossing of the two reference planes is in the correct location for the geometry of the luminaire. If there's a shade, make sure it's been assigned a translucent material.

Another common problem is when the light has an improper color, which can leave the rendering with a yellow cast. Click on **Family Types**, and look for the **Color Temperature** field. Change the light

Figure 13.5 *The Family Editor for a luminaire*

Family Types... define preset dimensions, materials, and other options for variations of this component

Re-imports the component—be sure to override parameters of those already in the model

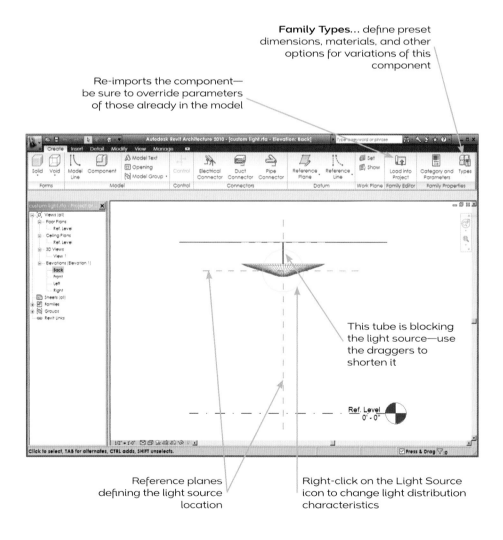

This tube is blocking the light source—use the draggers to shorten it

Reference planes defining the light source location

Right-click on the Light Source icon to change light distribution characteristics

source to be cooler—4800° Kelvin, for example, and the rendering should improve.

When you've figured out the problem, load the component back into your project and give rendering another try.

Custom Light Fixtures

Creating a custom light fixture is a matter of choosing which type of fixture you'd like to create and then generating the geometry around wherever the light source is supposed to be. I'm going to a make a simple floor lamp with a silly shade on it. The geometry has already been created in SketchUp. Have fun in creating your own fixture, or use the file *Custom_Lamp.skp* in the Online Resources for this chapter.

CREATING A NEW LIGHT FIXTURE

1. Choose **Application Menu>New>Family...** Choose **Lighting Fixture** from the list. (There are wall- and ceiling-based ones, too. This forces the component to connect to an appropriate host object.)
2. You're now in the Family Editor. On the **Insert** ribbon, choose **Import CAD**.
3. Browse to find the lamp you created in SketchUp (or use the file from Chapter 13 Online Resources, *Custom_Lamp.skp*). Be sure to place manually, putting the base at the intersection of the dashed green reference lines (Figure 13.6).
4. Open the Front elevation view.
5. The upper reference plane is where the light source is located. Drag it down to the center of the lamp shade (Figure 13.7).

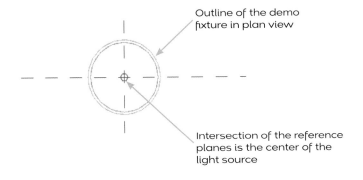

Outline of the demo fixture in plan view

Intersection of the reference planes is the center of the light source

Figure 13.6 *The custom lamp in the family editor-plan view*

Figure 13.7 *Aligning the light source with the model*

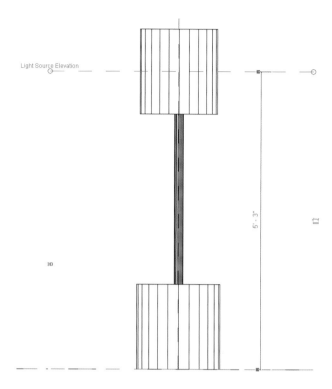

6. Save the new family onto your computer—I have a special folder for custom families in the root directory of my school work. See Chapter 13 Online Resources for my version of this file, *Custom lamp family.rfa*.

7. Click **Load into Project** on the **Contextual** ribbon.

8. Create a new material for the shade and the base.

9. In your plan, you should now be able to place the component.

10. As with other imported SketchUp objects, you control the assigned materials in the **Object Styles** dialog box—under the Imports in Families group.

11. Choose an appropriate material for the different parts of the lamp—or create a custom translucent one for the shade.

12. Render at a low resolution first to see if it works properly.

Note the pools of light on the floor and ceiling created by the lamp shade. Because Revit actually traces light rays from the source to different surfaces, the geometry of the light fixture makes a difference.

The light distribution for a given luminaire can also be changed. In the Family Editor, right-click on the yellow Light icon and choose **Options** (Figure 13.8).

Match the geometry of the luminaire and lamp with the closest

LOOK OUT!

If a custom lamp isn't working at all, make sure you've left an opening in the geometry for the light to come out! Also, make sure glass material you've chosen really is translucent.

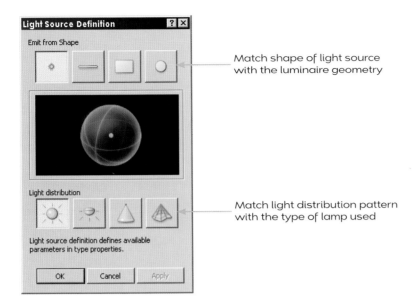

Figure 13.8 *Light Source Definition* dialog box

Match shape of light source with the luminaire geometry

Match light distribution pattern with the type of lamp used

patterns and click OK. For advanced users, IES light distribution files can be assigned to a family of lights. This will create a very precise, realistic representation of the light output of a particular luminaire. Assign the IES file in the **Family Types** dialog box.

Inserting Photos

It can be very effective to have photos in your rendered images, although you're generally limited to square images. Revit uses a Decal, found on the **Insert** ribbon, to map the image file onto an object that can be placed in a drawing. Create a new decal, then browse for the image file map. As with some rendered materials, Decals can be self-luminous (Figure 13.9).

You can also create a mask that will crop this image to a different shape—to fit in an oval frame, for example. If you play with transparency levels, you can get that screen-printed-on-glass look.

Click **OK** to place in the drawing—any orthographic view (including axonometric) will accept the decal, but not every type of surface will. Once inserted, the size can be changed by selecting and then dragging a grip one way or another. Render a view where the decal shows up to see what it looks like. If it's not rendering the way you like, select the Decals and get its **Properties**. Click on **Edit/New**, then on the **Edit** button next to the **AccuRender Attributes** field. This brings up the same dialog we saw when creating the Decal.

Figure 13.9 *Decal*
settings

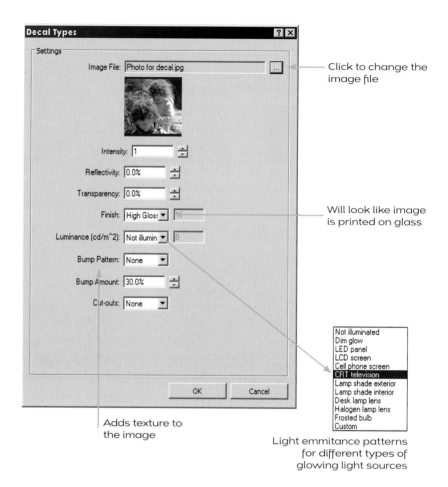

Click to change the
image file

Will look like image
is printed on glass

Adds texture to
the image

Light emmitance patterns
for different types of
glowing light sources

Rendering

Any view in perspective (and axonometrics, too) can be rendered. Revit's Mental Ray rendering engine can, at its lower settings can produce an image in a few minutes, depending on the complexity of the drawing. Settings can be changed to raise the quality of the image and reflections, and at the highest settings can take a dozen hours or more. Any perspective or axonometric view can be rendered—click on the little teapot at the bottom of the view window, or choose **Render Options** from the **View Control Bar**. This brings up the **Rendering** menu (Figure 13.10).

At this stage, we just want to see if the lights are working and the materials are rendering properly. For fastest operation, choose **Draft** as the quality setting. You'll also want to define the lighting scene—for this project, **Interior: Artificial** only is the best option. When you have windows or doors that you'd like to let in daylight, choose **Interior: Sun and Artificial**. Click the Render button at the top of the menu. Revit will generate an image that begins as fuzzy but will slowly become sharp.

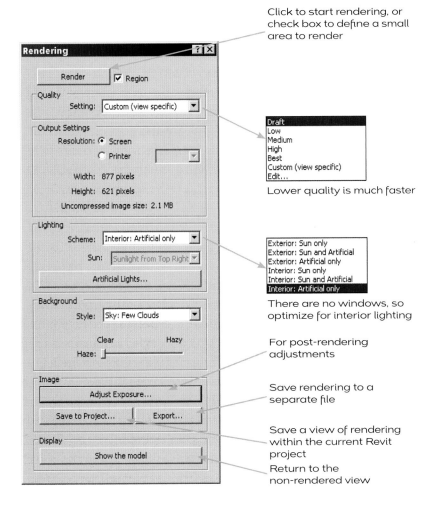

Figure 13.10 *The Rendering dialog box*

Click to start rendering, or check box to define a small area to render

Lower quality is much faster

There are no windows, so optimize for interior lighting

For post-rendering adjustments

Save rendering to a separate file

Save a view of rendering within the current Revit project

Return to the non-rendered view

Make changes to lighting and materials as needed. When it's working as you'd like, set up the rendering for high-quality output. Back on the **Rendering** menu, choose **Edit...** for the quality setting. This will bring up the **Render Quality Settings** dialog box (Figure 13.11). You can choose one of the standard quality settings, or Custom to specify exact settings. Click **OK** to finish, and try rendering again (Figure 13.12).

It may take quite a long time, and your computer will be tied up for the whole process. Consider rendering overnight, and be sure to turn off your screen saver and automatic hibernation options. This rendering will usually give a fairly good impression of the space if materials have been applied appropriately.

Using the **Exposure Control** dialog box on the Rendering menu, the rendering can be adjusted without having to re-render (Figure 13.13).

LOOK OUT!

If you are staring at a partially or completely gray image, in all likelihood it's the Phase settings. Interior projects often have a mix of existing and new elements, and Revit will override the rendering material in some views. Make sure the current view Phase is set to Project Completion and the Phase Filter is set to Show Complete. If everything is still gray, it's time to apply materials.

Figure 13.11 *The **Render Quality Settings*** *dialog box*

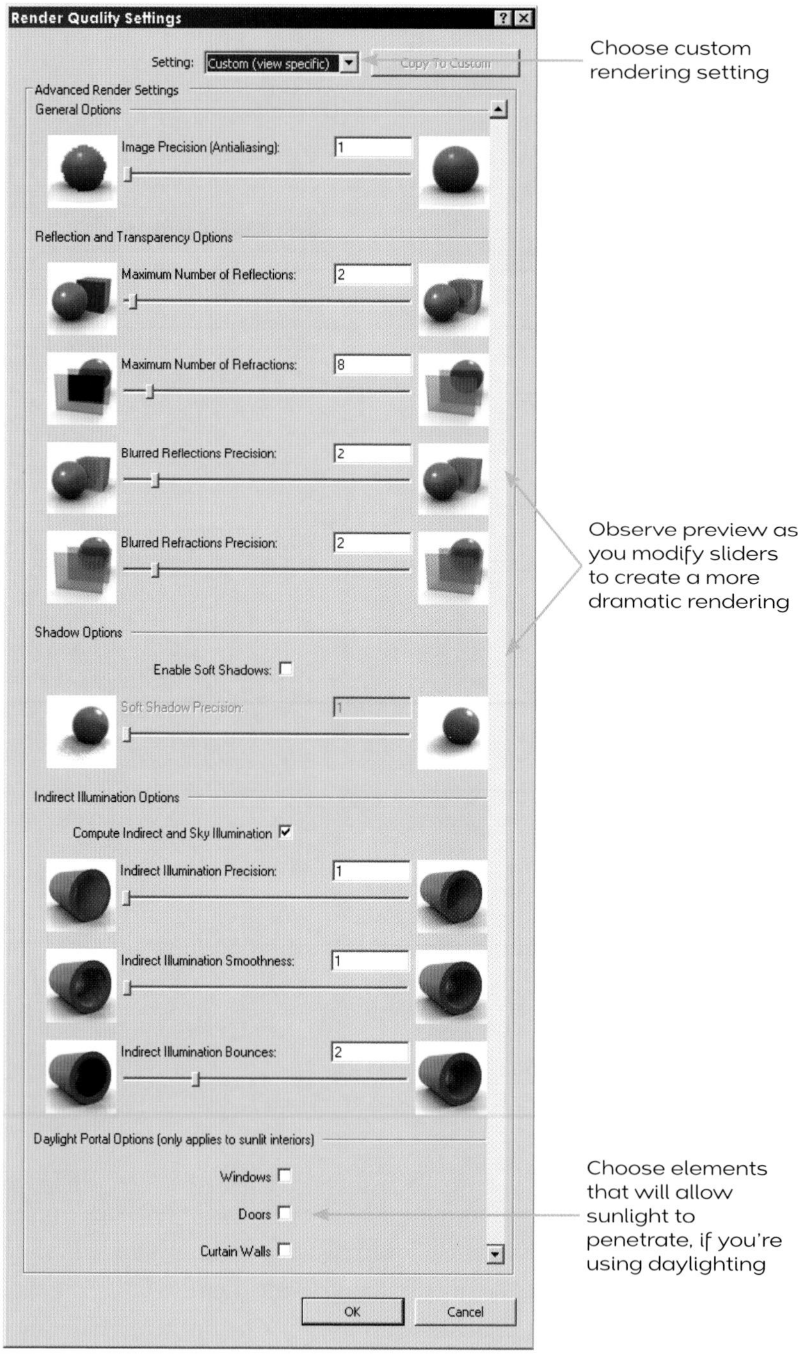

Choose custom rendering setting

Observe preview as you modify sliders to create a more dramatic rendering

Choose elements that will allow sunlight to penetrate, if you're using daylighting

Drag sliders and then click **Apply** to see the effect. Click **OK** to return to the Rendering menu. The rendering can be saved as a view within the Revit project, or exported to an image file. Choose the option you'd like on the Rendering dialog box. As before, choose the TIFF file format for the best resolution and retention of the original colors.

Figure 13.12 *The finished rendering*

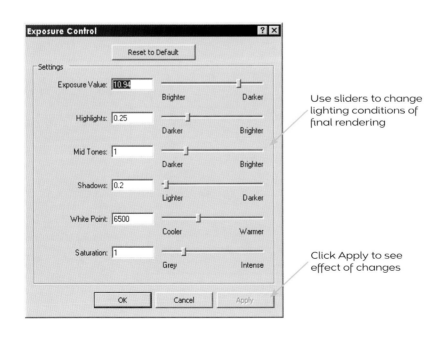

Use sliders to change
lighting conditions of
final rendering

Click Apply to see
effect of changes

Figure 13.13 *The Exposure Control dialog box*

Grouping and Dimming Lights

The character of an interior design is generally dependent on the quality and sophistication of the lighting. Particularly in spaces with complex use requirements, like conference rooms, dimming schemes are the best way to create preset scenes for different activities. Also, renderings can be used to study the effect of off-set dimming, where electric lighting is adjusted on or off based on daylighting conditions within a space.

The light output of a given luminaire can be controlled within the **Family Properties** dialog box. Revit also allows single or grouped luminaires to be dimmed, either decreasing or increasing output. On the **Render** dialog box, be sure you've chosen either the *Interior: Sun and Artificial* or *Interior: Artificial only* scheme. Click on the **Artificial Lights...** button (Figure 13.14).

Under the Dimming… category, you may enter a value from 0, where the luminaire or group is off, to 1, where the luminaire or group has twice the light output.

To group lights, click on the **New...** button under the **Group Options** area of the dialog box. Name the new group—I'll call the first one

Figure 13.14 *The Artificial Lights dialog box*

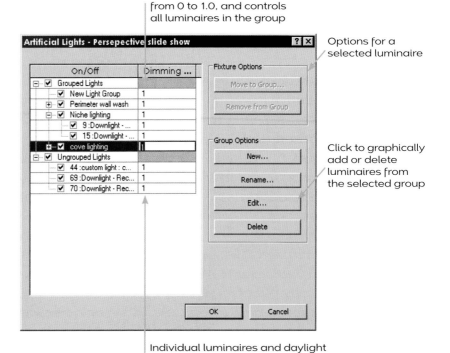

Dimmer can be a value from 0 to 1.0, and controls all luminaires in the group

Options for a selected luminaire

Click to graphically add or delete luminaires from the selected group

Individual luminaires and daylight sources can be dimmed individually or as part of a group

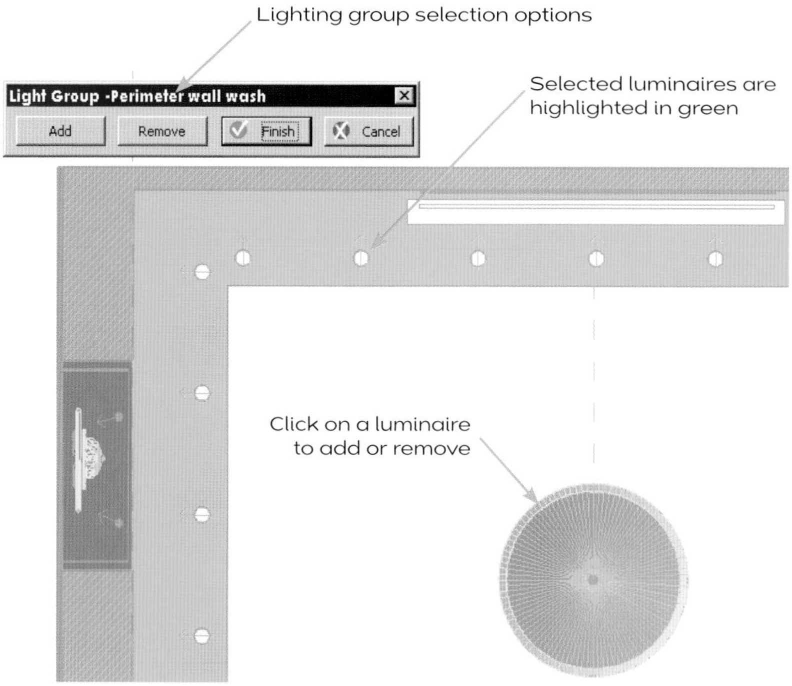

Lighting group selection options

Selected luminaires are highlighted in green

Click on a luminaire to add or remove

Light Group -Perimeter wall wash

Add   Remove   Finish   Cancel

Figure 13.15 *Choosing lights in a group*

Downlights—and then click on all the lights you want to be included; they'll be highlighted in red. If you can't see all the luminaires you'd like to include, switch to your Reflected Ceiling Plan view (Figure 13.15).

Enter a value and click the **New** button on the Options bar to make another group—I'll call it *Troffers*—and select the recessed fluorescent luminaires. Now click on the **Lighting...** tool to see a list of all the lights and light groups in your drawing. In this way, you can group together most of the luminaires that you'd like to dim en masse. An alternative method is to select a luminaire in RCP—there will be the same artificial lighting options available on the Options toolbar.

Once you've grouped different luminaires, just change the Dimming value for the group in the **Artificial Lights** dialog box. Re-render to see the effect.

Online Resources

- Revit model used in this chapter, *Conference room.rvt*
- Custom luminaire, *Custom lamp family.rfa*
- Examples of student work, *Revit Rendering.pdf*
- SketchUp file, *Custom lamp.skp*

Term Project Assignments

- Create presentation renderings of main bowling areas, indicating all lighting and materials.

Exercises and Further Study

- Render a view from a previous project.
- Render day and night scenes.
- Render scenes with dramatic dimming effects.
- Create custom fabric from a downloaded sample.
- Create custom materials for different paint colors, using paint chips from a specific manufacturer.
- Create a glowing material.
- Create a custom-screened material, such as a resin panel with bamboo rings in it.

14

Photo-Realistic Images with IRender nXt

LEARNING GOALS

- Understand different rendering settings
- Understand lightbulbs and lighting controls
- Create custom IRender materials
- Understand image adjustment and capture options

Wouldn't it be great if you could just turn on all those light fixtures you put into your SketchUp model? Well, you can, thanks to a handy plug-in called IRender nXt from Render Plus Systems (RPS). This plug-in takes the materials and geometry of your model and uses a rendering "engine" to generate photo-realistic images of your project. Besides lighting, IRender nXt will map SketchUp materials to a much more realistic-looking sample, and all without any changes to the model. You can even create custom lamps, luminaires, and mirror components.

Rendering is launched from inside any SketchUp view, and will open up a new window to preview and process the final rendering. Once it starts, you basically have to abandon the model for a while, and probably count on leaving your machine alone, too.

BIG PICTURE

Models need minimal preparation to use IRender nXt—just apply materials and be sure to have a light source somewhere in your view. Quality Options, controls, and exporting should look somewhat familiar if you've rendered with Revit. Sometimes it's easier to make a Revit model look good by bringing it into SketchUp, painting, adding lighting and mirrors, and rendering it with IRender nXt.

IRender nXt Setup

The first step is to load IRender nXt onto your machine. Download the software (the link is in the Online Resources) and run the executable file. If you don't have a license it will run in trial mode, but it will leave a watermark on your renderings after the trial period has expired. Once loaded, go to the **Plug-ins** drop-down menu and activate it—you'll see the IRender nXt toolbar (Figure 14.1).

Click on the **Options** tool to peek at the rendering settings. I usually check the radio button next to "Automatically load IRender nXt toolbars and functions" for convenience. On the lighting tab, be sure you've checked the box next to **Interior No Sun** or **Interior With Sun**, as this will optimize for electric light sources.

SketchUp models can often be in the 20–30 MB file-size range, and this really taxes your computer. The first step is to save a copy of your project just in case you get a bad Bug Splat. Then you can remove all the detritus from downloaded components and other junk, using the **Purge** command, which can often speed up the model quite a bit.

PURGING A SKETCHUP MODEL

1. From the Windows drop-down menu, choose **Model Info.**
2. Click on **Statistics** in the left frame.
3. Click on the **Purge** button. This will help IRender nXt work faster.
4. If your model was already in the 30 MB range, click **Purge** again.
5. Click **OK**, then save your drawing again (it should be a much smaller file size now).

Figure 14.1 *The IRender nXt toolbar with tool descriptions, courtesy Render Plus Systems*

- (IR) IRender Info - start up settings and general information.
- ● Full Ray Trace - starts a new ray trace of your current model and settings.
- Quick Ray Trace - starts a ray trace without resending the current model.
  (Use this when you have changed the view or other settings, but have not made any changes to the model.)
- IRender Options - Render window size, render quality, etc.
- Material Placement - Select and Edit materials and place them directly into components.
- Create Lamp or Light Fixture - Create a lamp, or a light fixture.
- Create Mirror - Make a mirror component.
- Load Sample models.
- Create Plant - create a SketchUp component from an AccuRender Plant. The component will automatically render as a Fractal Plant.
- Create Material - make a new SketchUp material from an AccuRender material.
- Animation - create movies, or batch images from SketchUp animation pages.
- Help - load the on-line Help pages.

This usually gets rid of the biggest impediments, and it will speed up your model, too. A more drastic step is to delete all components and other drawing elements that don't show in your current view. IRender nXt has no way of culling those objects otherwise, and will waste time running calculations.

Rendering a View

Let's take our file from the Chocolate Café and see how well it renders without any modification or enhancement. Just click the green **Go** button on the IRender nXt toolbar. A render window should show up shortly, and you'll see the image slowly develop from a rough view to a more refined rendering. This won't be a high-resolution image by any means, but should give you some idea if your lighting and materials are working. Wasn't that easy? Once the rendering is done, you can click the **Save** button and specify a file name and location—but you'll probably want to spruce things up a little before producing a presentation-quality image.

Advanced Rendering Settings

It can be so easy to get that basic rendering from your model, but so hard to get a perfect photo-realistic image. The first step is upping the size and quality level of the render window. Of course, there's a relationship between image size, quality level, and file size, just as in Revit: The more of the first two you have, the bigger the last one will be.

CONFIGURING IRENDER NXT FOR
HIGH-QUALITY IMAGES

1. Open your model and choose **Save As** from the drop-down menu. Name the new one *Copy for Rendering* or something clever like that, so you don't accidentally mess up the original.
2. Choose the scene or view you'd like to render.
3. Click on the **Options** button to configure for a test rendering (Figure 14.2).
4. Choose **Quality** settings based partly on how confident you are of the model settings and how much time you have.
5. Check on the **Interior with Sun** radio button to make sure you're set up for an interior rendering (Figure 14.3).

Figure 14.2 *IRender nXt*
Setup options

Interesting preset
coloration schemes

Add a background
image

Control rendering
of edge lines

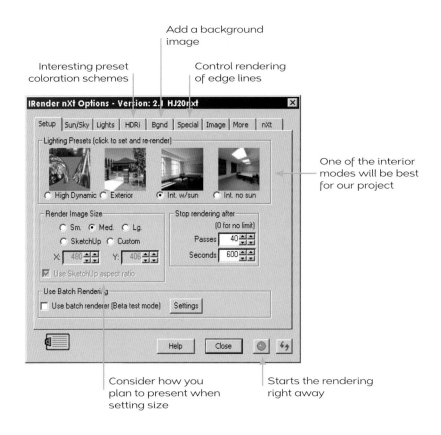

One of the interior
modes will be best
for our project

Consider how you
plan to present when
setting size

Starts the rendering
right away

Figure 14.3 *The*
Lights tab

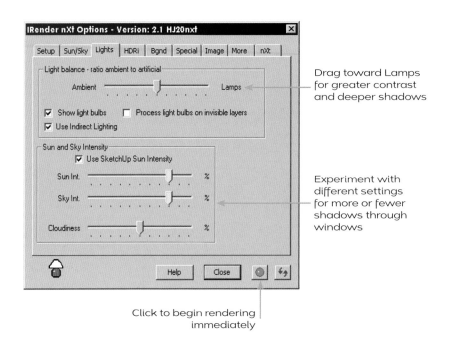

Drag toward Lamps
for greater contrast
and deeper shadows

Experiment with
different settings
for more or fewer
shadows through
windows

Click to begin rendering
immediately

6. The **Lights** tab has settings for the balance between lamps and ambient lighting, as well as sun and shadow intensity controls (Figure 14.3).

7. Set options for edge lines, blurriness, and number of bounces, and click **OK** when you're feeling composed.

8. Click the green **Render** button.

9. IRender nXt will trace up the screen over and over again, refining reflected lighting and shadows with each pass (Figure 14.4).

10. Once the image has rendered, adjust the brightness slider as needed.

11. Click the **Tone Operator** (it looks the same as the **Adjust** dialog box for a Revit rendering). Adjust brightness, contrast, and indirect lighting to taste.

12. **Save** the rendered image to your disk. JPEG and PNG are the only formats available.

These rendered views are not connected with the original model, and once you close the IRender nXt window, you'll lose an unsaved rendering. IRender nXt can also perform a batch render, where all of your scenes can be rendered and saved at once. This will certainly take a while, but it

Save image to JPG or PNG

Copy image to clipboard

Stop rendering

Tone adjustment operator

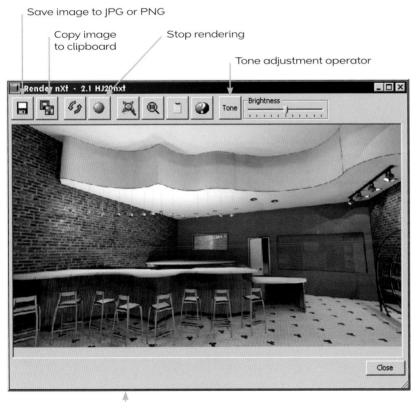

Doubling resolution will quadruple rendering time

Figure 14.4 *The Render window after completion*

will run automatically, so start it on a Friday and enjoy your weekend away from the computer.

Lamp Components

Custom lamps components can create some very sophisticated lighting designs, because they give such realistic optical control. Each "lamp" (a lightbulb, in common parlance) is assigned an intensity in Watts or Lumens and a color. Spots can have specific beam spreads and can be aimed at geometric locations in the model. Click the **Create Lamp or Light Fixture** button to see the available option (Figure 14.5).

These lamps are useful in a variety of ways, such as if you're trying some tricky casework or museum lighting. Insert a lamp inside the component you need to have lighting, and all instances will be functional. This is a good way to fix a luminaire that's not rendering as a light fixture within IRender nXt.

Traditional light fixtures (luminaires) can be created also, using a stan-

Figure 14.5 *The **Create Light Fixtures** dialog box*

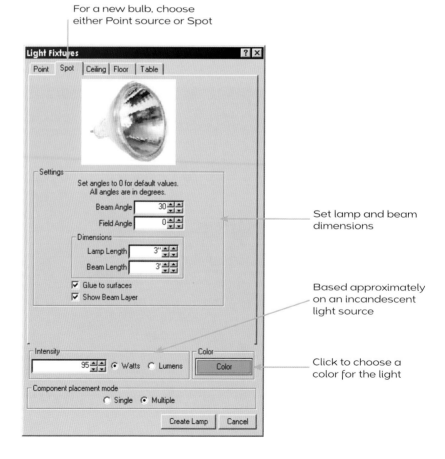

For a new bulb, choose either Point source or Spot

Set lamp and beam dimensions

Based approximately on an incandescent light source

Click to choose a color for the light

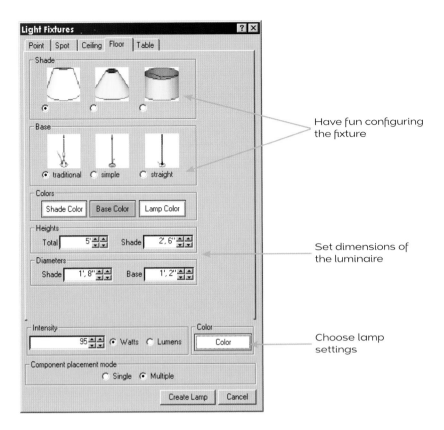

Figure 14.6 *Creating a table lamp*

Have fun configuring the fixture

Set dimensions of the luminaire

Choose lamp settings

dard kit of parts. The light source in each can be customized, just like the lamps above (Figure 14.6). You can really have some fun here, although anything custom will be easier to just model on your own. OK, so it's not high design, but it's fun. And the lamps do work nicely in the rendered view.

Once inserted into your model, a lamp component can be modified and aimed in place. Right-click on the lamp and choose **IRender: Aim Lamp...** Your cursor rubber-bands from the center of the lamp to the center of the beam—click on the location you'd like the lamp to focus on. To change the properties of the lamp, choose **IRender: Edit IRender Lamp...** All the original settings can be modified. Luminaire intensity can also be overridden from this menu.

Mirror Components

It couldn't be simpler to create a mirror component, complete with a frame. Click the **Create Mirror** tool, then fill out the dimensions and other features you'd like.

There are some tools for creating special objects that take advantage

Figure 14.7 *The **Create** Mirror dialog box*

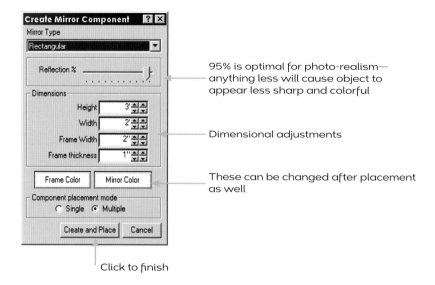

95% is optimal for photo-realism—anything less will cause object to appear less sharp and colorful

Dimensional adjustments

These can be changed after placement as well

Click to finish

of the powerful rendering features. The simplest is the **Create Mirror Component** tool—this makes a mirror with a frame of the size you specify (Figure 14.7).

This creates a component, just like any other in SketchUp. It will render as fully reflective, so be sure you check what parts of your model will be reflected. Mirrors can add a great sense of depth to a project, and can create some interesting relationships with elements in different parts of your design.

Reflective and Glowing Materials

To create custom materials of any sort, IRender nXt has some special tools for editing the materials in the model. Apply preset material characteristics such as plastic or mirror to any texture already in the drawing. Right-click on materials you'd like to change and choose **IRender nXt: Edit material...** (Figure 14.8).

I've taken one of the brick textures that come standard with SketchUp and clicked the Reflective default material. The intensity and sharpness of the reflections can be controlled with sliders, and the preview image reflects all changes immediately. The material can be made transparent or even to glow, although it won't be very bright. For a solid color, or when creating a new material, click on the **Advanced** button to access controls for adding a map to an image file of your choice (Figure 14.9).

Bumps can make for a particularly realistic effect on materials with a pronounced texture, like concrete or travertine marble. You could also use this dialog box to create materials of your own invention, so experiment.

MAGIC TRICK

*To see how your materials are working, select a bunch of objects (individual faces or whole components), right-click on them, and choose **IRender nXt: Render Selected**. This will render just those objects based on the current settings.*

Options and effects for
glassy materials

Makes the materials into
a light source

Preset material
characteristics

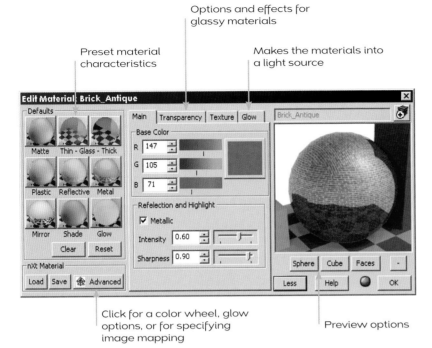

Click for a color wheel, glow
options, or for specifying
image mapping

Preview options

Figure 14.8 *The Edit
Material* dialog box

Click to browse for an
image to map to material

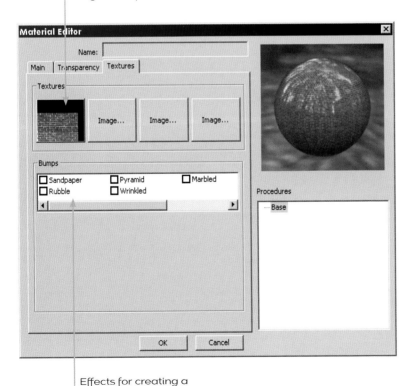

Effects for creating a
textured surface

Figure 14.9 *The
Advanced Material
Editor*

Rendering an Exported Revit Model with IRender nXt

If you're having trouble with rendering in Revit, know that many people turn to SketchUp for the greater view controls, style filters, and the ability to render materials if needed. You'll definitely want to save any files you're working on first. Then, to export your model from Revit, you must be in a 3D view—perspective or axonometric. Choose **Application Menu>Export>CAD Formats...** The big problem with former Revit models is that the lighting has to be re-created in IRender.nXt. If you only have a few views, though, it may still be worth it. An entire walk-through, though, may require too much re-modeling.

This will save an AutoCAD version of your project, which you can import into SketchUp and explode to edit. Be sure to choose a version of AutoCAD that SketchUp can handle from the **Save as Type** drop-down list. If you prefer the AccuRender rendering engine to the MentalRay engine provided with Revit, IRender is also available as a plug-in for Revit.

Animations

Exporting animations is also a simple operation, although it will tie up your computer for many hours. Click the **Animation** tool—the options

Figure 14.10 *Animation options*

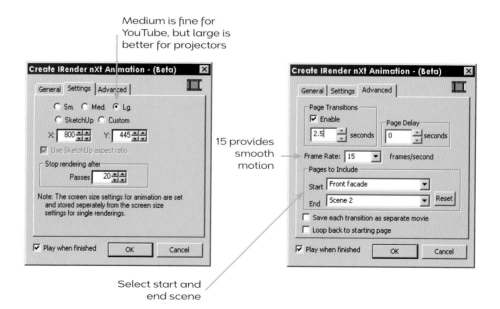

Medium is fine for YouTube, but large is better for projectors

15 provides smooth motion

Select start and end scene

similar to the basic SketchUp animation export. One nice advance is that you can choose which scenes to start and finish on. You can also set resolution and other goodies to produce a pretty impressive walkthrough.

You'll want to test each of the scenes before doing the final renderings, and it's really a bummer when they're not working properly. Also, this would be a good candidate for a lab computer or other machine, as animation export leaves the machine unusable for quite a long time.

Online Resources

- File used in this chapter, *Chocolate cafe rendering.skp*
- Examples of students' work, *IRender nXt examples.PDF*

Term Project Assignments

- Render main space of Chocolate Café

Exercises and Further Study

- View a scale figure through a mirror.
- Create a custom light fixture, insert an appropriate light source, and render.
- Create and aim angled colored lights for a nightclub effect.
- Render a view from a past project.
- Export a model from Revit, apply materials, fix lighting, and render a view.

15

Composite Drawings

LEARNING GOALS

■ Understand onscreen, projected, and printed resolution
■ Extract various parts of a perspective view for use in a composite
■ Understand general compositional strategies
■ Seamlessly assemble different images in Photoshop Elements
■ Render lighting and texture

BIG PICTURE

Compose the perspective view in Revit or SketchUp for your intended output first, and save those views, renderings, or scenes. That way, if you need to go back and retrieve some other part of the model, you won't have to re-create the angles and cropping of the perspective composition. Many compositing techniques will obscure details, so if you plan to use those techniques, don't stress too much over the minutiae in Revit or IRender nXt.

No single piece of software is foolproof for producing rendered images—something always goes wrong with a certain material, shadows, or some other aspect. Therefore, it's important to have a backup plan when your rendering crashes or just looks boring. Photoshop Elements provides many neat tools for converting bland images into subtle, high-quality presentation composites. This can be as simple as fixing irritating rendering glitches that would take hours to track down, or morphing images into a more expressive and less purely representational style.

Borrow pieces from the original model, such as linework, color shading, shadows, or photo-realistic rendering, and composite for effect. Filtering, which can produce a hand-rendered look, or mimic lighting, can be applied to the whole drawing or a selected layer. Another technique creates perspective in material images, which can be used with a layer mask to create flooring or other surface textures.

All of these techniques, such as lighting or materials, are independent of the original model, be it Revit or SketchUp, so you'll have to add them image by image where you need them.

Understanding Pixels

The first complexity in a high-quality rendering is how to specify the size and precision of the image you're working on. Most three-dimensional modeling programs (SketchUp and Revit) create walls, floors, and the like using vectors—mathematical formulas that describe the geometry of whatever you're creating. If you zoom way in on a table, for example, the software will make it nice and sharp because the vector information can be scaled to any view.

Pictures, called raster images to those in the know, have a finite dimension—there are only so many pixels in them, and you can't really make them more detailed. If you zoom in on a snapshot of your beagle, it will eventually begin to look broken up, or "**pixilated**." The trick for us is to extract enough pixels from our source (a model, camera, or scan) to be able to print or display on a projector without the image becoming distorted.

To complicate matters, images are described not only by dimension but also by density of pixels. This resolution is a tricky concept, since there's a difference between the requirements for computer monitors, digital cameras, and printers. Typical images are about 96 pixels per inch (PPI), which is tailored for your monitor. Web-based images are usually 72 PPI. Digital cameras measure total pixels in a given image (megapixels), and printers are labeled by the number of dots per inch (DPI) they can squirt out. All these are constrained by the reality that computers will get bogged down significantly as file sizes grow, until you can't draw a line without crashing your machine.

If you're just producing onscreen presentations, stick with 96 PPI and you'll be fine. You could even check the settings of the screen or projector for the actual pixel dimension, to tailor it perfectly. My computer, for example, has a maximum screen resolution of 1,920 × 1,200 pixels, but the projector I typically use is 1,024 × 768 pixels, so I might adjust a rendering or animation to the resolution of the device on which it will be presented. Files at any of these resolutions will also print fairly well, as long as you can tolerate a little graininess.

For printed presentation boards, however, we should work back from the maximum printing capabilities to figure out what image size and resolution we want. Each pixel on the screen has a certain "depth," which means it can be any one of hundreds, thousands, or millions of colors. Many printers have only four ink cartridges, though, so they need to combine them in different proportions to reproduce the particular color depth you see onscreen. Since each jet can only squirt one dot in one place at a time (that's the dots-per-inch rating), it takes about four little dots in combination to reproduce the color in one of those rich pixels you see on your screen.

BIG PICTURE

You need a few critical pieces of information even before the pencil hits the paper (or the mouse hits the pad, as the case may be). Determine how you will be presenting—print, projector, onscreen, or on the Web. If printing, you'll need to know the resolution of the printer and what paper options you've got. If you only have cheap lightweight bond available, you won't be able to use the highest settings on the printer or plotter. This will tell you the resolution you'll need when exporting images from SketchUp or Revit.

TABLE 15.1 DEALING WITH PIXELS

600	Printer output resolution, in DPI
4	# of pixels it usually takes to render 1 color
150	Maximum resolution needed in Photoshop document, in PPI
34	Width of desired print, in inches
5100	Total width of electronic image, in pixels

To get the best printed resolution, you'll need at least one-quarter the number of pixels in your electronic document. Take that number and multiply it by the intended size of your print, and you've got the target size of your electronic file (Table 15.1).

Plug in the ratings for your printer/paper combination and the widest dimension you plan to print. That gives you the desired pixel dimension you need to get from a scanner or 3D model. Cameras may just have broad settings (Medium, High, Super, and so forth), and scanners may only allow you to adjust resolution. In the latter instance, scan (in PPI) the maximum resolution of the printer (in DPI), if possible.

Why not just save at the highest available resolution? In a word, time. Photo-realistic renderings can take a long time, so only render the size you need. In the end, nothing beats experience and leaving time for a test plot.

UNDER THE HOOD

SketchUp export proportions are based on the size of the window on your screen. Maximize the SketchUp window before saving a scene, even if it means you'll have to crop later on. This way you'll be able to re-create the exact proportions of the perspective, making it easier to overlay a new export with the old ones.

Exporting Pieces of a Composition

Starting a perspective composition in Photoshop requires a little bit of advance planning. Let's do a large rendering of our Chocolate Café. While this was done in SketchUp, the concepts about exporting views with different settings to layer your composition apply to Revit and any other 3D modeling software.

Save views of all the pieces you think you might need from SketchUp, and then export at the correct resolution. This makes selecting areas and adding scale figures (and other features) easier when you get to Photoshop Elements. Sometimes an image is needed just to make selection easier in Photoshop, such as with lighting.

EXPORTING MULTIPLE IMAGES FROM SKETCHUP

1. Compose a perspective view of your Chocolate Café so it's perfect.
2. Save a scene with materials displayed.

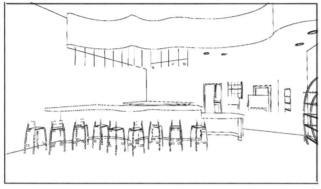
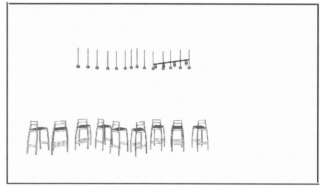

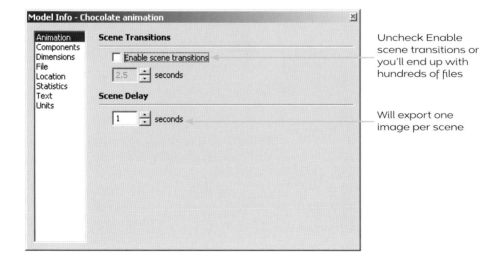

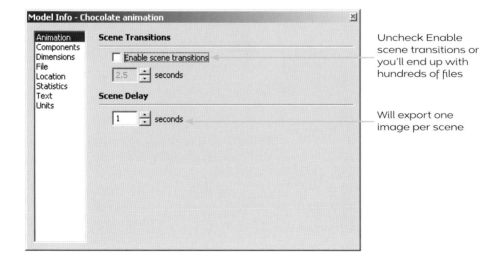

Figure 15.1 *Different exported scenes from SketchUp model*

3. Click on one of the sketchy styles and save another scene.
4. Using layers, hide everything but the pendant lights and save another scene (Figure 15.1).
5. Again using layers, hide everything but the bar stools and save a scene.
6. If there are other things you'd like to isolate, such as the service counter, do the same.

Figure 15.2 *Animation settings for exporting multiple still images*

Uncheck Enable scene transitions or you'll end up with hundreds of files

Will export one image per scene

7. To export all the scenes to separate image files, you'll use the Export Animation feature. Choose **View>Animation>Settings** to set up (Figure 15.2).

8. Uncheck **Enable Scene Transitions** and set the **Scene Delay** to one second.

9. Close the menu and choose **File>Export>Animation**.

10. Click on the **Options** tab (Figure 15.3).

11. Choose TIFF from the **Export Type** drop-down list.

12. Set the image width to 4,096 pixels, which is the maximum with this technique (the height will adjust proportionately), and click **OK**.

13. Click the **Create Folder** button to hold all the files you're about to create.

14. Click **OK** and wait for the export operation to be complete.

Remember that if you're not using a standard aspect ratio for your original drawing, you should write down the size (in pixels) that you've exported. This makes it easier to go back to your model later on and export additional pieces. An image width of 4,096 pixels will give enough resolution for about an 11 × 17 print to look sharp.

For images intended to be larger than 11 × 17, you'll need to export images one at a time from **File>Export>2D Graphic…** You can choose

Figure 15.3 *Export Animation*

For greater than 4096 pixels, export images one by one with a greater pixel dimension

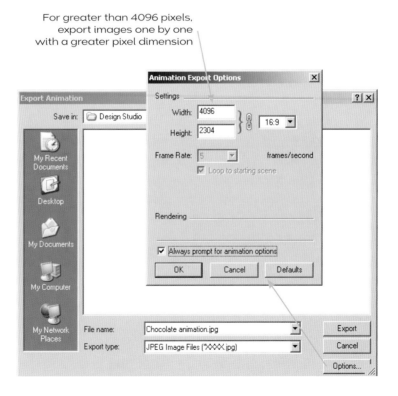

any resolution you'd like, but note that file sizes get vastly larger and processing gets slower as file sizes increase. Starting with a roughly 8,000-PPI TIFF file can lead to a Photoshop document that's well over 100 MB.

Drawing Prep in Revit

You can use a similar process for Revit-based images. Compose the view you'd like to use and change the view settings to Hidden. Make the image size the same as what you'd eventually like to print. Copy the view in the Project Browser and make the next one shaded. Render the same view and capture the rendering. You can also set up views where different elements are hidden. As in SketchUp, it's sometimes handy to have an image of just the furniture or of a scale figure. When exporting, you can select several views to export all at once.

Compositing a Perspective

Now that you have a folder full of images, it's time to start compositing. Why not just use computer-generated imagery? Well, you could, but often our modeling software is not entirely perfect in how it represents lighting or materials. Other times it is perfect, but the design isn't working right, so you need to touch it up.

SketchUp applies materials to curved objects very nicely, though, so it's often worth applying materials inside the program, even if the original model was done in Revit. Revit, on the other hand, is particularly bad at textured materials like flooring and carpeting, so use either custom AccuRender materials or make the changes in Photoshop. Both programs have integrated daylighting, and this is particularly useful for plan, section, and axonometric compositions.

The only time Photoshop Elements fails us is in creating a pattern on a curved vertical surface. This is so tricky that it's easier to do in SketchUp and export. In SketchUp, apply the material to whichever object is causing you trouble. Then select the object and choose **Render Selected** from the context-sensitive menu. This will give you a rendered version of the object (Figure 15.4).

Save the rendering as usual. Open in Photoshop Elements and use the **Magic Wand** to select all the black areas. Right-click on the screen and choose **Select Inverse**. You can then copy and paste your selection into the composite drawing.

MAGIC TRICK

Exporting image files from Revit doesn't always produce great results—the linework is often pixilated. Print the views to a PDF file first, then open the PDF with Photoshop Elements. Be sure to check the Adobe (or other virtual printer) Page Setup first, so that you have a decent sheet size and resolution. You can print multiple views this way, saving valuable seconds.

BIG PICTURE

Compositional strategies would be a great subject for another book. However, here are a few basic rules of thumb for interior views that might be helpful:

- *Have a balance of walls, floor, and ceiling areas.*
- *Use lighting and color intensity to draw viewers' eyes across the image.*
- *Use scale figures at various points (foreground, middle ground, and background are good spots) to give depth and life to the view.*
- *Use eye heights representative of various users (adults, kids, pets) and positions (people sitting, sleeping on the floor, and so forth).*
- *Consider the type of perspective: interior vistas, one- and two-point perspectives, distorted angles, and vignettes.*

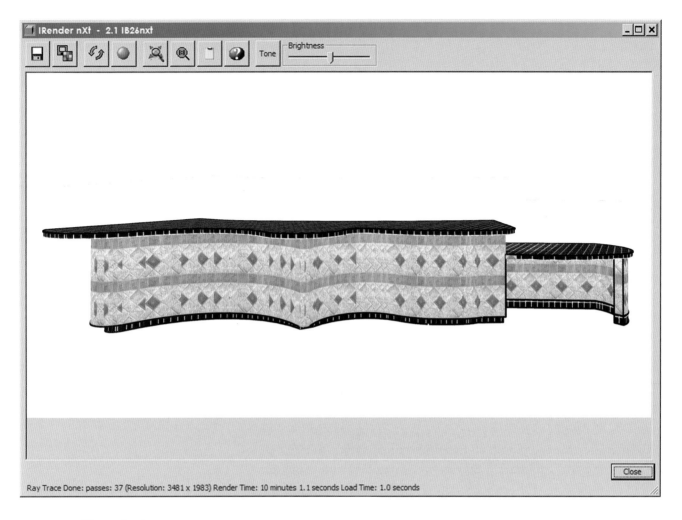

Figure 15.4 *The rendered curved service counter with tile applied to it*

The composition process in Photoshop Elements involves several distinct operations, so I've broken it into sections: assembling the pieces; modifying materials for perspective; filtering for lighting; and filtering for style.

Assembling the Pieces

1. Call up Photoshop Elements.
2. Choose **Edit and Enhance Photos.**
3. Click **Open**, then browse to find the JPEGs of your SketchUp scenes for the Chocolate Café. (Hold down **SHIFT** or **CTRL** to select more than one.) Click **OK**—all the images you have opened will show up in the Photo Bin at the bottom of the screen.
4. Let's use the most complete image (with materials) as our base. Click on the preview in the Image Bin to switch to that drawing.

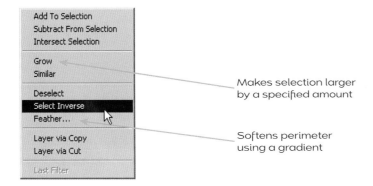

Figure 15.5 *All the black lines selected*

"Marching ants" surround everything that's selected

5. Right-click on the Background layer and choose **Layer from Background**.
6. Click on the line image of your perspective.
7. Use the **Magic Wand** to select all the white in the drawing (Figure 15.5).
8. Right-click on the Screen and choose **Select Inverse**—this selects all the black lines (Figure 15.6).
9. Press **CTRL+C** to copy.
10. Switch to the main drawings and type **CTRL+V**. The pasted selection comes in on its own layer.
11. Use the arrow keys to nudge the image into the correct position if needed, or click and drag on the target in the middle of the selection.
12. Switch to the drawing with just the furniture.

Add To Selection
Subtract From Selection
Intersect Selection

Grow
Similar

Deselect
Select Inverse
Feather...

Layer via Copy
Layer via Cut

Last Filter

Makes selection larger by a specified amount

Softens perimeter using a gradient

Figure 15.6 *Selection context-sensitive menu*

13. Use the **Magic Wand** tool again to select all the white area.
14. As before, right-click on the screen and choose **Select Inverse** to select the furniture.
15. Cut and paste into the main drawing.
16. Continue until you've gotten all the pieces assembled into one file.
17. Open a photograph of a person you'd like to include.
18. Click and drag on the **Lasso** tool until you see the **Magnetic Lasso.** This tool looks for edges between colors. Click to start the tool along the edge of the figure. Move your mouse slowly around the edge of the figure until you've completed the entire border. Click on the end-of-the-loop icon to complete the selection.
19. Right-click on the image and choose **Feather**. This blends the edges so the image looks more integrated with its new background.
20. Type **5** and click **OK** (this may take some experimentation to find the amount that looks good).
21. Copy and paste into the original drawing.
22. Other bits of entourage can be added in the same way, including paintings, furniture, or pictures of materials you'd like to use as painted textures.

There are many selection tools for different types of geometry, including ellipses, freehand and polygonal lassos, and the magic selection brush. Selections can be added to. Just hold down **SHIFT** and select another area. To subtract from the current selection, hold down **ALT**.

All elements of your composition should have a resolution similar to that of the original base image to avoid having pieces look pixilated. This won't be a problem for images we've exported from SketchUp or Revit, but for miscellany pulled off the Internet, it will be. Use filters on your search engine to look for only large file sizes, as discussed in Chapter 2. On manufacturers' Web sites, try to find the highest-resolution image of the product that you can—most finish product catalogs will have full-scale scanned images of their flooring, vinyl wall finishes, and so forth.

MAGIC TRICK

Select part of the image using whichever command you like. Using the Move command, hold down the ALT key—when you click and drag, it will make a copy. This is handy if you've decided you need to add just one more light fixture or piece of furniture but don't feel like going back to SketchUp or Revit.

Modifying Perspective Distortion in Images

When materials aren't showing up properly, or you just don't like them, it's possible to take an image file from the Internet or from a manufacturer and force it into the perspective of your drawing. You can save a selection of the area you'd like to fill for recall later, so that you can experiment with different textures. Adjustment layers in a special blending mode create a **Layer Mask**, which crops the pattern around furniture and other elements. Finally, you can create a new paint bucket texture from a selected image, which can speed up applying it again in the future.

MODIFYING PATTERNS FOR PERSPECTIVE

1. Find an image file of the flooring materials you'd like to use and open it in Photoshop Elements.
2. Copy and paste the image into your composition.
3. Make sure the layer with the flooring pattern is on top.
4. Select the flooring with the **Move** command.
5. If the area you need to cover is bigger than the sample you've got, make copies of the flooring next to the original in a tile pattern.
6. Select all the flooring layers. Right-click on the layers and choose **Merge Layers**.
7. Lower the opacity of the flooring layer if needed to see the lines of the drawing below.

Figure 15.7 *Transforming the texture*

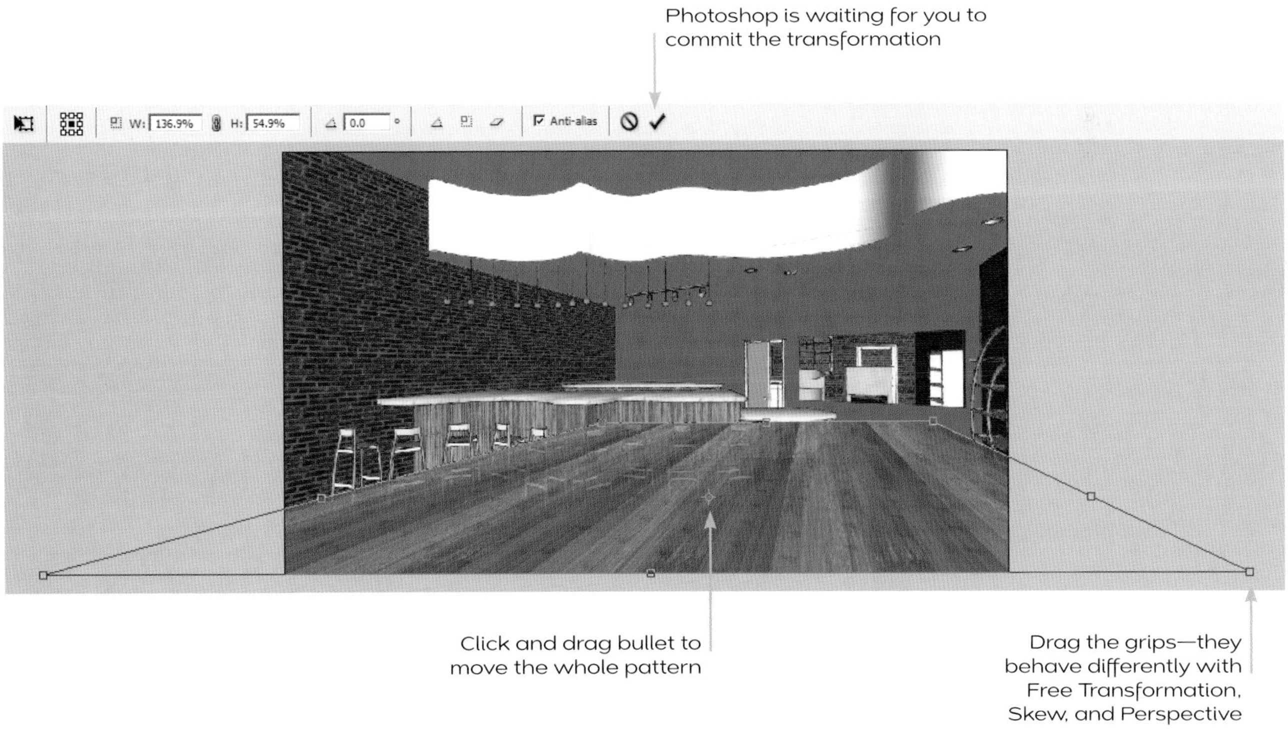

Photoshop is waiting for you to commit the transformation

Click and drag bullet to move the whole pattern

Drag the grips—they behave differently with Free Transformation, Skew, and Perspective

Figure 15.8 *Creating the*
Layer mask

Icon indicates layers will
be linked

8. Choose **Image>Transform>Perspective.** Use the grips to distort the selection.
9. Use the lines of the drawing to skew the image to the vanishing
   points as best you can, or draw in a line to represent the horizon.
10. In two-point perspectives, you may need to use the **Free Trans-
    form** tool to adjust each side for different vanishing points.
11. Use **Image>Transform>Skew** to modify the image in an irregu-
    lar pattern (Figure 15.7).
12. Click the **Commit Transformation** button when done.
13. Switch to the layer that has the whole image in solid colors.
14. Turn off any layers that might be obscuring your view.
15. Use the **Magic Wand** tool (with **Contiguous** selected) to select
    the floor.
16. Hold down **CTRL** and click to add areas, or **SHIFT** to delete areas.
17. Choose **Select>Save Selection** and name it *Flooring* or some-
    thing clever like that. This allows you to recall this particular selec-
    tion at any point.
18. Click on the **Create Adjustment Layer** button from the Layers
    Palette.

Figure 15.9 *The masked*
bamboo flooring

19. Choose **Brightness/Contrast.**

20. Leave the slider values unchanged in the dialog box and click **OK.** The new adjustment layer icon should show a silhouette of your current selection.

21. Move the layer with the flooring to just below the adjustment layer.

22. Hold down the **ALT** key and click on the border between the layers to join them (Figure 15.8)—the floor pattern will be cropped to fit within the white area of the adjustment layer (Figure 15.9).

23. To compare this to another material—Mexican tile, for example—turn off the first material and its linked adjustment layer.

24. Repeat the perspective distortion operation on a new material.

25. Choose **Select>Load Selection** and choose the Floor.

26. Create a new **Brightness/Contrast** adjustment layer as before.

27. Link it to the new material with **ALT** to form another Layer Mask.

This process can be repeated with almost any material you'd like. It's also nondestructive, in that the operation can be undone. Just **ALT+click** on the border between the joined layers and they'll become unconnected.

Layer masks can be used in all sorts of situations, even when you're not trying to distort textures in perspective. Floor plans, sections, and interior elevations all benefit from rendering with textures and layer masks. When rendering these orthographic views, be sure to create a new layer for rendering, as textures generally need to be softened with filters or lower opacity to balance with the lighter linework.

> **MAGIC TRICK**
>
> *Save selections for all of the different areas you plan to modify all at once—it's more efficient. CTRL+D deselects whatever you've got and allows for a new selection.*

Custom Patterns

Sometimes you need to cover a larger area of an illustration using a relatively small image—a vinyl tile sample, for example—and a pattern would make this easy. Custom patterns can be created using the current selection. Rectangular ones work best, since the selection will be "tiled" in an endless repeated pattern. Choose **Edit>Define Pattern from Selection…** to create a new pattern, and be sure to give it some name you'll remember. For example, you could use the same bamboo flooring used above. It now becomes available under **Options>Paint Bucket** (Figure 15.10).

If you need to resize the pattern, paint it onto some object—a rectangle will do and distort or transform the object. You can now add more subtle shadows at the base and under the countertop (Figure 15.11). The burn tool is good for adding shadows, but will only work on the currently selected layer. Be sure you're burning the right part of your project.

Figure 15.10 *Custom patterns*

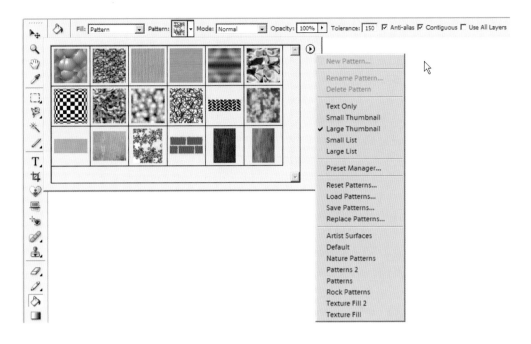

Figure 15.11 *The tiled counter without and with "burned-in" shadows*

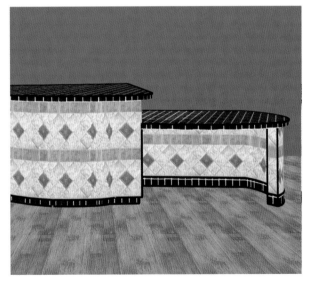

Adding Embellishments

As we saw in Chapter 4, filters are a quick way to make a drawing look less cold and technical, and can often make a drawing look more hand drawn. They are potentially destructive, though, and will only affect the active layer. For a composite drawing like ours, it's a good idea to create a "flattened" copy of your drawing to work on, then bring it back into the main composition for further manipulation. Opacity can soften the filter effect, and parts of the unfiltered layer can be selectively revealed using the Eraser tool.

APPLYING FILTERS TO A COPY OF THE COMPOSITION

1. Open your composition and turn off the layers for furniture and entourage.
2. Choose **File>Save As…** Choose **JPEG** from the Format drop-down list—this option automatically saves a copy.
3. Save the file in your project folder and click **OK**.
4. Back in your composition, choose **File>Place…** Browse for the flattened image, select it, and click **OK**.
5. Choose **Filter Gallery** from the Filter drop-down menu. (Refer back to Chapter 4 if you need a review.)
6. Click on **Graphic Pen** in the Sketch folder.

Figure 15.12 *The filtered layer*

Figure 15.13 *The filtered image being erased around the edges*

7. Drag the sliders to produce a result that's appealing in the preview window.
8. Click **OK** to apply—this can take a while (Figure 15.12).
9. Drag the opacity slider so that the effect is softened somewhat.
10. Drag the filtered layer below layers for furniture and other entourage, so that they stand out in contrast to the softer image.
11. On the layer with color, click on the **Eraser** tool.
12. Choose a heavy lineweight with an opacity of 25%.
13. Erase around the edges to reveal the linework underneath—it may take several passes to make the drawing look good (Figure 15.13).
14. **Save As** again to create another flattened copy.
15. Place the newer flattened version of your drawing in the composition.
16. Filter this copy using **Filter>Artistic>Colored Pencil...**
17. Change the opacity to soften the effect.

Leaving the furniture and entourage sharp can create interesting juxtaposition of filtered and photographic imagery. Selectively bleeding away the color from part of the drawing can be very effective, and can be used for effect with line drawings as well as the filtered one shown above.

Shadows

Sometimes our rendering software doesn't produce realistic results when it comes to shadows. Imported objects, in particular, can be unpredictable in how they behave in IRender nXt. Also, that lighting design you threw together in five minutes may just not work, but there's no time to fix and re-render. There are a few tools for fixing lighting in Photoshop. The sponge tool washes out (or saturates) colors in a given area, which is good for making objects fade into the distance. The **Burn** tool darkens lighting, which will create shadow effects—be sure to consider the location of light sources when faking them in. The **Dodge** tool does the reverse, lightening color and contrast, which is good for highlights. Again, consider the location of light fixtures and where highlights might realistically occur.

Lighting Filters

Lighting effects are similar to other filters in that they affect only the current layer. As before, you can merge several layers to apply effects across various elements, or make a flattened version of the whole drawing. If lighting is applied to the whole composition, it's best to apply the filter to a new, all-gray layer. You can then select the light distribution and create a brightness-adjustment layer—this has the advantage of being non-destructive, although it's quite a few extra steps.

APPLYING ELECTRIC LIGHTING

1. Select the area you'd like to work on, or use **CTRL+A**. If it's a selection, be sure to feather it heavily.
2. Choose **Filter>Render>Lighting Effects** (Figure 15.14).
3. Choose **Three Down** from the **Style** drop-down list.
4. In the preview area, click and drag the white circle at the center of the light source to move it.
5. Check the **Preview** button to see the effect of the lighting on your image.
6. If desired, click on the grips at either end of the ellipse to change the spread and depth of the light.
7. To add a light, drag the lightbulb into the preview area.
8. Adjust the sliders on the right to produce the desired result.
9. Click **OK** to apply (Figure 15.15).

Figure 15.14 *The*
Lighting Effects menu

Different pre-set
light distributions

Small preview
window—can't
be enlarged

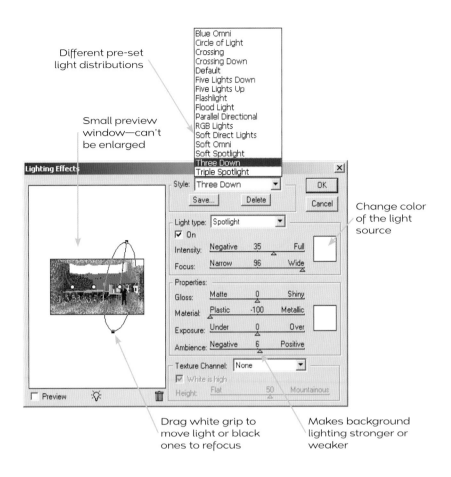

Change color
of the light
source

Drag white grip to
move light or black
ones to refocus

Makes background
lighting stronger or
weaker

Figure 15.15 *The lighting*
filter applied

10. If you don't like the effect, be sure to click **UNDO** right away.

11. Call up the lighting menu again—Photoshop Elements recalls where you had the lights last.

12. When done, adjust layer opacity to control effect on the layers below.

13. Click the **Add Layer** button on the Layers Palette.

14. **CTRL+A** to select all.

15. Make the foreground color a medium gray.

16. Choose **Filter>Render>Lighting>Effects.**

17. Add three **Omni** lights and move them over the pendants in the drawing.

18. Change the ambient level to fairly high and click **Apply.**

19. Use the **Magic Wand** tool to select all the gray area—you may need to change the tolerance to 15 or 20.

20. **Feather** to about 75 pixels.

21. Create a new **Brightness/Contrast** adjustment layer—the same kind we used to create a layer mask.

22. Lower the brightness and increase the contrast with the sliders (Figure 15.16).

Figure 15.16 *The applied lighting effects in the composition*

Lighting often makes the drawing a little too dark. You can increase the ambient level of the light fixtures used, or lower their intensity. You can also add a Brightness/Contrast adjustment layer at the very top of the layer stack. Add brightness to all layers below by using the sliders.

Losing Focus

There are a few other techniques to add finished depth to the illustration. A good drawing will have distinct elements in the foreground, middle ground, and in the distance. Of course, interior vistas are often limited, but in large or deep spaces, this sense of depth can be increased by blurring elements in the distance slightly and making the colors less intense. Objects and textures in the foreground, especially when rendered electronically, are often overpowering. Use **Filter>Distort>Glass** or an eraser with 5%–10% opacity to soften them. This is particularly true of the kitchen area in our composition, which is seen through a glass window (Figure 15.17).

You can also add an adjustment layer with a cooling photographic filter. These adjustment layers can be stacked on top of each other, so you can add a brightness layer too.

Sometimes you just need a quick but dramatic touch to an electronically rendered drawing. Try the **Lens Flare** rendering filter for a photographic look (Figure 15.18).

As before, don't become obsessive about detail if you know that you'll be using Photoshop Elements to render the drawings later on. It's easy to burn up hours putting soda cans on the shelves and toast in the toaster, none of which will be visible in a highly filtered 8 × 10 rendering. You can

Figure 15.17 *A blurred background*

Figure 15.18 *Rendered image with a lens flare*

download more filters from various online sites, and I've posted some with our Online Resources.

Printing and Export

OK, so it's time to present this beauty. If you've been working with a large file (somewhere around 8,000 PPI, TIFF format), you can do anything from 24 × 36 prints to onscreen presentations without the risk of the image becoming pixilated.

For electronic presentations, it's best to convert it into a JPEG for easy transfer and inclusion in a PowerPoint show, or a PDF if you work with that format. You could even just have a slide show of images—Photoshop Elements has a number of very nice tools for producing slide shows, with animation, music, and timed transitions. When you first call up Photoshop Elements, choose **Make a Photo Creation**. These sorts of presentations can be burned to a CD or DVD, and are very nice for automated presentations, but they are a bit beyond the scope of this book.

Printed images are of course the most popular, since they are the easiest for a reviewer or client to study in great detail. Printing a lone image straight out of Photoshop is relatively easy, but getting it to look right is a little harder. If your computers are calibrated to your printers, even better, since this ensures that what you see is what you get on paper. Advanced users with fancy photographic printers can apply ICC profiles to their image files, which calibrate the printer to a specific paper.

Just for fun, try printing the exact same image on regular 8.5 × 11 bond, matte photo paper, glossy photo paper, and watercolor paper. The colors will be vastly different on each. Anything soft like bond will tend to absorb color and soften detail, but will take pencils, pastels, and other traditional media quite nicely. Glossy photo paper, on the other hand, will give you the most vibrant colors but has a sheen that can take a long time to dry.

Of course, we all finish our projects with plenty of spare time for a test print and final adjustments, right? Just in case, though, use the quick and simple hand-rendering techniques presented to make up for the most common weaknesses of printed images.

Online Resources

- File used in this chapter, *Chocolate cafe composite.psd*
- Excel file for calculation of the resolution and paper size, *Resolution calculation.xlsx*
- Examples of student work, *Composites examples.pdf*

Term Project Assignments

- Create a single, high-quality 18 × 24 perspective with final materials.
- Critique one another's work.
- Develop a self-critique questionnaire or checklist.

Exercises and Further Study

- Render materials in a plan, section, or elevation.
- Create a wall-wash effect.
- Create a glowing television screen effect.

Unit 6

Portfolios

16

Physical Format

- Understand possible uses of a portfolio
- Understand possible organizational and layout strategies
- Understand implications of different binding alternatives
- Lay out and print documents of different formats

Everyone these days seems to have a portfolio and a journal of every experience since kindergarten. OK, that might be a bit of an overstatement, but considering how a project you've just completed fits in with your "body of work" is certainly a worthwhile exercise. You'll need to develop a way of organizing your work that is partly related to what you plan to do with it. Once you've come up with a strategy, you'll need to come up with a rough layout for each two-page spread. Then it's a matter of adapting individual projects or sections to this template.

BIG PICTURE

All of your work is already in electronic format of some sort, so creating the portfolio is a matter of collecting and formatting. Power-Point is a natural for multipage documents that combine graphics, text, and other goodies. Greater graphic control can be had in Photoshop, but that needs more advance planning.

The Design Portfolio

There are five main organization schemes for portfolios, each of which has implications for layout. These hold true even for the more creative hand-constructed binding devices, although page spreads may be more complex.

Archive: This has everything you've ever done, regardless of whether or not it's a design project or even if it's good. It includes everything from high school term papers to playbills from your dance performances in college. There's really no public audience for this. This is a great candidate for remaining solely within the electronic realm or boxes from The Container Store.

Chronological: This is a display of all your design work regardless of quality, and it tends to include only design-related works. This can include anything creative. The audience in this case could be a graduate school, grant, or contest application.

The Best: The most common approach is to choose your very best work from design school and work experience. This is the high-quality, bound presentation used in job interviews, and is meant to express who you are as a designer and a professional.

Skills: Meant to show a depth of skills in various aspects of professional practice, from space planning and schematic designs to rendering and construction drawings. This is generally what an employer is looking for, even though these types of portfolios are not always the most dramatic.

Handout: Often a smaller reproduction of one of the above schemes. Meant to be included with cover letters and résumés as a teaser to employers you're trying to interest.

Each of these schemes has different considerations for style and configuration. If you have used good file management and kept all of your work since elementary school, you're good to go and start with layout. Most of us, though, will need to do some collection and documentation first before we can move forward to the other steps in producing a portfolio.

ASSEMBLING A DESIGN PORTFOLIO

1. Catalog everything—and I mean everything.
2. Convert original items to electronic format whenever possible, while retaining the original.
3. Map your portfolio.
4. Design the master page layout.
5. Choose or design a binder.
6. Test map and layout on a few projects.
7. Revise as needed.
8. Choose which projects and other elements to include.
9. Adapt material to layout (or vice versa).
10. Design résumé and cover letter to match the theme.
11. Print, crop, mount, and so forth.
12. Assemble final product.

Students need to think about their portfolio right after they finish a project. It's relatively easy to keep track of electronic files, but there's a tendency to sit on, step on, or otherwise trash models almost immediately after final presentations. Good discipline is needed to take time and photograph models you worked hard on before leaving campus for summer break or graduation.

Documenting Physical Work

Reproducing physical work—models, paintings, hand renderings, and more—is usually the first step. For small flat work, a scanner is best. Scan at the 600 dpi minimum and save as a JPEG. For larger works, a photo studio is ideal. If you don't have access to one, pretty good results can be had at home.

PHOTOGRAPHING PHYSICAL WORK

1. Set camera in a tripod (or at least on a table) to avoid vibration.
2. Set the camera resolution and image quality to the highest quality level.
3. Set **ISO** to the slowest possible speed—64 is good.
4. Turn on **Auto White Balance** (AWB).
5. Frame so that the artwork fills as much of the viewfinder as possible, and use a zoom setting that's not too wide and not too close to avoid distortion. Move your camera closer or farther, or up and down, to achieve proper framing.
6. For flat work, align horizontally on the wall and don't worry about the backdrop—it'll get cropped in Photoshop.
7. Position the lights at approximate 45° angles to the wall on which the work will hang (Figure 16.1).
8. For models, use an ironed-flat bedsheet if a neutral studio backdrop is unavailable.
9. Position lights about 45° above models in addition to 45° away from the horizontal (Figure 16.2).
10. Rotate the model to best advantage, and take plenty of extra shots, since the LCD is so tiny.
11. Use either daylight-balanced fluorescent light sources or a combination of fluorescent and tungsten lamps, and clamp lights to stands or chairs.
12. Turn off any additional lights and block daylight (or wait until night).

Figure 16.1 *Photo setup for flat work*

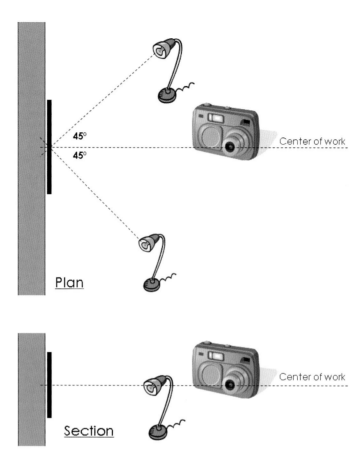

13. Look for spots in the camera window, and slightly adjust the position of the lights to eliminate glare. Sometimes a piece of tracing paper hanging over a fluorescent lamp does the trick, or change the angles or move lamps away.
14. Use the self-timer—this avoids shaking the camera.
15. Press the button and wait for the camera to take a picture.
16. If your camera allows you to, adjust the shutter speed to one stop slower and make another exposure—this is called bracketing.
17. Adjust the shutter speed to one stop faster and make another exposure.
18. Do the whole process over and over again for all of your work.

What you end up with is hundreds of picture files for dozens of different items. Your next step should be to cull the crummy shots, then move the pictures into the folders where the main projects are kept. Since my overall file structure is chronological, I can just make new folders for things like paintings, pottery, and sculpture that were done in an entirely nonelectronic class.

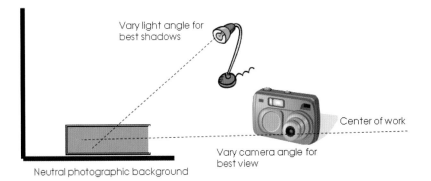

Figure 16.2 *Photo setup for models*

Vary light angle for best shadows

Center of work

Vary camera angle for best view

Neutral photographic background

<u>Section</u>

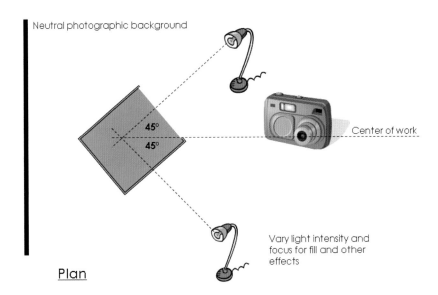

Neutral photographic background

45°

45°

Center of work

Vary light intensity and focus for fill and other effects

<u>Plan</u>

Mapping Your Life's Story

Now it's time to develop the "map" of your portfolio. This is an outline of what projects you think you'd like to include in the final design. Never put in a project that you're not proud of or that you don't think is very good—it can make for an awkward explanation. Strive for a balance of different types of work.

It's best to come up with groupings, rather than just ordering based on which you like best. Early on, a student will have mainly schematic design projects, so perhaps an organization by project type is best. For more experienced individuals, try to show a range of your skills: hand rendering, physical modeling, electronic rendering, construction drawings, lighting design, sustainable design, and so forth (Figure 16.3).

Figure 16.3 *A blank portfolio map representing two-page spreads*

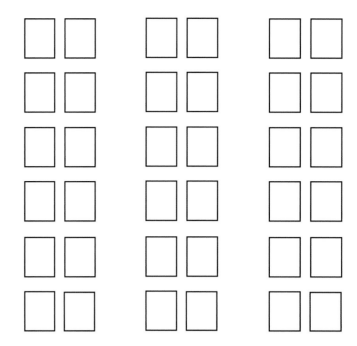

Figure 16.4 *A map example, using PowerPoint*

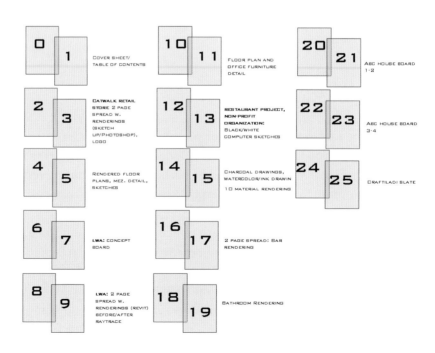

Take the blank form shown in Figure 16.3 to list each of the projects you'd like to include. You'll also want skill areas like sketching or rendering, where you place several original hand-drawn designs (keep the originals for yourself and scan or copy for the portfolio). Write in the name of the project, or draw the rough shapes of the images you plan to include (Figure 16.4).

Keep your eraser handy, as you'll soon want to start moving things around as more logical groups become apparent.

Choosing a Binding Device

You can't begin to design your portfolio until you have some idea of how the pages will be bound. There are many ready-made designs out there, most of which take standard sheet inserts. A few need you to punch holes into the final prints, and many need to be screwed together. Many students opt to design and build (or have built) some special creation (Figure 16.5). Even standard binding devices can be manipulated for a custom look.

See the Online Resources for links to some of the bigger portfolio resellers.

Figure 16.5 *A custom aluminum binder, courtesy Robyn Savitske*

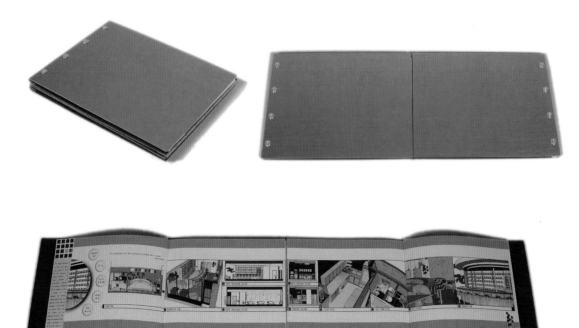

Designing Your Spread

Each two-page layout in a portfolio is called a "spread" and consists of a left- and right-hand page. Once you've purchased a binder, you'll know the size and possible orientations of the spread. Sketch out a rough diagram of how you can lay out that spread—don't think specifically about any project at this point, but more in terms of graphic composition (Figure 16.6). There are usually only about four elements on any layout:

- **Images**: Choose only your best, and use overlaps or iconic selections.
- **Titles**: Project data, view names, keys, and so forth.
- **Body text**: A *very* brief explanation of the project or drawings.
- **Graphics**: Lines, colors, or other devices that occur throughout the portfolio, which help to organize and navigate.

Each of these schemes should incorporate the four basic elements. Often the background graphics will provide an area for the text to occur, such as a block of color on one side or at the bottom. Titles can also

Figure 16.6 *Schematic layouts for portfolio spreads*

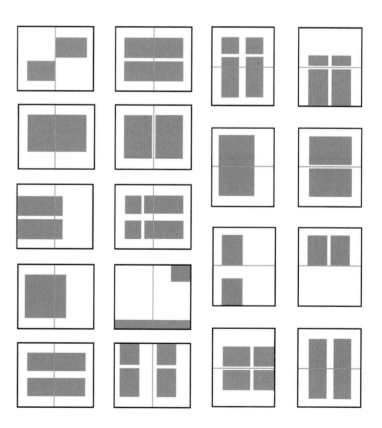

contain graphics, which give more flexibility to portfolios with a big variety of image sizes. You could also include a color graphic or space for a small icon of the project in one corner of the standard layout, to help navigate through the whole document.

Another consideration is how pages will be inserted or otherwise affixed to the binding device. Inserting paper directly by punching holes may seem easy enough, but you'll need to print double-sided and use a heavy-weight paper to handle the creasing and folding. There are plastic sleeve inserts, which are the easiest way to proceed, but you might get too much glare if you print on glossy paper. Some binders accept pre-punched adhesive strips, which solves the problem of how to handle folding your prints where they insert into the binding. In this case, using a glossy paper will give you the strongest colors—photographic matte tends to soften images a bit.

It's always impressive to see a handcrafted custom portfolio, with lovely double-sided prints creased to fold perfectly. That said, a sloppy portfolio or one that looks rushed and not well thought out will reflect on the impression you create. Be sure to mock up anything complicated before starting your electronic development, to be sure it's going to work for all sides of each sheet of paper.

Adapting the Template

Now take one of your favorite projects and try to make it fit into the layout. PowerPoint is the easiest to use, since you can control the Master Slide to manipulate the design. Handling the left and right halves of each page is a little tricky, though, and usually requires two files. For more artistic portfolios, however, Photoshop Elements is the best, and with a little planning, can be fairly efficient for a multifile project like this.

DESIGNING A PORTFOLIO SPREAD IN PHOTOSHOP ELEMENTS

1. Start a new single sheet or spread of the correct dimension for both.
2. Make a new layer.
3. **CTRL+A** to select all.
4. Paint a background color or gradient.
5. Use the drawing tools to add graphics such as bars and lines.
6. Insert icons if desired for organizing the portfolio (Figure 16.7).
7. Open all image files for this project that you'd like to use.

> **LOOK OUT!**
>
> *If you have access to a high-quality printer and paper, PowerPoint is not your best option, since there is a limit to the resolution it can print at. Use Photoshop Elements instead, and just copy a base file with your standard graphic to start a new page. More expensive programs, such as Adobe InDesign, offer even greater flexibility, but are more complex.*

Figure 16.7 *The background graphic scheme*

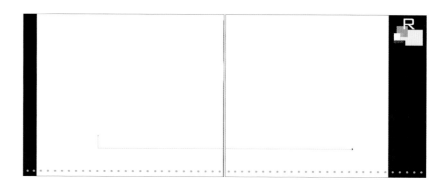

8. Copy and paste in the main image.
9. Add other images.
10. Adjust layer opacity as needed.
11. Change layer order to control overlaps.
12. Place text for the layout title.
13. Place text for titles.
14. Place text for project data and description.
15. If you are cropping, place light gray lines as guides for where to crop (Figures 16.8).

Repeat this procedure for each of the projects or thematic areas you'd like to include. Be loose as you compose both individual spreads and the whole portfolio, as you'll almost certainly go back in and make changes as things develop. Work in PowerPoint or Photoshop Elements, and

Figure 16.8 *The draft layout for a single spread*

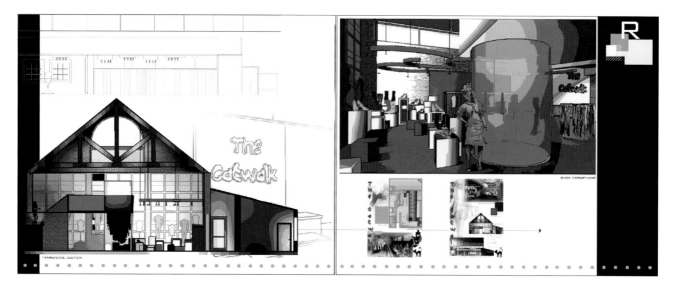

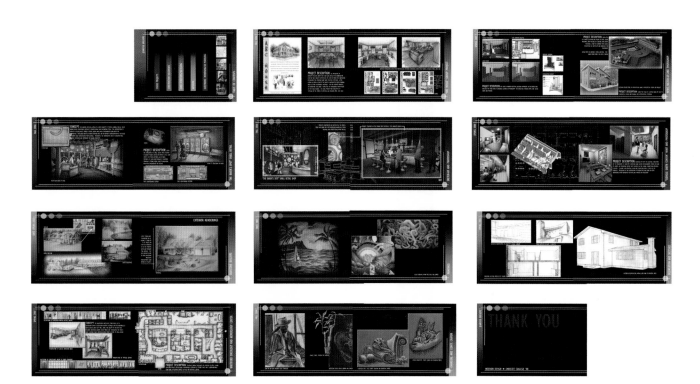

Figure 16.9 *A draft of the entire portfolio (courtesy Rachael Buchanan)*

create a template for the left and right pages as you go. Each spread can also be laid out in one slide or file, but allowance must be made for the portion of the sheet eaten up by the binding, if there is any. Look at the portfolio as a whole, in addition to each individual spread (Figure 16.9).

Try not to let the background distract from the elements of main importance: your work. Vignettes are often more effective than trying to squeeze too many larger images into a small area. And be sure to consider how the layout will function across the fold—some binding devices leave quite a bit of space there, which makes it harder to span with a single image. Finally, don't be afraid to take up a whole page or spread with an image—especially if it's a rendering or something you feel is your absolute best work.

The Table of Contents

As usual, I've saved the first piece for last: the table of contents. This is typically the page that your portfolio opens to. If you've grouped work into four or five headings, it's a good idea to use a color or graphic in the individual spreads to help navigate. Sometimes students will elect an

LOOK OUT!

Sometimes you want the background color or image to continue all the way to the edge of the face—called a full bleed. Many 8.5 × 11 home printers are capable of this type of printing, but not all larger printers and plotters. Check yours before printing, and adjust your page size accordingly. If you need to, buy larger paper and crop away the unprinted borders to the desired sheet size. Consider the extra time and expense this may require.

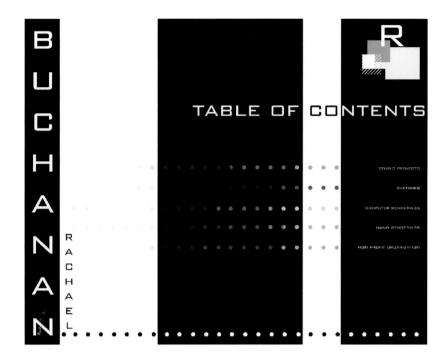

Figure 16.10 *The table of contents (courtesy Rachael Buchanan)*

image or vignette from one of the projects as the organizing graphic. Most of the time there are no page numbers, as they tend to make the design inflexible (Figure 16.10).

Remember that the portfolio is supposed to represent who you are as a professional and as an individual. So if you're very artsy and visual, use a more graphic table of contents. Thumbnail icons or colors representing each section are common organizing techniques. Avoid page numbers no matter what, as they are a pain to keep updated.

Paper options are the same as the rendered images printed in earlier chapters, although you should also take into account the effect of having plastic sheet inserts, if you choose them. Printing high resolution directly from PowerPoint involves overriding printing defaults to allow the printer's settings. Click the **Office** control button and choose **Power-Point Options** at the bottom of the menu. Click on the **Advanced** tab and scroll down to the **Print** group. Check the radio button for **Align transparent graphics at printer resolution**.

Résumés and Cover Letters

Résumés and cover letters should match the graphic look and feel of your portfolio, and should be included, usually at the end, so you can hand copies to your interviewers (Figure 16.11).

RACHAEL D. BUCHANAN
RBUCHANA@MAIL.ENDICOTT.EDU

SCHOOL ADDRESS: PERMANENT ADDRESS:
MAIL STOP #555   8 JONES ST.
376 HALE STREET   APARTMENT 16
BEVERLY, MA 01915   BEVERLY, MA. 01976
(978)232-3074   (978) 555-1212

OBJECTIVE: A FULL-TIME INTERIOR DESIGN INTERNSHIP DURING THE FALL SEMESTER, WHICH WILL PROVIDE MEANINGFUL INDUSTRY EXPERIENCE.

EDUCATION: BACHELOR OF SCIENCE, INTERIOR DESIGN (FIDER ACCREDITED), ENDICOTT COLLEGE, BEVERLY, MA.

DIPLOMA, GRADUATED 5/2001 GREENFIELD REGIONAL HIGH SCHOOL, GREENFIELD, MA.

EXPERIENCE: INTERNSHIP, JANUARY 2000   STUFFED SHIRT ARCHITECTS, MARBLEHEAD, MA
- ATTENDED SEVERAL PROJECT MEETINGS.
- PARTICIPATED IN ALL STAGES OF DESIGN DEVELOPMENT.
- GAINED EXPERIENCE WITH THE SWEETS CATALOGS.
- DESIGNED PRESENTATION BOARDS
            INTERNSHIP, JANUARY 2001   SAD SACK INTERIOR DESIGN. WAYLAND, MA
- PARTICIPATED IN DEVELOPING AN ELECTRONIC LIBRARY, CLASSIFYING ALL IMAGES FROM PRIOR PROJECTS, MATERIAL SELECTIONS, AND EXAMPLES OF DECK HOUSE AND ACORN HOMES.
- CONTRIBUTED IN A DESIGN COMPETITION WITH THE TOP DESIGNER AT DECK HOUSE, FOR THE NEW MODEL HOUSE BEING BUILT IN BOLTON, MA.
- WORKED AS AN ASSISTANT FOR THE REGIONAL SALES ASSISTANT MANAGER.
            CONSTRUCTION EMPLOYEE, JUNE 2000- MAY 2003   STILL STANDING BUILDERS, LAWRENCE, MA
- WORKED ON RESIDENTIAL CONSTRUCTION SITES.
- ASSISTED IN NEW CONSTRUCTION AND REMODELING. PROJECTS, INCLUDING: STRIPPING AND SHINGLING ROOFS, REPAIRING DECKS, SANDING AND STAINING WINDOWS, SIDING AND PARTITIONING.
            CUSTOMER SERVICE ASSOCIATE, JUNE 1999- DECEMBER 1999   WHOLE FOODS, WATERTOWN, MA
- PROVIDED CUSTOMER SERVICE AND SALES SUPPORT, WORKING IN ALL AREAS OF A LARGE RETAIL STORE.
- ASSOCIATE OF THE QUARTER- RECOGNIZES EMPLOYEE FOR SUPERB TEAMWORK, COOPERATION, COMMUNICATION, AND CUSTOMER SERVICE.

COMPUTER SKILLS: MS WORD, MS EXCEL, MS POWERPOINT, SKETCH UP, AUTO CAD, REVIT, PHOTOSHOP ELEMENTS

REFERENCES AVAILABLE UPON REQUEST

Don't try to make résumés fit into highly artistic and unusual formats, as this can leave them hard to read. But you should include some graphics—linework, colors, or even the little project icons from your table of contents.

Interviews

All this planning and effort in assembling a physical portfolio will give you more confidence when you present it to a potential employer. That said, it's a rare portfolio that's so impressive that it instantly lands you a job. Your ability to develop a rapport with your interviewer indicates how well you might get along in a particular office environment. Remember to talk to the person in front of you, not your portfolio. Make eye contact and try to sense if they're still interested or if it's time to flip the page. Always give them the opportunity to flip through your work, even if it means not getting to talk about everything you've done for the last four years. For a more in-depth discussion of presentation techniques, see *Design Portfolios: Moving from Traditional to Digital* by Diane Bender (Fairchild Books, 2008).

Online Resources

- A blank map file, *Blank map.tif*

Term Project Assignments

- Generate a map of all your past work.
- Purchase or construct a binding device.
- Develop organizational schemes and map out projects.
- Produce the portfolio spread for your Chocolate Café and Bowling Alley projects.
- Print and assemble your portfolio.
- Present your portfolio to a classmate in a mock interview.

Exercises and Further Study

- Generate alternative organizational schemes.
- Generate spread layout alternatives.
- Seek job descriptions that interest you and visualize bringing your portfolio to that job. This may guide your choice for binding, layout, and what kind of projects you will include.
- Arrange a 15-minute informational interview with a manager at a company you admire.

17

Electronic Format

- Understand different types of electronic portfolios
- Create a simple stand-alone portfolio
- Create a one-screen Web page
- Create a simple multiscreen Web page

So much of business communication happens electronically that it's an advantage to have your portfolio in an electronic format. There are two basic types: a single file, and a Web site. Both can be created using the work you created in the previous chapter, although the latter offers greater possibilities for larger images.

These documents should be self-explanatory, since they are generally looked at without the benefit of your presentation. This said, keeping descriptions to an absolute minimum is always a good tactic. On the other hand, you can add motion graphics and music, which expand your creative possibilities and enhance the experience of sharing your portfolio.

A Single-File Portfolio

The best format for a single-file portfolio is a PDF file. You'll need some way of taking the electronic images from your portfolio and printing them to a PDF file. This may require breaking some layouts into halves if your overall design had some folds or other pages printed nonsequentially.

BIG PICTURE

PowerPoint or Photoshop files from your physical portfolio layouts can be used to directly create a simple PDF file. Adding internal hyperlinks makes navigation easier, creating a stand-alone single-page Web site. More complex Web sites require creating separate files from each face layout but allow higher-resolution images to be exchanged more easily.

There are several virtual printers or converters that can create PDFs, some of which are free—see **Online Resources** for more information. I'm going to use Adobe Acrobat, since it's fairly common. If you worked in Photoshop Elements, you won't have the ability to create internal links, but these can be placed later using Acrobat.

CREATING AN ELECTRONIC PORTFOLIO USING POWERPOINT

1. If your project was done in Photoshop, open up the documents and save each as a high-quality JPEG.
2. Set up a new PowerPoint document with the same page size and orientation, and insert the images into new slides.
3. Create a table of contents, then select text for the first section.
4. Type **CTRL+K** to insert a hyperlink connected to that text (you could also click **Insert>Hyperlink**).
5. Click the **Bookmarks…** button to open a list of slides and other bookmarks in your file.
6. Select the slide number for the first face in the first section, and click **OK**.
7. Repeat the procedure for each section of your portfolio.
8. Click the Acrobat tab in PowerPoint, then the **Preferences** button (Figure 17.1).

Figure 17.1 *Acrobat preferences*

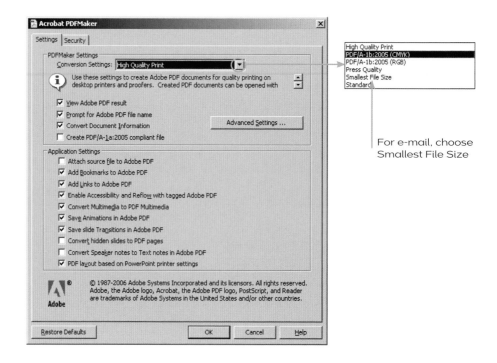

For e-mail, choose Smallest File Size

9. Make sure radio buttons next to **Save Slide Transitions** and **Save Animations** are checked, and click **OK**.
10. Click the **Create PDF** button.
11. If you're using another virtual printer, you may have to choose the page size that matches your portfolio (Adobe does this automatically).
12. If your exact size isn't there, see if there's an **Add** option somewhere.
13. Give the new size a name and change the dimensions.
14. Click **OK** to save (or print, as the case may be), then browse for a location to save the new file.
15. The file should open right up, and links will appear underlined and blue.

That's all there is to it. If the document is huge, be sure to choose a smaller file size under the conversion settings.

CREATING AN ELECTRONIC PORTFOLIO USING PHOTOSHOP ELEMENTS

1. If you started in PowerPoint, open up your Portfolio document.
2. Choose **File>Save As** from the drop-down menu.
3. From the File of Type drop-down list, check **Tagged Image File Format** (.TIF).
4. Browse for a location to save the files. PowerPoint will create a new folder for you. Click **OK**.
5. At the prompt, choose **All Slides** to create an image file of each slide.
6. Open **Photoshop Elements** and choose **Create**, which will send you into the main interface. If you've turned off the Welcome screen, choose **Create** from the side bar.
7. Choose **Slide Show** as the creation type and click **OK** (Figure 17.2).
   Set the slide show preferences however you like, but don't make the transition duration longer than the static duration—that's too quick to see the work (Figure 17.3).
8. Make sure to turn off cropping.
9. Click the **Add Media** button.
10. Choose **Photos and Files from Folder** option.
11. Browse for files and select (hold down **SHIFT** to select a contiguous group or **CTRL** to select noncontiguous files).
12. In the Slide Show Editor, change timing and transition effects if desired—just click on the number or transition icon (Figure 17.4).
13. Click and drag an image to change its location.

Figure 17.2 *The*
Photoshop Elements
creation setup screen

Click for different
creation options

This will create a slide show
with various simple effects

Creates a disk that plays on
your DVD player—send one
to your mom!

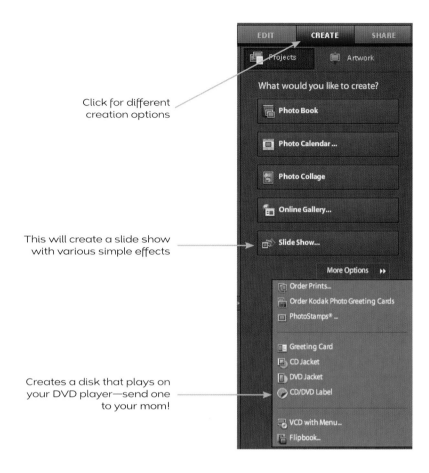

Figure 17.3 ***Slide Show***
Options *dialog box*

Time spent on a
given slide

Time on transition
effect (wipes, fades,
and so forth)

These options
apply to the whole
presentation, but
you can also change
individual slides

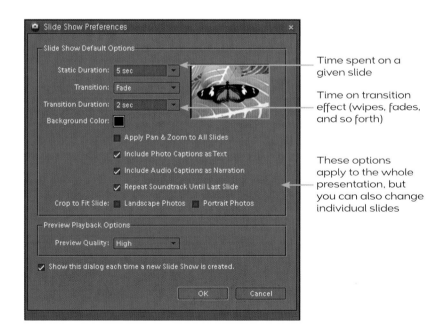

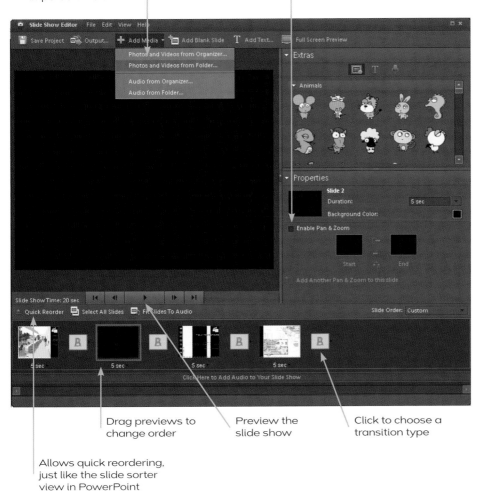

Browse for your files one at a time, or import a whole bunch

Enabling Pan and Zoom creates a Ken Burns effect

Figure 17.4 *Slide Show Editor*

Drag previews to change order

Preview the slide show

Click to choose a transition type

Allows quick reordering, just like the slide sorter view in PowerPoint

14. Add music using the **Add Media** button.
15. When you're all set, click the **Output** button (Figure 17.5).
16. Be sure to allow manual advance of slides.
17. Choose **PDF File** if you plan to e-mail, but remember that animations will not be included.
18. Choose **Movie File** to create your multimedia extravaganza.
19. Choose a file size (as a reference, YouTube videos are about 400 pixels wide).
20. Click **OK** to export.

You can also create computer- or DVD-based movie files, which are great if you're mailing out a disk to a prospective employer. Most people will delete any unsolicited file, so e-mail your portfolio only if you've been invited to.

UNDER THE HOOD

Converting a PowerPoint slide show into image files usually results in some lost resolution. To lessen this problem, you could double the dimensions of the paper in the **Page Setup** *dialog box. This will at least make the exported image four times as detailed and won't mess up the page layout or proportions.*

Figure 17.5 *Slide Show Output* options

Movie file format is better for YouTube or other types of automatic display

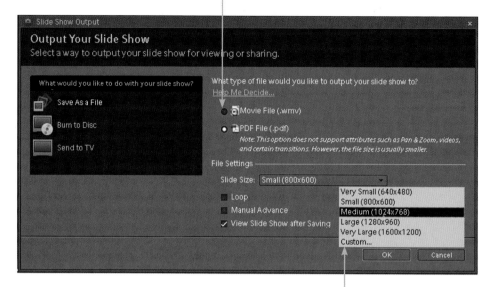

Small- to medium-sized PDF is best for e-mail, Large is best for online posting

Assembling the Single Document

RPS, the creator of IRender nXt, also makes a 3D PDF converter for your SketchUp files. Only users who have the latest Acrobat Reader will be able to use the features, but they are definitively slick. All saved scenes can be retrieved and printed, and view commands such as Zoom and Orbit are available within the PDF window. This can also be combined with other PDF pages to make a self-contained submission. Tech-savvy clients will appreciate these files as well.

CREATING A SINGLE PDF OF YOUR PORTFOLIO

1. Call up 3D PDF Creator—it will be in your start menu if you've installed IRender nXt (Figure 17.6).
2. Fill out the PDF Page information items you like, or leave them blank.
3. Click on the **SketchUp File** field to browse for your model.
4. Click on **Options.**
5. You can set the page size to 11 × 17 if your client needs to print.
6. Click the **Preview** button to see what the file will look like.

Figure 17.6 *The 3D PDF interface*

Add information
as you see fit

3D PDF will open your
latest file, or browse
to choose

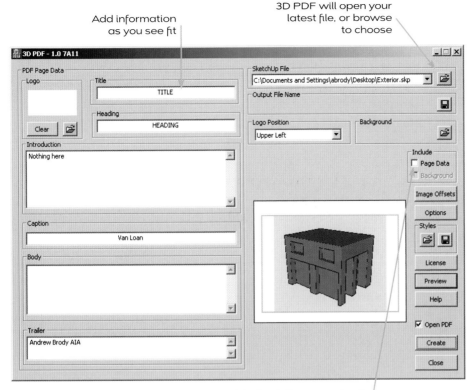

Uncheck if you want only
the model image to show

7. Click **Create** to save the file.
8. Open Acrobat and click on the **Create PDF>From Multiple Files...** button on the main toolbar.
9. Browse to find and add files for your main portfolio pages and the 3D PDF (you can add MS Office documents here, too, like your résumé).
10. Click **Next**, then reorder as needed.
11. Click on **Create Document** to complete the process.

Using this technique, you can allow someone to explore your projects on their own. You could also add in your résumé, references, hyperlinks to your MySpace page, or other random information.

Basic Single-Page Web Sites

Creating a Web page of your portfolio can be as easy as posting the file created above, which is adequate if you're just trying to avoid e-mail limits on attachment size. There are plenty of free hosting sites, and many have their own page-layout software to help you add text, files, and Web links. One that is relatively easy, and free, is from Microsoft. You'll need to sign up for a free account first, and the account is limited to 500 MB.

The interface is oriented toward business users, but it allows the creation of a simple, effective Web site without any additional software, knowledge of HTML, or continuing education classes.

CREATING A WEB-BASED PORTFOLIO

1. Go to the **Microsoft Office Live** page: http://smallbusiness.officelive.com.
2. Click the **Sign Up Free** button and fill in all the information.
3. Once you're logged in, follow the **Create a Business Web Site** link (Figure 17.7).
4. If you're feeling flush, you can purchase your own domain name (follow the **Register a Domain Name** link).
5. Follow links to the image gallery and upload any individual photos you might want to use.

Figure 17.7 *The **Office Live** Web site creation screen*

Add pictures and other documents to the different "galleries"

You'll have to pay for your own domain name if you want one

These are all the pages in your site

Click here to open the Page Editor

6. Follow link to the document gallery to upload your portfolio—just make sure it's less than 10 MB.

7. When you're done uploading, follow the **Design Your Web Site** link.

8. A new window will open up, with your homepage visible—this is the **Site Designer.** Choose a font, color, and navigation orientation here (Figure 17.8).

Figure 17.8 *The Site Designer screen*

Click to switch to the Page Editor

Choose which page you're editing

Preview in a Web browser

Global design options (well, just for your Web site, anyway)

Navigation buttons to other pages in your site

Click in a "zone" to edit, cut, and paste text

9. **Styles** change your color scheme.

10. Modify your header and footer with text, a logo, or a theme.

11. Change text style globally here (although there aren't many fonts available).

12. Just click in a field to type. Text-formatting tools are available for any selected text.

13. Click on the **Page Editor** tab to modify or add components (Figure 17.9).

14. **Layout** changes how many frames (called **Zones** here) you'll see.

15. Add modules for a slide show, which is a little nicer than just posting a single document.

16. Type out the text to receive the link—name it *My Portfolio* or something clever like that.

17. Select the text and click on the **Hyperlink** button (you can also select a photograph to receive the link).

18. Click the Document radio button, then **Select Document...**

19. Choose your portfolio document form the selection window and click **OK**.

20. The linked text (or photo) should appear with a blue highlight.

21. Click the **Save** button.

22. Click the **Preview** button to see what it looks like, then test the link to see if your file pops up.

This is about the most basic Web site you can get, but it's certainly better than clogging up people's e-mail accounts with great big attachments.

Figure 17.9 *The Page Editor screen*

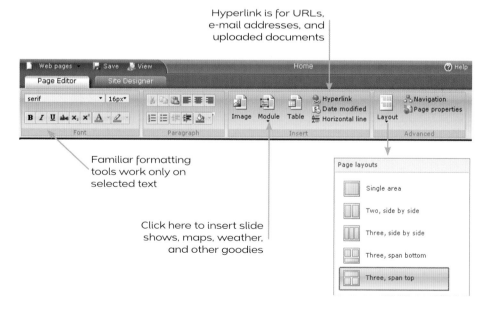

As you can see, there's the potential for some degree of customization, but basically this is a business-oriented Web site. You won't get snazzy mouse-over flash animations and cool sounds using this method. For that you'll need to find another service. That said, we can make our Web site a tad more interesting with a few extra touches.

A step up from the simple one-page site is one in which you have links to PDF files for each section. This allows you to give the person browsing your site a little more flexibility in choosing what they look at. The process is the same as that above, except that you add icons for each of the main areas in your portfolio. These may be interspersed between text, but you can't use a single picture of the whole table of contents—there needs to be an image or text to attach the hyperlinks to.

Sophisticated Multidocument Web Sites

A superior online portfolio has a gallery of photos that visitors can click on to enlarge. This requires creating icons for each of your sheets at a very small size, which will load quickly. If you've been working in Photoshop, you'll also need to convert all those files into JPEGs. The icons get loaded into the picture gallery, but the higher-resolution images are loaded into the document gallery, where they can be used in hyperlinks.

CREATING A PHOTO GALLERY USING PREVIEW ICONS

1. Open Photoshop Elements and choose **Edit and Enhance Files.**
2. Choose **File>Process Multiple Files** (Figure 17.10).
3. For the source folder, browse to find your original documents.
4. For the destination folder, create a new one called *For Web Page.*
5. Make the final file width 300 pixels, and the resolution 72 DPI.
6. Click **OK**, and Photoshop will go wild opening and resizing images.
7. Back at **Office Live**, upload all the icons into your photo gallery.
8. Upload all of the full-sized JPEGs into the document gallery.
9. Click on the **New Page** button in the **Page Manager** (if you're in the **Page Editor**, choose **New Page** from the **Web Pages** drop-down list).
10. Choose **General** for the style and click **Next.**
11. Give it a short name, like *Table of Contents*—this is what will appear on the navigation buttons.
12. Allow the parent to be *<Top Level>* and click **Finish.**
13. Add another page for, say, rendering, but make the parent be the table of contents page.

Figure 17.10 *The Process Multiple Files dialog box*

Choose source and destination folders

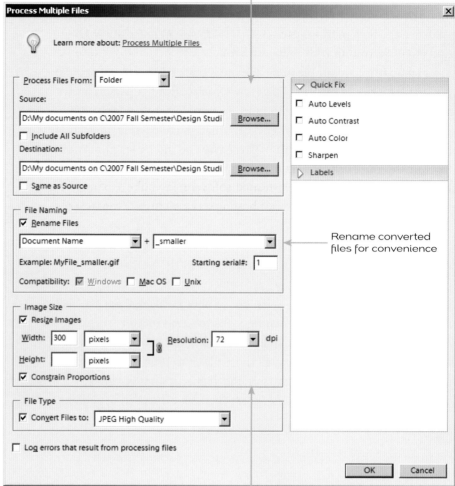

Rename converted files for convenience

No more than 300 pixels wide for a 34"-wide two-page spread

14. Add others for other sections of your portfolio.
15. Edit the new table of contents page, and make any stylistic changes that tickle your fancy.
16. Add text instructing the user to click on the pictures to see the gallery for different sections.
17. Insert an icon for one of the sections. Add a title, too.
18. Select the photo and click the **Hyperlink** button.
19. Choose *A Page on my Website.*
20. Select the Rendering page from the list and click **OK.**
21. Repeat the process if inserting icons and linking to the other sections.

22. Now open up the Rendering page.
23. Insert an icon for one of the individual sheets.
24. Select the photo and click the **Hyperlink** button.
25. Click the Document radio button, then **Select Document...**
26. Choose your portfolio document from the selection window and click **OK.**
27. Repeat ad infinitum, or until you run out of sheets.
28. Save and preview your site.

Office Live is free and relatively easy to use. You can use whatever service you like, and those that come with your Internet provider often have better support and more sophisticated software. If you're looking for a more artistic interface, another free hosting service is http://mosaicglobe.com. We'll stick with the Microsoft product, however, because it's simpler to integrate with our workflow. For a much more in-depth discussion of creating Web sites for interior design, see the book *Design Portfolios: Moving from Traditional to Digital* by Diane Bender (Fairchild Books 2008).

Online Resources

- Examples of student electronic portfolios and Web pages using the WindowsLive system (*Student Web pages.pdf*).

Term Project Assignments

- Develop Web pages using Office Live (or any other service provider you like).
- Post single PDF version of physical portfolio to a Web page.
- Post multiple-file version of your portfolio using image previews.
- Post gallery-style portfolio, with icons for faces leading to larger-size images.

Exercises and Further Study

- Convert image files to small-size JPEGs for use on your Web page.
- Select three Web pages from young designers you admire and attempt to emulate those. Find out which programs they used and observe why their organization and presentation are appealing and professional.
- Have a classmate critique your electronic portfolio.

GLOSSARY

Accelerator key Keystroke or combination of keystrokes that activates a command or operation. Also called a *keyboard shortcut*.

Backup What you were planning to do the day after your computer crashes, losing months of data.

BIM Building information modeling.

Block From AutoCAD, a group of drawing elements gathered into a named mini-drawing; often has parametric elements.

Bookmark A reference point in a document, such as in Word, that can be referenced in a hyperlink.

Building Information Modeling (see BIM) A method of designing a building with parametric elements combined into a single database.

CMYK color Printers and the matching software configuration that use secondary colors of cyan, magenta, yellow, and black to reproduce the entire color spectrum.

Combination drawing A collage of related drawings and images, typically of a single project.

Command A tool or operation.

Component From SketchUp and Revit, a group of drawing elements gathered into a named mini-drawing; often has parametric qualities.

Composite drawing A single drawing created from combined pieces of other drawings.

Composition The careful arrangement of visual elements, such as elements of perspective, cropping, text, images, diagrams, and lines, to produce an overall effect.

Context-sensitive menu A menu accessed by right-clicking on some object, area, or selection set.

Conversion Changing a file from one type to another for use in another program, generally through Export or Save As menus.

Cropping Choice of the amount of image or view to display; related to composition.

Dialog box A menu that has selections for the user to input.

Directory structure A hierarchy of folders within folders, organized according to some scheme—usually chronological by year or semester.

Drop-down menu List of written commands typically found at the top of a software window.

DWG file format AutoCAD native file format, although many programs will accept through import and export.

.EXE file Executable file—basically, a program.

Export To extract an image or model from one program, typically to another file format.

Eye level Height of the station point in a perspective.

File format The type of document a program saves to;

most programs have a "native" format that retains formatting and other features.

Filter A tool for selecting or deselecting model elements based on specified criteria.

Fly-out A hidden menu accessed by clicking on an arrow, typically leading off to one side.

Folder Virtual storage containers, each with a unique name, for different types of electronic files; use in a directory structure to organize your work.

Foreground In perspective, entourage and other elements that appear nearest to the station point.

Function key F1, F2, F3, etc., on the keyboard.

Gradient The even transition from one color or hue to another.

Grid A set of reference lines, typically used for assistance with layout.

Grip A point along a model or drawing element that allows selected elements to be modified by clicking and dragging.

Ground plane Typically, where a 3D model is started; defined by red and green axes in SketchUp and a level reference in Revit.

GWB Gypsum wall board, otherwise known as drywall.

Hatching A repeated pattern, often associated with a material.

Highlights The brightest spot in a composition, often on highly reflective surfaces or where a light source is in the field of view.

Horizon line The line in perspective where sky and ground appear to meet.

Hyperlink A reference to a location on the Internet or another computer.

Import To bring a drawing or modeling element into a project, typically from a library or another program.

ICC Profile Color-image conventions created by the International Color Consortium, used to calibrate the image you see on your screen with the printed output, based on your chosen printer and paper.

Interoperate The ability of different programs to read model information and assorted data from one another.

Layers A system for organizing drawing or model elements.

Mapping Applying a raster-based image to a vector-based object such as a surface or solid.

Materials takeoffs A systematic count of some project element, such as doors by type, or area of flooring by material, typically for the purpose of pricing and ordering. Most often produced in a schedule format.

Menu A list of choices, such as red wine or white.

Minimize/Maximize Hiding/revealing a program window without actually closing the program.

Modeling—solid A system for producing 3D objects that relies on graphic massing more than parametric definition.

Orthographic A drawing without perspectival distortion, including plans, sections, elevations, and axonometrics; typically set to some reference scale.

Parametric A modeling element characteristic that can be defined by changing a value (or choosing from a submenu) within the elements properties.

Perspective A system of representing three-dimensional space on a two-dimensional surface.

Photo-realism Rendering a model view using raster-based mappings to achieve a highly realistic appearance.

Picture plane The location on which perspective lines are projected from the station point past a building element.

Pixel A pixel (short for picture element, using the common abbreviation "pix" for "picture") is a single point in a graphic image.

Pixilation (or pixelization) Visible distortion of an image where, due to lack of resolution, individual pixels are visible.

Plug-in An adjunct to the base configuration of a piece of software, often from outside sources.

Preferences Program-wide settings controlling a variety of characteristics about the interface.

.PSD file format Photoshop document—the native file format to Photoshop CS and Elements.

Radio button A user-controlled check box.

Raster-based graphics Image construction based on a two-dimensional grid of pixels.

Rasterize Convert a vector-based document (a Revit file or a PDF) to a raster-based image (a JPEG, TIFF, etc.).

Remote backup A copy of all or selected files on a main computer to some location (another computer, server, or removable media) far, far away.

Rendering Adding color, materials, and (typically) lighting to a model view.

Resampling Changing the size of a raster image wherein the software interpolates characteristics of missing pixels.

Resolution Density of pixels per inch (PPI) for an electronic image or dots per inch (DPI) for a printed image.

.RFA File Revit family file extension.

.RGB color Relative percentage of red, green, and blue in a given color.

.RTE file Revit template file extension.

Rulers Reference lines on the side and top of a screen with measurement markers.

.RVT file Revit project file extension.

Scaled output A printed orthographic view.

Selection set Currently selected objects or elements.

Shortcut In terms of software, a key or keystroke combination that activates a command.

.SKB file SketchUp backup file. Change the name to .SKP to open.

.SKP file SketchUp native file format.

Station point The location of the viewer in a perspective, relative to focal point and picture plane.

Texture Representation of finish quality of a material.

Tiling A repeated pattern, where an image can cover a surface in a grid pattern based on the image size.

Toolbar A collection of buttons representing tools or operations. Can often be moved and customized for specific tool themes.

Vanishing point The point on the horizon at which parallel lines appear to converge.

VCT pattern Vinyl composition tile—typically, 12" square.

Vector-based graphics Image construction based on geometrically constructed drawing elements; scaled drawings.

Virtual printer Software that converts documents to another file format while retaining the original graphic formatting, hyperlinks, and sometimes multimedia content. Most commonly works via the print menu.

Webmail E-mail accessed by logging in to a specific Web page.

Workflow The process and order in which the different steps of a task are accomplished.

INDEX